Right Back Where I Started

A Memoir in Music

David Itkin

Number 19 in the North Texas Lives of Musicians Series

University of North Texas Press
Denton, Texas

Printed in the United States of America.
10 9 8 7 6 5 4 3 2 1

Permissions:
University of North Texas Press
1155 Union Circle #311336
Denton, TX 76203-5017

The paper used in this book meets the minimum requirements of the American National Standard for Permanence of Paper for Printed Library Materials, z39.48.1984. Binding materials have been chosen for durability.

Library of Congress Cataloging-in-Publication Data

Names: Itkin, David author
Title: Right back where I started : a memoir in music / David Itkin.
Other titles: North Texas lives of musicians series no. 19.
Description: Denton, Texas : University of North Texas Press, [2025] | Series: Number 19 in the North Texas lives of musicians series | Includes index.
Identifiers: LCCN 2025021127 (print) | LCCN 2025021128 (ebook) | ISBN 9781574419658 cloth | ISBN 9781574419702 ebook
Subjects: LCSH: Itkin, David | Conductors (Music)--United States--Biography | BISAC: MUSIC / Genres & Styles / Classical | BIOGRAPHY & AUTOBIOGRAPHY / Music | LCGFT: Autobiographies
Classification: LCC ML422.I87 A3 2025 (print) | LCC ML422.I87 (ebook) | DDC 784.2092 [B]--dc23/eng/20250505
LC record available at https://lccn.loc.gov/2025021127
LC ebook record available at https://lccn.loc.gov/2025021128

Right Back Where I Started is Number 19 in the North Texas Lives of Musicians Series.

The electronic edition of this book was made possible by the support of the Vick Family Foundation.

Typeset by vPrompt eServices.

For my parents, always remembered.
For my siblings, holding us together.
For my children, original and bonus,
keeping me honest.
For my friends, I don't tell you often enough.
And for wifey, there are no words.

You are all loved more than you know.

L'Chaim.

Contents

Silence is everything. Without silence there is no music, because empty air is the canvas upon which music is made. And when that canvas is overwhelmed, when the noise is ever present, there is no space in which to create something new.

Chapter 1

Rumblings and Fumblings

I always wanted to be a conductor—except when I planned to be an opera singer, a lawyer, a rock star, a writer, an actor, a composer, a director, or a furniture merchant. At some point in the distant past, I think I wanted to be a cowboy. Along the way, tiny stones on the path altered the flow of events, and each pebble—each choice—led to a unique destiny.

Every decision spreads before us a new web of possibilities. But those same choices preclude other pathways whose existence will remain forever a mystery. And the most important of these difficult decisions are made when we are least equipped to understand their significance.

But our youthful handwringing was unnecessary. Our paths are neither straight lines nor winding roads but circles so vast we believe we are moving in one direction. And like each journey around the sun, the longer we move forward, the closer we are to our starting point.

Fourth Child of Three

At the peak of the baby boom, in spring 1957, I was born as a replacement for our family's meticulously planned third and final child. The original me was stillborn, and I became aware of her existence only decades later, courtesy of a momentary glitch in the family's secret-keeping orthodoxy. This tragic loss was—by my grandfather's command—never spoken of again, and I was ushered into the world two years later to fill a hole in an allegedly perfect 1950s Pacific Northwest assimilated American Jewish family.

In recent years my sister, Marianne—the second child—has privately wondered how her turbulent early life might have been ameliorated by the presence of the lost little girl. I have often mused on the same question. But no good comes from wondering what might have been, because this delicate branch on our family tree was too fragile to support its own weight.

I wasn't supposed to be born, so I was "special." In my view, though, the strange gap between my siblings' ages and mine made me the perennial outsider. And my place as the odd man out wasn't mere perception. Of the five members of our family, I am the only one with a unique birthday. My parents were born on October 5 (seven years apart), and my brother and sister were born on December 11 (two years apart). Once up to speed on the facts of life, I tried to figure out if Valentine's Day, my parents' anniversary, or some other romantic occasion fell nine months before the date on which my siblings were born. But the math never worked out, so I finally had to accept that our odd family structure was just the first of many cosmic jokes at my expense.

As the only child who didn't live through adolescence during the 60s, I was automatically the "good" kid. Furthering this comfortable myth, my parents repeatedly reinforced the idea that I was an artistic phenom. But their efforts to demonstrate the unconditional approval that had eluded my siblings didn't feel like validation. Though it was surely unintentional, their message to the replacement child was clear:

perfection is the only standard. Being reminded daily that you're a wunderkind who can do no wrong is exhausting, especially when it's not the truth.

In a pitiful effort to maintain my perfect son status, I drove safely down the center of every road, rarely veering from whatever course I believed would garner parental approval. But we cannot search for our true selves or learn who we are as artists by playing it safe. Sex? Drugs? Alcohol? Maybe take a risk occasionally, or extend my intellectual or artistic reach beyond my grasp? Not their good child. My years of personal and artistic exploration were being saved for my mid-20s and beyond, a period during which I worked hard to discover just how flawed I could become. But during that period of purposeful imperfection, I would begin to understand that both life and music have more to offer than treading carefully from one predetermined step to the next.

Being the odd man out—combined with my place as the baby of the family—also had its advantages. With fewer middle-class Jewish expectations forced upon me—medical school or some equally predicable path—I was freed to explore the possibilities of who I was meant to be rather than trying to fit this round peg into a square hole. This is not to say that I took advantage of that opportunity wisely and courageously. On the contrary, my self-imposed requirement for an error-free existence meant that for many years I modeled my choices on my parents' strict servitude to convention.

My father was a furniture salesman who wanted to be an actor, and my mother was a travel agent who'd wanted to be a doctor. Both had their ambitions thwarted and tried to hide their frustrations, like shameful family heirlooms locked in a forgotten cabinet. But despite their best efforts, their disenchantment with the hands they'd been dealt seeped from every pore.

Their three children escaped the house of unspoken dreams—the eldest by distance, the middle child into nonconformity, and the replacement into music. But it took the third child decades to realize

The three Itkin kids, c. 1961. From left, David, Marianne, and Hank.

that, without the honest emotions and introspection he was taught to avoid, his quest was pointless.

So this improbable story of a half century on concert stages from Portland to Shanghai, from Dubai to Ljubljana, and a hundred places in between—this quest to find the truth—began with an amateur piano teacher named Mrs. Shapton and an elementary-school band director everyone called Pinky.

Like many middle-class children of our generation, my brother, sister, and I took piano lessons at our parents' insistence. My brother, Hank, was diligent if uninspired and later switched to the trumpet, where he was also diligent and uninspired. In his senior year of high school, he was elevated to drum major of the marching band, but this promotion may have been—by his own admission—no more than a wedge to remove him from the trumpet section. My sister dabbled at the piano and the flute, then took up the guitar—under the unlikely combined influences of 60s counterculture and the Campfire Girls—and still plays to this day.

This is all to say that the much-touted Jewish musical gene was, perhaps, not distributed equally across our generation.

Regarding that mythical gene, my second wife—yes, the third time *is* the charm—once observed the stark contrast between congregational singing in a Christian church versus the disorganized groaning that passes for music in a synagogue. Hymn singing is usually pleasant and reasonably organized, while the Jews sound as though we are singing different songs, or perhaps the same song in different keys, simultaneously.

Based on her observation, she concluded that the gentiles spread the musical gene evenly across the population while the Jews concentrate it in a few individuals. To support this theory, she mentioned Bernstein, Gershwin, Billy Joel, Irving Berlin, Streisand, Horowitz, Mendelssohn, Mahler, and so on. While odd, and somewhat ethnocentric, the evidence is difficult to rebut.

While I may have gotten the long end of the gene, my diligence as an 8-year-old piano student was nowhere near as laudable as my brother's. After a half dozen lessons, during which my teacher regularly lamented my lack of progress with technical exercises, she gave me my first real piece of music, a sonatina by Muzio Clementi. Following an introductory lesson on the piece, she phoned my parents in a state somewhere between elation and panic.

According to my mother, Mrs. Shapton played through the piece once, then I sat down and played the entire thing without one missed note. I was, according to the teacher, a savant too gifted for her pedagogical skills. While I vaguely recall the piece being rather easy, either Mrs. Shapton, my mother, or both were indulging in unfathomable levels of exaggeration. Banished for reasons I didn't understand, I continued lessons with a talented high school student. But I wandered away a year or two later, bored with both the exercises and the repertoire and tired of his complaints about my work ethic.

In truth I *was* practicing. I was at the piano every day but spent my time playing what interested *me*. The fact that I was recalcitrant about scales and arpeggios is an irony too rich to ignore, because as a professional conductor and teacher, I am an uncompromising hammer about technique. I imagine a psychiatrist would say I'm still trying to compensate for past mistakes. But psychobabble aside, there is no question that quitting piano lessons, and having to pick up those pieces in college, was the dumbest decision I've ever made.

As a youngster, I wanted music to be an escape from the confusing mixed signals I received at home: follow the rules . . . no, be creative . . . but don't paint outside the lines. The scales and simple piano pieces I was given did not allow for the self-expression I sought, and I was far from mature enough to make the connection between technique and art.

So what was I looking for? Approval? I had plenty of that from my parents, even if it seemed to be based on fiction rather than fact. Artistic fulfillment? I'm not sure I would have understood what that means. A real sense of who I am? Perhaps—but I wouldn't have known where to begin.

~~~~~ Rock Star ~~~~~

At Fernwood Elementary School, on the northeast side of Portland, the teachers annually showed their softer sides by auctioning off various personal services to benefit the school's extracurricular programs. In the second grade (1964), I begged my mother to bid on the band teacher's offering: three beginner lessons on any instrument. She was the highest bidder for the services of Clement "Pinky" Williams, and much to my parents' chagrin, I chose snare drum lessons. A few years later, I transitioned to the drum set, beginning a lifelong search for my inner rock star.

In seventh grade I was recruited as the drummer in a country cover band called The Tiny Bubbles. The invitation came from twin Vietnamese boys in my school whose dad was the rhythm guitar player and lead singer. If the image of a middle-aged Vietnamese immigrant singing country music in fractured English backed by three junior high kids conjures images of Saturday Night Live, then you fully understand The Tiny Bubbles.

The next year, 1970, with The Tiny Bubbles in my rearview mirror, I started a rock band with two classmates. We wrote some of our own material, masterminded by the fantastically talented bass player, but mostly covered current pop/rock hits. For several months we played gigs at school dances around town but then parted company over our supposedly compelling artistic differences. We were 13 years old, so everything was incredibly important. It seemed our breakup would shake the rock and roll world to its foundations, as had the Beatles' parting that same year, but it passed with hardly a whimper.

Like falling from one adolescent crush to another, I immediately formed a new band in which I was the keyboard player and lead singer. Our name, Light of Creation, may have sent mixed messages to potential buyers who thought we were a Christian group, though we managed to get some bookings over the next year or two. Sadly, the approaching commitments of theater and honors classes soon engulfed me, and my days as a rock and roll animal were done.

But no musical experience is valueless, no matter how it may appear at the time. Playing rock music with amateurs is a never-ending lesson in quick thinking, cool headedness, and public improvisation. And more to the point, I'm not convinced that a musician who has never been onstage in a rock concert can thoroughly understand the primitive, pulse-pounding sensuality of Stravinsky's *Rite of Spring*.

The Cool Kids

I played in the marching band (trumpet) and the orchestra (timpani) at Woodrow Wilson High School from 1971 to 1975. But my goal was the jazz band, because that's where all the cool kids were. With his teaching hours entirely committed, our instructor scheduled jazz band in the hour before school began, so attendance was, technically, optional. To us, however, that hour was sacred, and we were there at 7:00 a.m. sharp, four days a week, rain or shine.

I took public transportation to high school because the school bus didn't circulate as far as our neighborhood. Not that it would have mattered, because I was headed to rehearsal more than two hours before the bell. To arrive at jazz band on time, I left home at 6:15 a.m. and walked about a half mile to the bus stop, where a twenty-minute ride deposited me within a block of the school. I am tempted, here, to channel my father, waxing eloquent about how I walked to and from the bus in knee-deep snow, uphill—both ways. In truth, it was downhill in the morning and uphill on the way home, but this was Portland, Oregon, so it *was* raining most days.

Now that I was one of the cool kids, a senior saxophone player offered to pick me up in the morning with other "jazzers," sparing me the rainy walk and bus ride. His James Dean vibe was not limited to his unkempt hair or the tiny used sports car into which we crammed six or seven people—without seatbelts. A rebel without a clue, he drove sixty miles per hour on curvy, wet, residential streets, where no amount of gasping or pleading could slow him down. I felt lucky to arrive at school alive and took the bus thereafter, further galvanizing my sadly unadventurous self-image.

My three years with the Wilson jazz band, initially as fourth trumpet and later as pianist and leader, were transformative. Not long after I took over as pianist in my junior year, our teacher started playing hooky from the early morning rehearsals. After a few months, he abandoned the group to my leadership, affording me an extraordinary opportunity to hone my rehearsal and aural skills. I was also selecting the repertoire and trying my hand at arranging, all of which taught me boatloads I could never have learned in a classroom.

But something about the pairing of jazz and me didn't fit. Our parents were belt-and-suspenders types, driving home their play-it-safe philosophy at every opportunity. My brother and sister, both faithful children of the 60s, rebelled against these constraints. And I, seeing how that turned out, ran in the opposite direction, always choosing the safest, least audacious path. With that mindset I should have loved the security and simplicity of scales and arpeggios.

But inexplicably I gravitated instead to the inherent unpredictability of jazz and rock.

At 17, when I was already playing semiprofessionally and doing little with my time other than music, my high school counselor asked what my plans for college and beyond looked like. I replied that I was thinking about law school and was dumbfounded when I heard what had come out of my mouth. I was so terrified of the unconventional, so doubtful of my own abilities, that I couldn't speak my true intentions aloud. Pulled left and right, I couldn't have said if I was my parents or my siblings. And it would be years before I understood that those two directions are not mutually exclusive, because discipline is not conformity and rebellion is not imagination.

Grandma Belle

My maternal grandmother was born Belle Bloom in Taunton, Massachusetts, in 1895. She hoped to become an opera singer, but in the second decade of the twentieth century the road to an operatic career still led through Europe. So when a bullet struck down Archduke Franz Ferdinand, igniting World War I, her dream died with him.

She married Louis Gevurtz—the aforementioned enforcer of family secrecy—in 1919 but never forgot about the opera. Never making it to the stages of Europe, she was nonetheless the diva of our family, with four children, twelve grandchildren, and an army of great-grandchildren.

For Belle, music was like breathing—necessary and nonnegotiable. Without realizing it, she taught me about the joy of music. She showed me how to be part of it, and to let it be part of me. She quietly guided my understanding that music isn't about intellectual machinations or ego but about how the music speaks to you, and, finally, how you might learn to speak through it.

In the spring of 1973, I turned 16 and obtained my driver's license. This was, by coincidence, the same year my grandmother gave up driving due to her failing eyesight. By this time I was deeply involved

The extended Gevurtz family one year before the author was born, 1956. Itkin family at far left. Louis and Belle Gevurtz at center, standing.

in jazz and show music, and the last thing I wanted for a 16th birthday was to chauffeur my grandmother to symphony concerts. I thought of her as little more than our very short, very wrinkled matriarch (think Yoda with a great cheesecake recipe). But if I wanted access to a family car, I was going. So the deal was made, the tickets purchased, and in the fall of 1973 Grandma and I began attending concerts of the Oregon Symphony.

On the first outing, I was as dressed up as my I'm-way-too-cool-for-this attitude would allow, and I immediately recognized that I was out of my element. Not only was I decades younger than the next oldest person in the hall (a phenomenon that, sadly, hasn't changed much in the intervening half century), but I was, as my mother had warned, terribly underdressed. These people, whoever they were, took this seriously. And whatever was in store for me would be unlike anything in my experience.

While growing up I had heard the Portland Junior Symphony (now the Portland Youth Philharmonic), an orchestra of talented young people under the direction of local icon Jacob Avshalomov. As I understood it from bits of adult conversation, the Portland Junior Symphony was a marvel and the equal of nearly any professional orchestra. They were, in fact, very good, but civic pride might have overstepped reality just a bit.

My extended family attended the Junior Symphony's concerts because my cousin played trumpet in the group. He was the guy who everyone thought would end up a musician. At 16 he earned a spot in one of the country's premiere youth orchestras, and he had the musician's unruly temperament to boot. But it was not to be. Instead, he enjoyed a fine career as a physician, one of the few paths (the others being musician, actor, accountant, and lawyer) looked upon with favor in Jewish families.

As the iconic good child, I wanted to skirt conflict by doing as I'd been asked. But I had no desire to attend the symphony every month. A dramatic, instantaneous transformation from wannabe rocker to classical geek makes a great story, but it's not mine. And while the seeds were firmly planted on these outings, they were some years growing strong roots.

I have little memory of specific pieces played or great artists who performed while I sat next to my grandmother at the Oregon Symphony. My recollections are most vivid in terms of the music itself. The sounds and ideas enter and transform us if we allow them, and this was how Grandma heard the music. She did not analyze or criticize, but neither did she passively let the sound contact her eardrums and be forgotten. She heard music by letting it inside, an ability far in my future. Unlike my father—who enjoyed live music but whose closed eyes signaled a nap rather than concentration—Grandma's fluttering lids indicated a state of rapture and openness unlike anything I had witnessed. Faint sounds periodically emanated from her closed lips, a sign she was following the music and humming along in her mind.

My God! I thought, *Is this what music is supposed to do? I thought it was about playing the right notes.*

It took me years of study and apprenticeship to emulate Belle's brilliant simplicity in my relationship to music: Let it in, allow it to touch the most vulnerable part of you, then release it back into the world, new and changed.

When our concertgoing relationship began, I was already deeply involved in learning about, and trying my hand at, orchestration and composition, so the palette of sounds in a big orchestra fascinated me. Awestruck by the possibilities, I began to understand the breadth of this sonic universe as compared with the meager fare in the school and theater orchestras for which I had been writing.

When the music began, I felt driven to write down what I heard. Tracing short sections of music staff on empty areas in the program, I catalogued the different instrumental combinations and noted novel harmonic, rhythmic, and melodic ideas. After each concert I tore out the pages, saving them and referring to them later as I learned more about orchestration and repertoire.

In the late 1990s, I found those scribblings tucked away at my parents' home in Oregon. Gazing at my scrawl was like looking into the past, seeing the ideas of great composers filtered through my inexperienced, 16-year-old brain. Now I picture Grandma Belle and me sitting inches apart but divided by light-years in our responses to the music. I scribbled away, a pseudo-intellectual, while she basked, reveled, and felt. Somewhere, somehow, someday, I would have to fit the two pieces together.

During our comings and goings, grandma often talked about opera. I heard her, but I didn't get it. Talking about opera is, as the saying goes, like dancing about architecture. But the thrill of opera, however foreign to me at 16, was percolating inside me somewhere, waiting for its moment to surface. It did so, quite by accident, during my freshman year at the University of the Pacific.

One Saturday afternoon in spring 1976 I found myself with nothing to do. I could have read the music history text I'd hardly opened, worked on overdue compositions, read the novels assigned in my literature class, or practiced the piano. But from my perspective I had nothing to do, so I set off on a bold adventure.

I smuggled a big cup of coffee into the music library, randomly pulled a score and a recording from the shelves—I'd heard the words *La Boheme* somewhere—and headed for the listening room. A reading of the synopsis and some of the Italian text complete, I turned back to the first page, donned the headphones, dropped the needle, and promised myself I wasn't moving until the fat lady sang. My newly acquired singer pals at college said opera was great, and I was going to find out why.

If asked to list my most important musical experiences, primary among them would be my first orchestra concert as a professional, my first Beethoven's Ninth, my first Mahler's Second, my inaugural concert as music director of the Arkansas Symphony, conducting *Peter Grimes* at Indiana University, and that muggy California afternoon in the Quonset hut we called the music library.

Hearing *La Boheme* for the first time, I was overcome by the discovery that any human creation could be so beautiful, perfect, and transformative. With no guide beyond dumb luck, I selected the recent (1972) recording with Mirella Freni and Luciano Pavarotti, conducted by Herbert Von Karajan. From beginning to end, their performances, and Von Karajan's leadership, seemed to my young ears the definition of incandescent perfection. And in one of those rare moments when our youthful judgment is proved correct, that recording stands the test of time as one of the greatest.

On my next visit home, I told grandma about my discovery. Immediately, in her soft, 80-year-old voice, she began to croon the aria from *La Boheme*, "Mi chiamano Mimi." I couldn't believe it. She knew about this all along and had kept it secret? But she hadn't. She had led me to the water, but the choice to drink had to be mine alone.

Belle had *Opera News* delivered every week to my dorm. Her gift was partly responsible for my five-year custom of listening to the Saturday afternoon Met radio broadcasts. During those years no

Belle Gevurtz, c. 1980. Photo by Hank Itkin.

social event or obligation could pry me away from my ritual. It was like observing Shabbat, but with strangers screaming in Italian.

By the time I left the University of the Pacific for the Eastman School of Music in 1978, it was increasingly difficult for Grandma to go to the symphony. Her eyes were bad, as was her arthritis. But whenever my mother told her she didn't need to go if she wasn't up to it, Grandma would respond, "My arthritis hurts just as much at home, so let's go and enjoy the music."

But there was substantially more to her aches and pains than arthritis.

In the early 70s, while visiting family in Palm Springs, she was in a disastrous car accident from which she was not expected to recover. From the outset of her hospitalization, we were told that even if she did survive, an elderly woman with multiple broken bones and other injuries would certainly not walk again. To keep this fragile little woman from contracting pneumonia, she was suspended from a device resembling a meat hook, attached beneath her sternum. This traumatic procedure was supposed to keep her lungs from collapsing and allow her ribs to heal in something approaching normal positions. They did heal, she did survive, and for many years afterward she walked just fine. We were hardly surprised.

Grandpa Louis had died in 1967, and by the mid-1980s my grandmother started to disappear a little bit at a time. I was the family's only remaining hope for producing a musician, and Belle never tired of hearing what was happening in my life. When I visited her, we always discussed my musical projects, but as the years went by this became increasingly difficult. As she passed 90, she had little memory of our symphony trips or even of her own musical experiences.

Then, on an otherwise unremarkable visit, a remarkable thing happened. I knelt next to her chair as we did in those days, hoping she might recognize me through her cataracts. As always she asked, repeatedly, what I was up to. I told her each time that I was a musician, a conductor, though I knew a minute or two later she would ask again.

The third or fourth time, she responded in a nostalgic tone, "I used to sing opera, you know."

I was pleased, and a bit stunned.

"I know," I smiled.

"*Tosca* was my favorite," she continued. Without another word she started to sing. In a low, small voice, but entirely recognizable, she sang the aria from *Tosca.* "Vissi d'arte, vissi d'amore"—I lived for art, I lived for love.

She sang the entire aria, every note from beginning to end, exactly as it should be. She remembered not only the notes but also every word of the Italian.

In that moment at her knee, I experienced the same awe I'd felt in that California Quonset hut. Her final lesson, however inadvertent, lives with me each day: Purity of musical intention, innocence of spirit, and the joy that comes from giving and receiving the gift of music cannot be faked.

The author with his father and brother following Mahler Symphony No. 2 in 1996, the weekend Belle passed.

In April 1996, forty-eight hours before I conducted my first Mahler's Symphony No. 2—the *Resurrection*—Belle died at the age of 100. Though we were two thousand miles apart, she was with me that weekend in the concert hall, as she's been with me for nearly thirty years every time I've stepped onto the stage.

By chance my parents and my brother were visiting Little Rock for the Mahler performance, so we were together when we got the news. Rather than dashing to the airport to catch a flight home, they stayed as planned, missing Grandma's funeral.

I was surprised by their decision, but Mom said, "She'd want us to be together, and she'd want us to share the music."

I'm certain my mother was right.

Barrie, the Furniture Man

Though he played many characters during nearly sixty years on the amateur and semiprofessional stage, my father, Barrie, was best known for one role: Sholem Aleichem's unlikely hero, Tevye the dairyman.

When I was young, he played the character several times in Arnold Perl's play *Tevye and His Daughters*, long before *Fiddler on the Roof* was even a glimmer in Broadway's eye.

At last, in 1972, *Fiddler on the Roof* was produced in the Northwest. Based on his experience with the character, Dad was a perfect fit for the role. But logical as it may have seemed, several hurdles existed between him and Tevye's musical incarnation.

Though not keen on the idea of auditioning, which he had not done in years, he subdued his pride. Dad being cast in the role surprised no one, but a bumpy road still lay ahead. *Fiddler on the Roof* is, after all, a musical—Dad's first since his student days. And though the role is designed for an actor who can sing somewhat, not the other way around, he was still expected to sing the right notes at the right time.

Dad had a pleasant singing voice, which was not surprising since he possessed the instantly recognizable, mellifluous baritone speaking voice that made him a favorite for commercial voice-over work. The notes of Tevye's music were well within his range and he could sing in tune—with himself. Singing in the same key as the accompaniment was a different matter. At age 14 I was enlisted to help him learn the notes, saving time and potential embarrassment in rehearsal. For several weeks we got together for an hour each day in the narrow window between his return from the furniture store and his departure for rehearsal.

I would begin playing the accompaniment—boom-chuck, boom-chuck—and Dad would sing, "If I were a rich man," almost invariably in the wrong key. I would change the key, but no matter where I played, he sang elsewhere.

Frustrated, he repeatedly asked why the orchestra couldn't play in the key where he was singing. It was hard for him to accept a 14-year-old's explanation about why he needed to pick one key and stick with it. Eventually we made progress and Dad learned to hear the accompaniment with a more discerning ear.

One would assume that my days of helping a singer find the right notes are far behind me, but that supposition is somewhat optimistic.

Despite their often-repeated reputation, most professional singers are diligent and well-trained musicians. Unfortunately, there are outliers, so helping my father at 14 turned out to be a preview of coming attractions.

By the time the show reached dress rehearsals, he could find the first pitch of each song nearly every time. In his defense, this task was more challenging onstage than in our living room. Not only was it difficult to hear the orchestra from the stage, but the semipro band often played out of tune, so there were moments when anyone would have had trouble locating the correct note.

On opening night, as Dad's first song approached, Mom's fingers were wrapped so tightly around my forearm she nearly cut off the circulation. The orchestra started and Dad began to sing—in the wrong key. I was panic-stricken. My first coaching job and I had failed! But the nightmare lasted only a phrase or two. Then, as though planned from the outset, he drifted into the correct key, and all was right with the world.

Of the dozens of plays in which he appeared, only one other was a musical. Most movie musicals are adaptations of Broadway shows (*The Music Man*, *West Side Story*, *The Sound of Music*, etc.), but there are exceptions. Among the most notable is the 1958 hit *Gigi*, starring Leslie Caron, Maurice Chevalier, Louis Jourdan, and Hermione Gingold and directed by Vincent Minelli, with a gorgeous score by Frederick Loewe.

From the time he was decades too young to play the part, Dad dreamed of a stage version of *Gigi* so he could play Honoré, the role created by Chevalier. In 1973 the film was adapted for the Broadway stage, and in the late 70s the same theater that had produced *Fiddler* staged the new *Gigi*.

By the time Dad took the stage as Honoré Lachaille, I was at school in California and could no longer lend my services as an in-home coach. His Achilles' heel in *Gigi* was the fact that several new songs had been written for the stage version, and some songs that appeared in the movie had been altered. This meant, to his eternal consternation,

Barrie Itkin's acting headshot. The mustache was a temporary anomaly.

that he couldn't learn the music by simply memorizing what he heard in the film.

I never let Dad forget how embarrassing it is to be a professional musician whose father can barely match pitch. He knew I was joking—I hope—though he never entirely accepted the fact that this was his problem and not the fault of the pianist.

Watching my father onstage, I learned about expression and communication in ways no music school could ever teach. I remember lying prone on the lighting rail, looking down from thirty feet above the stage, watching him do *Fiddler* for the umpteenth time. From that awkward vantage point, I tried to understand how he manipulated the audience to feel every joy and sorrow along with him—trying, also, to comprehend the gap between artifice and truth. His acting method, learned decades earlier in New York and Los Angeles, spawned an outpouring of emotion that seemed to me crafted rather than genuine. This disparity between the real and the

The author's father onstage in Tennessee Williams's *The Night of the Iguana*.

artificial would later help to define my direction as a musician, but the lessons had a downside, as well. I was getting my first tutorial on the dilemma of separating onstage Dad from at-home Dad; they seemed disturbingly alike.

But for all our parents' flaws (and every parent has them) there were many valuable lessons, as well. In our widely separated teenage years, my brother and I were both afforded the "opportunity" to work summers in the delivery department at the furniture store. The experience of doing manual labor all day, surrounded by teamsters whose language, opinions, and behavior shocked me, was not optional. Dad undoubtedly thought this would toughen us up, instill a solid work ethic, and give us an appreciation for the educated, white-collar life toward which we were striving. And guess what? He was right.

Suzanne Itkin with her children on the Oregon coast, c. 1962.

Barrie Itkin with his children, c. 1970.

My generation tends to view the millennials as soft, whiny, and entitled. And I suspect this is also how the Greatest Generation (my parents) saw *their* children. Naturally, I think we're right and my parents were wrong, but that's probably true of every generation. Similarly, my parents thought the music of the 60s and 70s was a hideous noise, and I think most of the popular music of the last twenty years is unoriginal, meaningless rubbish.

The difference, this time, is that while our kids applaud the unique artistry of Rihanna, Taylor Swift, BTS, and Ariana Grande, my contemporaries were talking about The Beatles, Carol King, Earth, Wind, and Fire, Aretha Franklin, Elton John, Chicago, Stevie Wonder, The Beach Boys, Jimmy Hendricks, Simon and Garfunkel, and a host of other greats. On *this* subject my generation *is* right, and our kids are wrong. And that's really all there is to say.

Trying to Be Like Dad

Though I enjoyed it, I knew acting was not my path. I wasn't tall, I wasn't handsome, and, frankly, I wasn't very good. But the theater was in our DNA, and a few minor obstacles weren't going to keep me from trying my hand at the family business. More important, years as an actor and singer taught me what it means to communicate and connect with an audience and the qualities of grace and professionalism onstage.

By seventh grade I had taken acting classes for several years and had performed in shows both with and for children. One day Dad mentioned that an upcoming semiprofessional production required a boy between 10 and 12 years old. I was at the audition in a heartbeat and, much to my surprise, was cast as Roger in Edward Albee's *Everything in the Garden*—four weeks of rehearsal and a seven-week run.

I don't know if my father was unfamiliar with the play or simply didn't want to make an issue of it, but this piece is definitely R-rated, despite containing none of the raunchy language or violence found in many contemporary Broadway dramas. The play revolves around suburban housewives who balance their family budgets by dabbling in the oldest profession, and the story's central couple has a son—me.

Nearly a decade later, as a young adult, I would still be somewhat underinformed regarding relationships and sex. But in seventh grade, this was true on a grand scale. It's not that I didn't understand about the birds and the bees, but subtle language about suburban prostitution went way over my head. It was method acting without the method, because the son wasn't supposed to know what was going on anyway. I knew my stage "mother" was in trouble because my "father" had found a lot of cash stashed in a drawer. But apart from that, I was in the dark.

Not long after rehearsals commenced, my (real) mother discovered what the play was about. Avoiding conflict, as always, Dad had earlier offered an abridged summary, something like, "He plays someone's son, I don't know." Now familiar with the details, Mom wasn't angry, but she wasn't pleased, either.

My parents cannot have been thinking clearly when they decided to bring my grandmother, Belle, to opening night. Grandma retained an early twentieth-century suspicion about theater people even though her beloved son-in-law, my father, was one of them. And her concerns were not eased when she was dragged to this "dirty" play. What my father chose to do was his business, but getting her grandson mixed up in this nonsense was a bridge too far. Outside my hearing, Grandma voiced her disapproval to my parents, and it wouldn't be the only time. In the spring of 1972, when a freshman in high school, I landed my first major role in a semiprofessional production.

I became aware of *You're a Good Man, Charlie Brown* at age 11 and had dreamed of playing Snoopy ever since. Heedless of the fact that this was an open audition for real, grown-up actors, I dove in. Following a daunting process lasting nearly a week, I got the role and was soon in rehearsal with a cast who were all in their mid to late 20s. At 14 I was a little out of the loop both socially and artistically.

The director and choreographer, a petite powerhouse of a woman named Sheri, ran a tight ship and insisted that every line be memorized perfectly before she would begin staging a scene. This led to some long, frustrating nights if one or more of us arrived less than perfectly prepared.

In the Red Baron scene, Snoopy is the only character on stage, fantasizing in a lengthy monologue that he is a WWI flying ace. I assumed that since I was the only one called to rehearsal the director would not be so inflexible on the memorization issue. I was wrong.

The first thing Sheri said after walking into the theater was "double-time," meaning she wanted me to recite the speech as fast as possible, proving it was unerringly committed to memory. In the second or third sentence I omitted one word, and she stopped me—"Top!" meaning, "start over."

On the second try I made it to the fourth sentence, then drew a long breath—an unsuccessful ruse designed to allow myself an extra second to think.

"Top!"

After sixty minutes, with each effort worse than the one before, I was in tears. But she wasn't finished. Sheri kept at it for another half hour, then suggested we "take a break" and walked out of the theater. After fifteen minutes she returned and, without referencing the preceding events, staged the scene. Half an hour later, with my 14-year-old wits in tatters, I was on the way home.

It took a few years for the wisdom to penetrate, but I learned a lot that day—lessons that some of us are not fortunate enough to absorb until much later.

Lesson 1: Being "kind of" prepared for rehearsal is an oxymoron; either you are, or you aren't.

Lesson 2: The discipline of our craft is not negotiable. It is the foundation of everything we do.

Lesson 3: Those who pick and choose when they will be prepared and when they will fake it will not be professional performers for long.

The author as Henrick in Sondheim's *A Little Night Music*, 1977.

I saw the rock musical *Godspell* in 1972 at Ford's Theater in Washington, DC, and fell head over heels. In the fall of 1974, one of the smaller Portland theaters auditioned a local production, and I was ready to rock. The director and choreographer, Richard Hurst, was a man with whom I'd worked previously, and the music director was Vera Long, the same woman who had led *You're a Good Man, Charlie Brown*. I hoped my familiarity with both individuals would help my chances, but it turned out to be a double-edged sword.

By that time I was in some demand as a percussionist for theater productions. I had just finished playing drums for *Anything Goes*, with Vera as music director, in the same theater where *Godspell* was being produced. A week before the *Godspell* audition, Vera asked me to play drums for the show, which left me in a bind: say yes and take the sure thing or roll the dice at the audition.

Nearly a hundred amateur and semipro actors flooded the theater on the first day of auditions. Every man there danced better than I did and looked more like the mid-20s hippies the show requires. Each day more people were excused, but with each cut I seemed to be moving farther toward the bottom of the pecking order. I was stunned a few days later to find I had been cast, as I was sure my refusal to play in the band and/or the strengths of the other men auditioning would be my undoing.

I was correct that the other men were superior dancers and had a better look for the show, but I had one thing they didn't. Near the end of the show, when voices are likely to be fatigued, one of the disciples must sustain a D above high C. And this was before regional theaters routinely amplified every performer—meaning we had to sing over the rock band unaided. So thanks to my dependable high D, I was in.

In my zeal to conquer the audition, I hadn't given much thought to a 17-year-old Jewish kid spending twelve weeks singing about Jesus. Though it was an oversight at the time, the reason I didn't ponder the issue is still valid: it's theater, and in the theater we do what the work demands of us regardless of our personal relationship to the subject matter.

The same is true in music. I've been asked many times how I can put my heart into the vast and important body of repertoire inspired by Christian faith and practice. The answer is simple: this is art, and my spiritual beliefs are not relevant. More important, from my perspective, is the fact that the Verdi *Requiem*, the *St. John Passion*, *Godspell*, or the songs in a Christmas pops concert speak to ideas and ideals understood instinctively by all people, regardless of what religion, or lack of religion, they practice.

My personal sanguinity notwithstanding, I also hadn't given any thought to my family's reaction. For the most part, and despite the director's scheduling of group church visits for the cast, my parents dealt with it in stride. Their attitude suggested they didn't consider *Godspell* an existential threat to the People Israel—a good call on their part. My parents shrugged off my quasi-religious theatrical experience until we ran head-on into an event that would live in infamy in Itkin family lore.

About two weeks before the show opened, I realized that the final dress rehearsal was scheduled for Kol Nidre night, the start of Yom Kippur, the most important day in the Jewish calendar. Up to that point in history, no Itkin child living at home had ever missed a High Holiday service. It was unthinkable.

One evening at dinner, I airily dropped the fact that I wasn't free the night of Kol Nidre. I hoped against hope that the remark would be met with an equally casual response, "Well, if you've got rehearsal, what can you do?" No such luck.

Glancing sidelong at my mother, whether for moral support or permission I couldn't say, Dad told me it was out of the question. And his flat refusal to discuss the situation sparked the only unpleasant scene with my parents I can recall. There was screaming and yelling, stomping out of rooms, and doors slamming—a real soap opera.

Though the argument and its subject matter were inconsequential in the big picture, one remark from that high-drama exchange has stuck with me like a stone in my shoe. My father was a kind, gentle man. Unfortunately, in fraught situations he had the habit of choosing his words as though he were in a play, where the dramatic moment is paramount and any consequences for what he said evaporated when he stepped off the stage. I was about to find myself, once again, trying to figure out if this was actor-Dad or home Dad speaking.

Frustrated by my stubbornness, he announced, "If you do this, you won't really be my son anymore."

That is a watershed declaration even in a religious household, and we were not one. Our observances were the Jewish equivalent of attending church on Christmas and Easter, so his threat made no sense. This paralyzing moment was just my father's ham-fisted way of trying to please my mother and close the deal with a dramatic gesture. A quarter century later, he confided that he didn't believe in God and never had, throwing the *Godspell* versus Yom Kippur battle into an even more suspicious light.

When the smoke cleared, it was obvious I had lost, destined to be tossed out of the show, the family, or both. But as with so many things in adolescence, the situation was not nearly as dire as it appeared. Terrified, I spoke with the director who, following unconvincing attempts at intimidation, made lemonade from lemons by adjusting the rehearsal schedule to allow for a night off on Yom Kippur. I should have realized it would all work out. But in my anxiety, I had failed to recognize two things. First, the director was a reasonable guy. And second, there still wasn't anyone else who could sing the high D.

So I was not excommunicated from the faith, the family, or the show, and everyone was happy. Well, almost everyone.

What we failed to foresee, again, was Grandma. Picturing it now, it's difficult to imagine my Jewish, opera-loving grandmother sitting for two hours in a small, hot theater while a dozen actors clad in tie-dye sang loud rock music about Jesus. But it happened—and Mom, Dad, and I were a long time living it down.

Adding injury to insult, when the show was over Grandma stumbled down the crumbling concrete stairs leading out of the theater. Alerted in the dressing room, I flew to the lobby and out the door. I found her sitting on the bottom stair, calm and alert, holding paper towels against a nasty gash in her calf and telling everyone to stop making such a fuss.

The task of theater is illusion, creating a smoke-and-mirrors universe where up is down, black is white, and fiction is fact. But life can feel equally insubstantial. Our memories of childhood are often inaccurate, colored, and redacted by time and emotion. From this vantage point, I peer through the haze and pick out moments of my father's blatant theatricality. And while so doing, I cannot help but wonder about the rest. Were our visits to synagogue and his veiled threat to disown me the only performances he gave, or were there others? Was he the funny, easygoing man I remember, or was it all a

The author (*seated*) as Henrick in Sondheim's *A Little Night Music*, 1977.

role? Was it an illusion all the way to the end—right to the moment when, standing over his wife's grave, he magically uttered a farewell worthy of Shaw, one perfect tear threatening to break loose down his cheek?

It's not important that I don't know the answer. What horrifies me is the idea that perhaps he didn't either.

I am not a psychoanalyst, and I don't know if my father's infatuation with the stage was pure love of theater or a desperate need to be someone else. I'm not certain if his strange pronouncement, "you won't really be my son anymore," was genuine or just more theatrics. But I do know he rarely looked honestly into the mirror, rarely took stock of his words and choices—a trick I learned only too well.

They say that no matter what we do, we grow up to be our parents. But the struggle to escape that destiny and shape our own path starts with a candid look at ourselves. It begins with the admission that we have not changed—that we are who we have always been.

The Once and Future Tenor

For a long time, I battled the stigma of being a singer turned conductor. The slur implies that singers are musically ignorant, not very smart, and unfit for maestro status. This bias—ridiculous at its core—is somewhat justified, though not usually the fault of the individual, because many undergraduate singers received little or no musical training during their precollege years.

Bearing this cross, I began my conducting training at a considerable disadvantage, having to be better than my peers just to be equal in the perception of others. The irony is that I am not a singer turned conductor. I am a percussionist, pianist, and trumpeter turned conductor, turned singer, who then returned to what he does best. Despite these obstacles, being a singer has provided me with a wealth of valuable experiences I would never trade for a more traditional path. My time as a singer connected me with wonderful colleagues and gave me a unique perspective on both vocal and orchestral music.

Toward the end of my junior year in high school, I landed my first opportunity to conduct in a semiprofessional situation. I was the percussionist for *How to Succeed in Business Without Really Trying* when an altercation took place between the conductor and the director. Overnight the conductor was gone, and we were leaderless less than two weeks before opening a new production.

Summoning chutzpah that amazes me even now, I maneuvered myself from the drum set to the podium. The management allowed me to take over rehearsals with the caveat that I had to convince the musicians to play those sessions without pay. Then, if the group was up to snuff under my leadership, I would open the show as conductor and the orchestra would receive their back pay. Contrary to expectations—that I was a placeholder who would be removed after the opening weekend—I stayed on for the show's entire seven-week run.

At that time the theater's vocal director was Ruth Dobson, a woman of substantial ability and background who was also one of the most respected voice teachers in the area. She, along with

How to Succeed's director, evaluated the rag-tag orchestra's progress during my first days of rehearsal, causing me inexpressible levels of anxiety.

When preparing the orchestra for an opera or other music with vocalists, I often find myself unconsciously singing along during rehearsal. Apparently I already had this habit fifty years ago, because a week or two after the show opened, my mother received an unexpected phone call. While checking up on my rehearsal, Ruth had heard me sing a passage and was impressed with the natural quality of my voice. Further, she told my mother she would like to teach me if I was interested. This was a complete, and not entirely welcome, surprise.

Among my friends at the time, there was a line in the sand between "us" and "them." That is, there were musicians and there were singers. We were a highly segregated musical community where young musicians rarely crossed the line. But despite this blockade, I was emboldened by one line-crosser of my early acquaintance; my friend Benjamin Whiteley, a talented singer and pianist, went on to an impressive career as a Broadway conductor.

Adding to my line-crossing concerns was the fact that in elementary school I'd been dubbed a "listener." That was the term for children whose singing gave every indication they were tone deaf. Those days were long gone by the time Ruth phoned my mother, but I assumed I still had the same ugly, crackly voice of a sixth grader. I also thought I had a very small baritone range. I look back in wonder at the serendipity of her phone call and the fact that she took me under her wing to show me that, to my amazement, I was a tenor.

Ruth was invaluable in helping me navigate the high D in *Godspell*, and my all-too-brief time studying with her culminated with the Oregon state solo contest in the spring of 1975. I resisted entering, but she finally wore me down. Classical singing was my dirty little secret, not something I wanted paraded around. I'd never sung anywhere more public than her studio recitals, so entering the competition would mean exposing myself to an audience of voice teachers and peer singers, not to mention being outed as one of "them."

The author with friends Ben Whiteley and Gary Harper, clowning as usual, c. 1975.

After winning the local stage of the competition, I headed to the statewide contest, held that year in Bend, Oregon, in the high desert about three hours from Portland. Against my teacher's recommendation, I sang a different song than the one with which I'd won the local round. The new piece was Luigi Dallapiccola's transcription of Alessandro Scarlatti's "Gia il Sole dal Gange," an exercise in florid, elegant singing that taxed my six months of lessons to their limit.

Beverly Sills, the great American soprano, once opined that anyone who says they're not nervous before singing is either stupid or lying. Experienced artists channel those jitters into a heightened state of focus that enhances rather than diminishes their performance. This is a skill learned over time, and just because we have not mastered it at age 17 does not mean we're in the wrong profession.

On the other hand, our bodies are wise and happy to tell us when we're going wrong. If we drink too much, we get sick and learn to exercise moderation. If one glass of wine makes us ill, however, perhaps that's a message that alcohol is not for us. Despite being panic-stricken, I acquitted myself adequately at the state solo contest. I wouldn't realize until years later that the debilitating stage fright I always suffered before singing, which I never experienced when conducting, was a message I needed to heed.

But the other tenors were more than just adequate. Another senior amazed everyone singing, "Vesti la Giubba" from *Pagliacci.* Only in hindsight could I understand what a bizarre choice that was for a teenager. Nonetheless, by 18-year-old standards he was incredible, singing with a clear, even tone and showing off secure high notes. In addition, there was one other tenor who was at least as good as I was, so it seemed third place was my best-case scenario. I had expected the state competition to be an embarrassment, so a bronze medal didn't sound so bad.

The awards ceremony dragged on like a Yom Kippur service, and I thought they'd never reach our part. When it finally arrived, my heart was in my throat, knowing third place was my only shot. They announced the bronze medal winner and, lo and behold, it was a guy I hadn't figured in the mix at all. I was crestfallen. With two winners yet to be announced, there were still two tenors who'd clearly bested me. They announced second place and, sure enough, it was the boy I'd figured to edge me out. No one doubted who the winner would be.

Then it happened. They announced the gold medal winner: me. It was absurd. There was no universe in which I beat the boy who sang like an angel. I was euphoric on the drive back to Portland, but despite my elation I couldn't shake the feeling that something was wrong. Had the judges slept through wonder boy's performance? Had they disqualified him for some unknown reason?

Like most things that seem too good to be true, it was.

Two days later my high school orchestra conductor beckoned me into his office. He closed the door—never a good sign—and told me he'd had a call from the state competition director saying there had been a mistake. Vesti la Giubba boy's scores were not tabulated at the close of competition, and I had come in second. But rather than revoke my medal, they issued a duplicate first prize to the other singer. Officially, and as far as any of my school peers knew, it was a tie for first place. I guess after fifty years I can come clean.

~~~~~ From Two Sticks to One ~~~~~

There's an old joke: What do you do with a drummer who can't keep time? Take away one of his sticks and tell him he's a conductor.

Though focused on improving my piano and improvisation skills in the jazz band back in my sophomore year, I was offered my first paying job as a drummer—The Tiny Bubbles notwithstanding—in spring 1973. From the 1960s to the 1980s, Portland's historic Benson Hotel was home to the only professional dinner theater in the city. A gifted harpist one year my junior, Jenny Lindner was playing a production of *The Fantasticks* there, and she gave my name to the music director when a more experienced percussionist backed out. Jenny and I attended different high schools, but we'd become acquainted via the young musicians' grapevine—without the assistance of social media—and I was flattered she had recommended me.

Jenny became a dear friend and colleague, and she played for the first several productions I conducted during the following two years. Though she arrived before I did, we would be classmates at the Eastman School of Music as well, beginning in 1978.

Our professional careers never dovetailed due to her stay-at-home nature and my many wanderings. Nonetheless, we were graced with one last opportunity to make music together nearly forty years later. In July 2017 Jenny came to Idaho to play in the orchestra where I was music director for the McCall Summerfest. At our opening concert, we played Rimsky-Korsakov's *Scheherazade*, a work we had both performed many times but never on the same stage.

Scheherazade has been one of my favorites since listening to my mother play it endlessly on the stereo while we did our Saturday

morning chores. It is a tale of teenage love and glorious adventures, some of which come to sudden, tragic conclusions.

In Idaho it was a bittersweet performance. Two mornings later the festival's president phoned to tell me Jenny had passed away in her sleep. She was 59 years old. I was 60, and with the first passing of a childhood friend, I was forced to accept the fact that we were no longer teenagers.

Not long after *The Fantasticks* in 1973, I was asked to play percussion for other professional and semiprofessional productions, including *Anything Goes*, *Carousel*, *Funny Girl*, *Celebration*, *Dames at Sea*, and *Jacques Brel Is Alive and Well and Living in Paris*. In the spring of my junior year, I was engaged to play for the 1960s Broadway hit *How to Succeed in Business Without Really Trying*. Through the Byzantine series of events described earlier, I ended up conducting *How to Succeed* instead of playing in the orchestra. The Portland

Civic Theater then asked me to conduct Stephen Sondheim's sophisticated concept musical *Company*—I realized only years later that the dialogue about sex and drugs had gone completely over my 17-year-old head—followed by the PG-rated *Guys and Dolls*.

Just before *Guys and Dolls* closed, I celebrated my 18th birthday. So with around fifty semipro performances as a drummer behind me, and an equal number conducting, it was time to go to college.

Chapter 2

Figuring It Out

~~~~~ California Dreamin' ~~~~~

When applying to music school as a composition major, as I did in spring 1975, a prospective student must also audition in a performance area—a specific instrument or voice. I intended to audition on percussion, which I had played for nearly ten years. But Ruth, my teacher, convinced me to declare voice as my performance area.

Despite being a composition and music theory major, I was far more interested in singing when I arrived at the University of the Pacific that fall. My first teacher at UOP, Shirley Thompson, was precisely what one might imagine when conjuring the exotic, sophisticated, late-career opera singer. Though American born, she had trained and spent her career in Europe and played the expatriate role to the hilt. A short, solid mezzo-soprano with straight, jet-black hair, she sported the eye makeup and bearing of the diva she was.

Despite my elementary technical level, we connected immediately. I adored Madame Flora, a nickname I gave her halfway through my freshman year after she appeared as a guest artist in a student production of Menotti's *The Medium*. In the title role, she played Madame Flora, a con artist hosting bogus seances whose personal demons drive her to believe the spirits are real. Worse than any horror movie, and bolstered by Menotti's extraordinary music, her performance was so frightening I was afraid to go to my next lesson. After that I never called her Miss Thompson again. She will always be Madame Flora to me.

One of the many things Madame Flora improved was my nonexistent upper register. This difficulty is common for an 18-year-old tenor, because many of us don't have the high notes kick in until we're in our early 20s. She was so good that one day near the end of my freshman year I managed to sing some high C's in a practice room. They were, perhaps, not God's gift to music, but they were there, and I was very excited. (This discovery may seem chronologically backward considering the importance of the high D in *Godspell*, but a high note in a rock musical is not the same as doing it *legit*.)

My high C discovery occurred only a few weeks after my first exploration of *La Boheme* in the music library, and since that first flirtation with opera I had delved deeper. Among those that caught my fancy was Verdi's *Il Trovatore*, with its famous tenor aria featuring seven high C's. The day after my practice room breakthrough, I began learning the aria.

Won't Madame Flora be impressed, I thought, *when I bring it to my next lesson?*

One of the many things about which I still knew nothing was the concept of Fach. It's a German term that essentially means "all tenors are not created equal." When I learned about Fach at my next lesson, I felt I'd been scammed, the victim of an operatic bait and switch.

In addition to being classified by range (soprano, tenor, etc.), singers are also categorized by vocal weight and color. Put them together and you get the Fach factor. A singer's Fach is usually described with an adjective preceding their voice type. For example, one might be a dramatic tenor or a coloratura soprano. At my loudest and heaviest, I was a leggiero (light) tenor, but Manrico of *Il Trovatore* is most certainly not.

Pumped up like a prize fighter, I strode into my next lesson, *Il Trovatore* at the ready. I told Madame Flora I'd brought something new and placed it on the music rack in front of her. She glanced at the score, looked at me, and released a howl of laughter that was surely heard at the opposite end of the building.

"*You're* going to sing this?" she gasped, fighting for breath, "This I've got to hear."

I was suddenly less excited about singing the piece, but I was too far in to get out. Trembling, and pretty sure my high C had fled, I sang.

When it was over, she said, "I have to admit, that was pretty good. Now get out!"

Grabbing the score off the piano, she headed through the door of her studio. Just outside she hurled the book down the staircase and gave me a look suggesting I was probably next. She wasn't angry. That was just how she made a point. At my next lesson I brought more appropriate repertoire, but she never called me by my name again. To Madame Flora I was always Manrico.

By my second year in California, I'd realized that the composition major was not for me. Perfectly mirroring my risk-averse personality, my writing was not weird enough to suit my instructors. My compositions radiated the fact that I was far more interested in the anatomy of instrumental and vocal ensembles than in creating cutting-edge music. Considering how things turned out, I guess that wasn't surprising.

In my sophomore year, I was cast in the tenor role for Mozart's *Cosi Fan Tutte*, to be produced the following fall. On the strength of this encouraging event, I reapplied to the Eastman School—this time as a voice major—and was accepted, matriculating the following January.

Picking a Lane

As a midyear, undergrad transfer student, I was assigned to the teacher nobody else wanted—a nice man who spoke almost no English and munched a smelly tuna sandwich throughout my lessons. After one semester I was accepted into the studio of the department chairman, John Maloy—a master teacher, role model, class clown, and all-around great human being. If you want the definition of real charm, it is a man who can refer to his wife as "Charlotte, the harlot" without anyone doubting he meant it with affection. As much as I'd learned from Madame Flora, it was Mr. Maloy who imparted a real understanding of the technique of the voice.

As fate would have it, during a portion of my four years with him, his studio also included a charming soprano named Renee. Despite an obvious abundance of talent, she was not the darling of the Eastman opera department and seldom got the big roles that make one a star at school. (The Eastman diva of the moment was another talented soprano whose story illustrates the outsized consequences of what may appear to be innocuous choices in young adulthood. After a meteoric start, this first-rate talent managed to screw and bad-mouth herself out of what could have been a fine career.)

After leaving Eastman my next several years were consumed with keeping my own life and sanity on track, so I lost touch with the world of opera—much to my grandmother's long-distance chagrin. One evening, several years after finishing school, I was flipping channels and stumbled across a live MET telecast of Verdi's *Otello*. What luck, I thought, and settled in to watch the rest of the performance.

Placido Domingo was singing the title role and, recent revelations notwithstanding, he was always one of my favorites. As the Act III conversation between Otello and Desdemona progressed, I realized I was having a strange déjà vu feeling. Then it hit me. The soprano looked amazingly like my old classmate Renee. How weird was that? At the conclusion the credits rolled, and my jaw went slack.

I knew she was doing well, but with my head buried deep in my own sand, I hadn't realized that my studio-mate, Renee Fleming, had become a star of that magnitude.

I immediately called another Eastman friend, "Oh, my God, you'll never believe this. I just saw Renee on the MET telecast singing Desdemona with Placido Domingo!"

My friend, a professional singer who had his finger on the pulse of that world, replied, incredulous, "No kidding. She's a monster star. Where have you been?"

I have always been thrilled, from afar, for her amazing and well-deserved success. My only regret is that we never reconnected as professional performers.

Coming to Eastman on the heels of a leading role at UOP was a bit of a comedown; I was back in the chorus. In my four years at Eastman, I was given only one leading role, Ernesto in Donizetti's *Don Pasquale*, conducted by David Effron, with whom I was also studying conducting. Mr. Effron had taken me into his graduate conducting class with some reluctance. I was, after all, a singer—you know, one of *them*—but he benevolently overlooked that defect in my character.

Mr. Effron was always supportive of my conducting, but that knife cut both ways. He was often derisive about my singing, sometimes in public, which was his ham-fisted way of pointing me in a different direction. His method aside, he was correct.

While I was working with him in my role as a singer, he did pay me one compliment. He mentioned that I made his job easier because I always seemed to have my eye on him at just the right time. The irony of his praise was that—being compelled to remove my glasses for the role—I could barely find him in the pit, let alone see if he was throwing a cue in my direction.

The period surrounding *Don Pasquale* was difficult. Though the experience boosted my confidence, I was already well along the path to accepting the fact that I would never be an opera singer. The evaluation of many knowledgeable people was correct: my voice was both too small and not sufficiently durable for opera on a big stage.

Adding to my personal doubts and David Effron's not-so-subtle attempts to redirect me, I began feeling ill during the final week of rehearsals. Two days before my first performance I made the mistake of mentioning my condition to Effron, who told me it was all in my head. In his defense there was ample justification for this response. Even I had to admit that my perfectly timed sore throat before nearly every singing performance was more than just coincidence. Paired with ongoing bouts of crippling stage fright, these illnesses were yet another message from the universe that I had, perhaps, chosen the wrong path.

This time, however, I was genuinely ill. I had mononucleosis and spent the ten days following the production in bed. But no one should be blamed for doubting I was sick, because I had sounded that warning once too often.

During the previous year, 1980–1981, the Eastman School was searching for a choral director, and this faculty vacuum left the choral conducting program devoid of graduate students. Nonetheless, in fall 1981 the school needed to provide Donald Neuen, the new director of choral studies, with an assistant. With no graduate choral conductors around, someone in administration decided that a singer and a conductor in the same body equals a choral conductor, and I was offered that assistantship during the second year of my master's degree.

But it's not that simple. Being a choral conductor isn't just waving your hands at singers instead of instrumentalists. It's a highly specialized craft requiring a unique skillset, much of which I did not yet possess. Ironically, this unexpected and questionable appointment was the single element that made the first four years of my professional life possible.

My year as assistant to the director of choral studies also propelled my ongoing quest to separate the genuine from the feigned. Ever since questioning my father's relationship to both acting and real life, I'd spent a great deal of time trying to locate the line between truth and showmanship.

Don Neuen was a real gentleman, but this didn't keep the two of us from getting along like two strange alley cats in a bag. While I'm sure I learned some things from Don, our fundamental differences as human beings and as musicians prevented me from being open to the entire experience.

Early in our association, Don took me into his office and offered sage wisdom to his doubtful protégé, saying, "David, a great choral conductor is half evangelist and half cheerleader."

Innocent as a lamb, I asked, "Which parts are musician or conductor?"

My question sent our relationship careening off a steep cliff. But despite my insolence, I am still haunted by the combined weight of his pronouncement and my question. Though I believe my father's theatrical motives were pure, Don's description struck close to home. And I found it difficult to toe the line as his assistant because, from my youthful vantage point, his ideas had nothing to do with our craft.

I've had the good fortune to work with several extraordinary choral conductors—including Robert Shaw, William Dehning, Jerry McCoy, and John Erwin—and what these artists do bears no resemblance to either evangelism or cheerleading. But as with my rock and roll adventures, no musical experience is without value. Sometimes, developing a strong sense of what we believe is wrong leads to our ultimate understanding of what is right.

Chapter 3

Four Years, Five Jobs

~~~~~ Out of the Frying Pan ~~~~~

In spring 1982, the last semester of my master's degree, I suddenly realized I had no idea what to do next. I wasn't ready for apprentice programs with big opera companies, and David Effron had discouraged me from applying for the doctoral program in orchestral conducting at Eastman. He recommended that, after seven years in college, I should get out into the real world for a while. It was the best advice I ever received. But I was annoyed—and scared.

My willful blindness during the preceding seven years had taken on Herculean proportions. Despite my ability to project an annoying degree of confidence, there was not one minute during which I truly believed I would have a career as a singer or conductor. Consequently, I'd neither thought about nor made tangible preparations for what would happen after graduation. I was being thrust, utterly unprepared, into the cold, cruel world, thoroughly convinced that I was unwanted and unemployable.

Goethe wrote, "At the moment of commitment, the entire universe conspires to assist you." At 16, brashly offering myself as a replacement conductor at the Portland Civic Theater, I'd already learned how accurate those words could be. And despite my consistent hesitation, I would discover their truth again and again in the years that followed. As my master's graduation approached, I was further inspired to action by my mother, who echoed Goethe: "You've been in college for seven years, now get off your ass and find a job."

I made a beeline for the school's careers center, the existence of which was unknown to me until that moment. In a closet-sized room along an out-of-the-way basement corridor, I scoured three-ring binders stuffed with job advertisements, but nothing seemed to fit my eclectic credentials.

Ready to give up, I stumbled on an ad from the Marist School in suburban Atlanta, a private, Catholic, seventh through twelfth grade school looking for a choir director with expertise in musical theater. While I didn't see myself as a choral conductor, I was, at that moment, graduate assistant to Donald Neuen in the Eastman choral program. Ironically, I looked as healthy on paper as a choral conductor as I appeared undernourished as an orchestral conductor.

Fed up with their band director's all-thumbs efforts to teach the choirs, the Marist School had set its sights on hiring a credentialed singer and choral conductor rather than a candidate with a music education degree, so I seemed like a shoo-in. And there was another weapon in my arsenal that sealed the deal. As our interview wrapped up, the principal mentioned their desire to start a strings program.

"Will that be a problem?" he asked.

I told him string instruments had never been a problem before, so I didn't see why they should be in the future.

My response was a bit disingenuous. I'd studied the violin several years earlier, but only for the purpose of being conversant in string techniques from the conductor's point of view. Needing to put my money where my mouth was, I spent the pre-Atlanta summer in Rochester, taking two violin lessons each week, practicing three hours a day, and working two part-time jobs to make ends meet.

Ecstatic at being offered the job, I called my parents. My father was genuinely pleased and, I suspect, somewhat relieved I wasn't staying in school any longer.

After absorbing the details, he asked, "Atlanta? In Georgia?"

His incredulity was understandable. West Coasters of my parents' generation, particularly among the Jews, thought of the South as the other side of the moon. At best Atlanta was a place to change planes on the way to Florida.

To my amazement, the following September I was an employed grownup, and the Southerners were welcoming and helpful to the new kid. I settled as smoothly as possible into duties for which I felt entirely unfit while finding additional employment singing at a big synagogue during the High Holidays and at the Episcopal cathedral during the rest of the year.

Over time my Northern roots began to show. Students whispered racist jokes they thought would amuse me, and when I gave a disapproving look, they offered the standard, "I don't mean anything by it." Parents mentioned "the war," and I was often confused. Where I grew up, "the war" meant World War II. In Atlanta of the 1980s, "the war" meant the War of Northern Aggression (a.k.a., the Civil War), and they talked about it like it happened last month and their immediate family members had taken part.

Cloning my most recent educational experience, I lectured to seventh and eighth graders about music history, expecting them to take notes and be tested on the information with no additional study aids provided. Avoiding this kind of stupidity is why would-be teachers get degrees in education and student teach before they are thrown into the deep end.

I valiantly tried to make music history cooler to teenagers by adding a section on rock and roll. However, at 26 I felt like a dinosaur when one of my junior high students asked, in complete sincerity, if it was true that Paul McCartney had been in a band before Wings.

My high schoolers liked me, but they weren't above conning me. Early in the year, a few boys asked if the school's prohibition against liquids on the stage could be overlooked during choir rehearsal. They needed water while singing, or so they said.

Eight months later, in a chat with a graduating senior, I learned the truth. Each time one of the boys raised his cup, he was not drinking, but spitting juice from the chewing tobacco tucked into his cheek. I don't know which was more ridiculous—that they indulged in this disgusting habit or that I fell for it.

My other major responsibility was the spring musical. First task: select a Broadway show the students could handle but that wouldn't offend the school's conservative sensibilities. I proposed Cole Porter's *Anything Goes*, a show I loved, in part because it had been my senior musical. The principal assigned another priest to read the script, and we were approved.

The cast and orchestra were doing a terrific job in rehearsal, having fun, and learning their music and stagecraft. Then, without warning, I was called into the principal's office, a location in which I found myself far too often for a variety of reasons upon which I would prefer not to dwell.

"I understand," he began, sternly, despite being only a few years my senior, "there is an out-of-wedlock child in this story?"

I smiled, realizing whatever he had heard was a misunderstanding.

"No," I said, "when the plot becomes knotty near the end, one of the couples puts on disguises and pretends the woman is pregnant so the man can avoid marrying someone else. It's all part of the comedy."

He didn't see the humor.

"But they refer to an unmarried woman being pregnant?"

"Well, yes, but—"

"You have to change it," he commanded.

I explained that I couldn't change it, because without that plot element the play has no resolution. And besides, I asked, why were we talking about this one week before opening night? Didn't the priest he'd assigned to approve the script read it?

Realizing we were at an impasse, he told me to do whatever I could to tone down references to out-of-wedlock pregnancy and then excused me from his office.

I changed a few lines to avoid repeated references to the taboo subject. Nonetheless, two weeks later he called me into his office and fired me. Technically, my contract was not renewed for the following year. Same thing.

By fortunate coincidence I had already applied for a position at Cottey College. After I moped around my apartment for a week trying to figure out how to tell my parents I'd been fired, the college called and offered me the job.

While working at the Marist School, I never needed a watch. School started at 8:15, and at 7:45 every morning I had an excruciating stomachache. I have never been so happy to be fired. That year I gained enormous respect for our colleagues who teach junior high and high school music. They're far braver than I am.

Beyond the obvious benefits of gainful employment, the only real upside to my year in Atlanta was the opportunity to work with Robert Shaw. Mr. Shaw was music director of the Atlanta Symphony and retained personal charge of the symphony's chamber choir, a group of thirty-two singers selected from the larger Atlanta Symphony Chorus. My work schedule did not allow time for the large choir, and Mr. Shaw was kind enough to make an exception, allowing me to audition solely for the chamber choir. Though the group did only two concerts that year, I treasure the unique opportunity to have worked with, and learned from, one of the legends of our craft.

The Missouri Blues

In August 1983 I moved from my swanky suburban Atlanta apartment into a filthy, falling-down, two-room rent house in Nevada (pronounced neh-VAY-duh), Missouri, that one of my new colleagues had helped procure from the town's sparse rental options. The tiny, ancient structure boasted dirty, threadbare carpet, loose wall paneling exposing meager insulation, no dishwasher, and no central heat or air conditioning.

The window-mounted air conditioner was in the bedroom, so I slept comfortably during the summer, though the rest of the house was sweltering. The heating unit, a small space heater mounted to the wall, was in the living room. In the dead of winter, I slept on the living room floor, changing positions every few hours when one end of me was freezing and the other roasting.

Early in my time at Cottey College—a women's junior college with about four hundred students in a town of less than ten thousand, in the middle of nowhere—one of my new colleagues invited me to join him and other faculty for dinner. The piano professor, Michael, said he'd pick me up at 5:00, but offered no other details. I couldn't figure out why they needed to chauffeur me in a town less than one mile across, nor did I understand why we were eating dinner at 5:00 on a Saturday. But it would all become clear very soon.

Michael pulled up in front of my shack at 5:00 sharp, with two other faculty onboard. As far as I knew, the only restaurants in Nevada were the McDonald's, the Dairy Queen, and a mom-and-pop steak joint from which I'd been warned away, so I was interested to see what secret haunts the town had to offer.

Michael hopped on the highway heading north and we were quickly beyond the city limits. I let a few minutes pass and finally asked what was going on.

"We're going to Kansas City. Didn't I tell you?" he replied.

We drove ninety miles, each way, for dinner, because that's what you did when you lived in Nevada. There was, as I'd surmised, nowhere to eat in town, and the travel time didn't bother anyone because there was nothing else to do.

On another occasion Michael spontaneously dropped by my office and asked if I wanted to join him for lunch at Wendy's. I was puzzled and suspicious because I'd never seen a Wendy's.

"Are we going to Kansas City?" I asked.

"Of course not," he smirked.

To reach Wendy's we drove twenty miles each way to Fort Scott, Kansas.

In addition to a joyous immersion into the choral repertoire for women's voices, that year afforded me an unusual singing opportunity. During the fall semester, an opera buff in the English department invited me to see *Tosca* at the Kansas City Community Opera. This was an amateur company with minimal sets and production elements, accompaniment by two pianos, but the singers did well, and their performance was quite enjoyable.

Afterward I went backstage and introduced myself to Joseph Fair, a retired opera singer who was the group's director and producer. Hearing my background, he asked if I was interested in singing with them, and I gave a polite, noncommittal response.

He called a couple of weeks later and asked if I would sing the role of Turiddu in Mascagni's *Cavalleria Rusticana* that spring. I'd mentioned the type of roles that suited my voice during our brief face-to-face, but he'd obviously missed Madame Flora's lesson about Fach. He assured me that since the theater was small and there was no orchestra, I would be fine in this role far outside my comfort zone.

But there's more to Fach than how much noise you can generate. It's also about color, weight, sound, and style. As a five-foot, eight-inch leggiero tenor, no one would mistake me for a Turiddu. But after some thought, I said yes, because with no orchestra to battle, I figured it wouldn't do my voice any harm. And when in the rest of my life was I going to sing a role like that one?

Joseph—who had, apparently, attended the Benito Mussolini School of Theater Management—was one of those people who thinks he knows everything, a big fish in a microscopic pond who's used to having his own way. The four Cottey students who sang in the chorus were constantly aggravated with him, but he and I ran afoul on only one occasion.

In a run-through of the confrontation between my character and his nemesis, the villain lit the stogic he'd been chewing as a character device. In seconds a cloud of smoke billowed from his cigar, filling the small stage. As he finished his next line, waiting for me to sing, I stood momentarily mute.

"Hold it!" I finally choked out. "What's going on?"

The baritone looked blissfully innocent as Joseph came harrumphing down the aisle to ask why I'd stopped. I told him—quite politely under the circumstances—that lighting a cigar in an opera was ridiculous, and I wasn't singing my final aria in a cloud of smoke.

Joseph drew himself up and proclaimed, "Anyone who can sing this role professionally could sing it with smoke on the stage."

I replied that anyone who could sing the role professionally wouldn't still be standing there. A tense silence ensued, then he turned his back and stalked up the aisle. We took a break and the cigar disappeared, never to return.

I've never known for certain if the baritone was taking a deep dive into his character or just being a jerk. But if, channeling the villain, he lit that cigar just to get under my skin, it worked like a charm.

To the North Country

As the spring semester of 1984 got underway at Cottey College, I began searching for a summer gig to tide me over until fall. My salary was $13,000, and without summer employment, things would get very lean very quickly. As manna from heaven, I received a call from Brian Tidwell, a friend from Eastman School days who'd found his niche in musical theater and other popular genres.

An outstanding pianist, arranger, and conductor, Brian had spent most of the preceding year playing keyboards on the national tour of *Evita* and called to inquire if I could sit in for him during the summer. The show was slated to play eight weeks in San Francisco, and I considered his offer for about four seconds. Did I want to spend the summer in San Francisco being well-paid to play the synthesizer for three hours a day? Hell, yes! We were both delighted with the deal, and he said the tour manager would be in touch.

But days, then weeks slipped by without word. Finally, an abashed Brian phoned in March. I hadn't heard from anyone, he said, because a protracted dispute between the tour's producers and the San Francisco musicians' union had resulted in an entirely new orchestra being hired from the ranks of local union members. Long story short: my dream summer gig had vanished.

With the clock ticking, I went back to the drawing board. One evening, alone in my Missouri hovel, I received a call from a man representing the Fort Totten Little Theater in Devils Lake, North Dakota. Following a ten-minute conversation, I was hired as music director for their summer production of Rogers and Hammerstein's *Carousel.*

They had engaged a director from New York, and we would hear auditions when we arrived in North Dakota in early June, casting from whatever locals turned up. The ensemble (I shudder to refer to it as an orchestra) was made up of local volunteers who came and went without warning, but they were window dressing for a two-piano arrangement of the score. I planned to play one piano part while conducting, with another pianist playing the other. For the eight weeks I would be paid a total of $1,000.

The task of identifying a set designer would usually fall to the director, but they had hired an odd duck, Lou S., who was apparently no help. Jumping at the chance, I contacted my best friend from high school, Gary Harper, a gifted artist and designer whose talents were, in my opinion, going to waste designing warehouses for his father's company. Despite his $600 compensation, he grabbed the opportunity to spend the summer together doing *Carousel*—a show close to both our hearts.

In addition to Gary, two of my Cottey College students also volunteered. One sang in the chorus and the other played the second piano part.

The semester in Missouri ended, and I loaded up my Mustang, heading north. Also on board was Salome, the cat who had wandered onto the front steps of my dilapidated rent house a few weeks earlier.

Two things about Salome deserve mention. First, she was with me from 1984 until she passed away, too soon, in 1996—a steadfast companion who slept next to my head from Missouri to North Dakota, Virginia, Indiana, Alabama, and, finally, Arkansas. Second, I'd never taken a cat on a lengthy car trip. Money was tight, and the animal carriers in the store were expensive. And what could that plastic thing do that a carboard box and some kitty tranquilizers couldn't? I found a box, cut holes for air and light, and in she went. What could possibly go wrong?

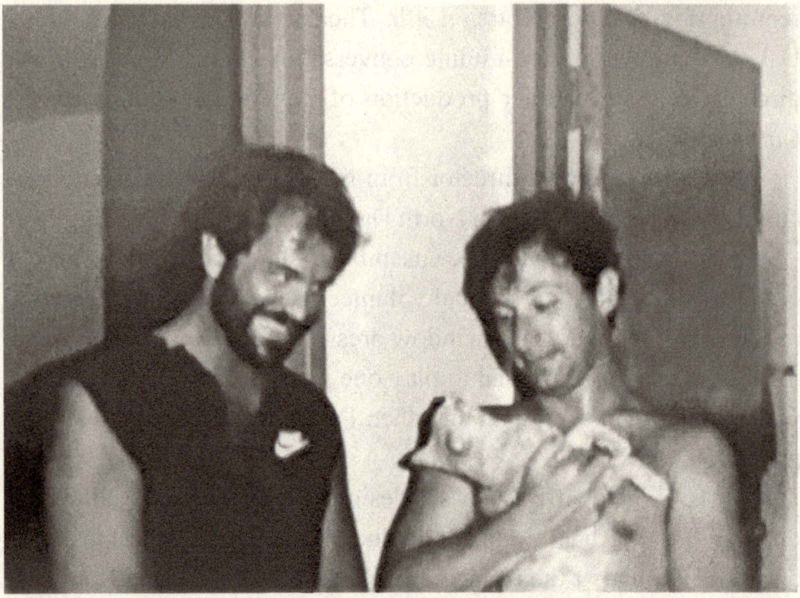

Gary Harper glares menacingly while the author holds Salome, North Dakota, 1984.

We weren't ten miles out of Nevada, Missouri before she had clawed the airholes three times their size and was near to making her escape. Ninety minutes later we arrived in Kansas City, a stopping point I was lucky to reach alive with her crawling under the pedals, clawing at my face, and meowing at the top of her lungs. There, I paused at a friend's house to let the drugs wear off, clean my car (tranquilizers cause animals to lose muscle control), and go to a pet store to buy a proper cat crate.

I couldn't afford a hotel, so I drove straight through, arriving in Devils Lake very late that evening. I was shown to my quarters, an apartment for married students at the local college that Gary and I would share. Despite its Spartan, minimum security prison decor, it was clean, spacious, and more than adequate.

Gary arrived two days later. After entertaining me with a saga of his flying retreads in the Columbia Gorge, he said, "Hey, Snoop,

I have to show you something." (The reason he has called me Snoop for the last half century is a reference to my experience in *You're a Good Man, Charlie Brown*, which he saw at least four times.)

He pulled a yellow flyer from his backpack, "Look at this—this is crazy. Some guy where I stopped for gas handed it to me."

In the Northwest in the 1960s and 70s, we grew up in a place and time where outspoken racism and its kissing cousins were nearly unheard of. I knew what anti-Semitism was, but apart from some idiot on the grade school playground, I had never experienced it firsthand. We had one neighbor who used the "n" word, and our parents told us never to go near his house. That's how it was. There were no Proud Boys, no institutionalized xenophobia, no normalizing of hate speech. Were we a bit sheltered? Perhaps—but blissfully so.

I took the paper and read. It was a neo-Nazi tract, shoved into Gary's hand in northern Idaho, purporting to tell the facts about the Holocaust: that it is a hoax perpetrated by a worldwide Jewish cabal. And, it turns out, we also control the world economy when we're not busy manufacturing fake concentration camp photos.

"Do these idiots really think someone would believe this?" he asked, taking it from my hand and tossing it into the trash.

I watched the paper fly into the bin. *Into the trash*, I thought, *into the showers*, *into the ovens*. Nearly a half million Americans died to stop these people, and now their spawn live in Idaho, unmolested? Free speech is never more important than when we disagree with the message. But when our nation has sacrificed so much to defeat a clear evil, mightn't that be an exception? Gazing at the crumpled paper, I wondered if, even from my left-leaning perspective, perhaps there's a little too much free speech.

The following day, we met Lou, the director from New York. Though we were in rural North Dakota doing what amounted to amateur theater, he talked as though we were mounting a Broadway revival. Unfortunately, talking is all he ever accomplished.

We launched into auditions, casting reasonably experienced amateurs for every part—except one. There was no one for the role of Billy, the male lead, requiring a handsome, brawny younger man with a strong baritone voice and large vocal range. Finding him in North Dakota was proving difficult but, at last, we located a candidate. He read a scene for us—badly—and sang—borderline.

Lou and Gary turned to me, "Can you get him to sing this part?" one of them asked.

"Maybe," I answered, though this was overselling it a bit. I countered, "Can you get some kind of acting out of him?"

"No problem. I can teach anyone to act," Lou blustered in a whiny voice.

But the discussion was academic: we beggars were in no position to be choosers. So the handsome North Dakota stud who couldn't sing much and had hardly set foot on a stage was our Billy Bigelow.

My students arrived from Missouri, rehearsals began, Gary spent untold hours drawing and building—without, it should be noted, the legions of helpers he was promised—and everything seemed to be proceeding smoothly.

My biggest challenge in the early going was getting our male lead up to snuff. Our rehearsals were little more than voice lessons, but that was to be expected. My real concern was getting a rural kid with no real experience in theater or music to understand and project the important ideas in his only solo piece, the famous "Soliloquy."

In this extended musical number, Billy, who has just learned he'll soon be a father, shifts from seeing himself as the best pal of a son to understanding his role will be as protector and provider for a daughter. When he imagines his child as a boy, he is allowed to remain a child himself, conjuring rough-and-tumble adventures and carefree days. As the father of a girl, he realizes, he must grow up and make sacrifices.

> She's got to be sheltered, and fed, and dressed in the best that money can buy.

I never knew how to get money, but I'll try, by God, I'll try.
I'll go out and make it, or steal it, or take it—or die!

At 27 I was still enduring my own slow transition from adolescent to adult. Billy's "Soliloquy" pains me each time I hear it, and the passage of years only intensifies those feelings. Maybe that's because I know how difficult that part of a man's life can be. Or perhaps it's because I know that, like many of us, nothing in Billy's plans will come true.

I attempted, with modest success, to explain to our inexperienced leading man that communicating Billy's elated, apprehensive state of mind mattered more than the high notes. Fifteen years later it would be my turn for fatherhood, with all my hopes and fears on the line. And, as ill-equipped as Billy, I would fare little better.

One week in, with opening night two weeks away, Gary and I were simultaneously alerted to the fact that, while we labored at our respective construction and music teaching tasks, the director had accomplished almost nothing. At the break between afternoon and evening rehearsals we pulled some cast members aside.

"What's going on?" I asked, "Why didn't he stage anything last week?"

"He did," we were told. "He stages a scene, then the next day he stages it again, differently, and the next day a third version. We have no idea what's going on."

Armed with these specifics, we took Lou aside later that evening and, as diplomatically as possible, expressed our concerns regarding his lack of tangible progress. Our leader, deeply affronted, explained to the two idiots that this was "a process" and we needed to butt out and let him "create."

More, rather than less, concerned, Gary and I retired to our bunker, poured alcohol, and attempted to strategize. One option was to do nothing. This was, in a certain sense, the most professional response, because how the director did his job was not, technically, our concern. On the other hand, when the show was not ready to open on time, I would be the one out in public with a production that was falling apart.

Early the following morning, Gary and I met with key members of the theater's board of directors. We gathered for breakfast in an out-of-the-way diner—a conclave that felt uncomfortably like the opening salvo of a coup. Overnight the chairman had called selected actors to see how they felt about the situation and discovered that their concern was even greater than ours.

After filling in the leadership, the chairman asked, "OK, suppose we let him go—then what?"

A very good question. One which, in our haste, Gary and I had not thoroughly considered. After a brief silence, my friend piped up. "You know, David comes from a theatrical family. His father is a director. David could do it!"

Bug-eyed, I turned to him with a look that clearly asked, "What the hell are you doing?" but said nothing. In truth, we had kicked around the idea the night before, while drinking, but I didn't recall volunteering for the job.

But, as with casting the male lead, we had what we had. And what we had, for better or worse, was me. A few hours later, Lou was put on a train (yes, a train) back to New York, and we all got to work.

I was suddenly thrown deep into the stew of zany personalities who inhabited the cast. Gary, who in addition to designing and building the sets played the role of the Starkeeper, had kept me in stitches with anecdotes about the group. But up close and personal with this crew was an entirely different matter.

We had the trailer-park Earthmother (think Roseanne, but twice as coarse and half as funny); the middle-aged chorister couple who wanted this experience to be, somehow, about church; the handsome male lead whom every woman under forty wanted, but who was, I'm pretty sure, in the closet; and the darling ingenue who spent half the summer trying to get the new director into the sack. And that's just scratching the surface.

With considerable assistance from the cast, my students, and Gary, we sorted out the mess, I staged the remainder of the show, and we opened on time and in reasonably good shape.

The cast of *Carousel*, Devils Lake, North Dakota, 1984.

The memories of our earliest artistic outings are influenced by time, naïveté, and the rose-colored lenses through which we view cherished friends and experiences. So working with this oddball group of amateurs made me question my own recollections of copious amateur and semiprofessional theatrical experiences in my teens and early 20s. Were we this bad? Were the productions I remembered fondly as both actor and musician this disorganized and amateurish? Surely not. We were much better than these North Dakota rubes, weren't we? I am, in all humility, determined to answer "yes." But in truth, who knows? Perhaps the past is so loaded with emotional smoke and mirrors that we can never say for sure.

But this is a tale of travel, and, unwilling, travel we did.

The day following the first of four Thursday-through-Sunday performance weekends, I was offered a job as director of choirs and chair of the voice department at Virginia Tech. I had interviewed at Tech a few months earlier but had heard nothing until that day. Following a brief negotiation by phone, I accepted.

Next, I needed to inform the Dean at Cottey College that, contrary to expectations, I wouldn't be returning in the fall. When a faculty member gives notice during the summer, the school must scramble for a replacement. This is inconvenient and time-consuming, but it does happen. In fact, it happens with some frequency, and it's not the end of the world.

The dean, however, did not see it that way. He berated me on the phone for some minutes, telling me I was irresponsible and ungrateful. When he realized I wasn't changing my mind, he ordered me to clear out my office and teaching studio immediately. I reminded him I was in North Dakota, returning in three weeks, and promised I would do so as soon as I arrived.

No, he said, that was unacceptable. If I didn't have my things cleared out in forty-eight hours, they would empty my teaching spaces and deposit everything into the trash. They had no need for my office or studio during the summer. This was pure spleen, and Gary could read on my face that all was not well.

When I hung up, I filled in the details. "This is ridiculous! There's no way I can do this when we have a performance Thursday night."

In his typically sanguine manner, he replied, "Sure we can."

Tuesday morning, the four of us found ourselves in my Mustang heading south, arriving in Nevada, Missouri, late that night. We slept in my hovel, Gary on my bed, with my students and me scattered variously on the living room floor.

We were exhausted from the long drive, and I was sure I'd be asleep before my head hit the pillow. Suddenly, I felt a tap at my shoulder. I opened my eyes to see one of the girls crouching next to me, the T-shirt she wore as pajamas riding up onto her hips. In the near darkness, not three feet from her schoolmate, she brought her face close to my ear and I realized, both thrilled and horrified, that she was about to continue a conversation she'd initiated some days earlier.

The intense working environment of theater, as well as our geographic separation from the college, had naturally led to a more casual relationship between me and the Cottey students. In North Dakota they called me by my first name, which they would never have done at school. And this, in turn, led to generally less guarded communication. At some point during the rehearsal process, the young lady who now crouched beside me had confided, not happily, that she was still a virgin. And being boyfriend-less at a women's college, she hoped to find just the right person, someone she could trust, with whom to rectify that situation.

That conversation had left me very uneasy. I was only 26 when I arrived at Cottey the previous fall, and it had taken all my willpower to avoid entanglement with any of the 18- to 21-year-old students, the older of whom would not have been considered an inappropriate age for me under other circumstances. Her admission—or was it an offer?—had terrified me. She was still my student during that conversation only days earlier. But there, in my darkened living room, following my resignation, she was not.

At 27 I was still working to overcome the influence of my parents' alternately puritanical and willfully blind attitudes about sex. When my former student made her midnight approach, every judgmental, Victorian remark my mother had ever uttered resounded in my ears. As a sophomore in college, I'd briefly renewed a relationship with a former girlfriend from high school, and my mother made her disdain clear when she discovered that, in the interim, "the bloom" was "off the rose" for the girl in question.

Selecting from the long list of reasons to decline—former student, other people nearby, her first time, and my mother sitting in the room—one word galvanized my waning resolve. She'd said "trust," but at that moment it didn't mean "discreet"; it meant "no."

Early the following morning—with a young woman who'd been among my favorite students no longer speaking to me—we four boxed everything in my studio and office and transported it to my house. When we'd finished, my tiny abode looked like a warehouse, boxes stacked everywhere, with just enough floor space remaining for another night's sleep.

That night I laid in the dark staring at the ceiling, listening to both girls breathing peacefully and silently congratulating myself for my good behavior twenty-four hours earlier. A few days later, I would learn that my favorite student had driven to a bar and gone home with a 30-something North Dakota cowboy. I get it; sometimes the good girl wants the bad boy. But watching it play out before my eyes, with someone I cared about and nurtured, was almost more than I could bear.

When I heard what she'd done, I took her aside to ask if she was all right, hoping for some insight into what was, from my perspective, a dangerous, reckless decision. She turned her back, telling me it was none of my business. Scant hours earlier we might have been lovers, and now we were utterly estranged. And who knows, perhaps if I'd said yes, we would have finished in the same place, even if for different reasons. They say, "the heart wants what it wants," but after all these years, I still don't understand what that is.

In *Carousel* nice-girl Julie Jordon falls in love with ruffian Billy Bigelow, and it doesn't end well. Why weren't we paying attention?

So I left North Dakota bearing two more things I didn't want to know. First, that this nice girl had consummated her plan with a stranger. And second, that no matter how noble our intentions, casting oneself as a knight in shining armor is pure self-delusion.

A Momentary Hokie

The Spartan living situation and geographic isolation notwithstanding, I enjoyed my work at Cottey College. But one year was enough, and shortly after returning from North Dakota, I was on my way to Blacksburg, Virginia, where I would spend two years as choral conductor and chairman of voice at Virginia Tech.

Arriving in August 1984, I was assigned to teach twelve private voice students, oversee two adjunct voice teachers, teach a course in foreign language diction, and lead the Virginia Tech Concert Choir and the Virginia Tech Meistersingers. This teaching load would never be allowed now, but I was in no position to argue, nor did I wish to.

I suddenly had a job that almost universally requires a doctoral degree in choral conducting, and my only credential was a master's degree in voice. By that point I was confident in my craft, but dipping my toes into the world of big university choral conductors made me feel like a trespasser.

The choirs were a mix of music majors and nonmajors. This was relevant to my work only as it concerned my not-so-surprising discovery that the nonmajors (mostly engineering students) read music far better than the voice majors. I quickly learned to arrange my groups by intermixing the two, seating a student with a better voice and larger range next to one who read well.

I struggled with only one serious challenge while working at Tech. The New Virginians were the institution's show choir, the darling of university administration and the ridiculous tail wagging the music department dog. They performed pop and Broadway songs with a ten-piece backup band, choreography, and gaudy costumes. In other words, they were an amateurish cruise ship show with a cast entirely under 22 years old.

The New Virginians were given substantial resources in faculty, facilities, and funding, far beyond the programs that served greater numbers of students. I was one faculty member teaching more than eighty choral singers and a dozen voice students, while their four full-time faculty/staff positions served a total of twenty-six students. This disparity between resources allocated and numbers of students served was repeatedly justified with the explanation that the New Virginians gave the university a "modern" look and was their most powerful recruitment tool. Further, it was strongly implied that, since I was the new kid, it wasn't my business to second-guess how the university spent its money.

And perhaps it was not my place to comment on the big picture, but the activities of the New Virginians affected my choirs on a day-to-day basis. There were perhaps six students in common between my groups and the show choir, but these were among my best and brightest. During their tours they were chronically absent from my rehearsals, and when present they were either hoarse from recent performances or saving their voices for an upcoming scream-fest. That *was* my business, but no conversation with the New Virginians' director or my department chair brought any compromise.

With no relief in sight through normal channels, I decided, foolishly, to take my case to the court of public opinion. It's not as though I didn't realize I was making waves; I simply didn't understand it would be a tsunami.

In the spring of 1985, the end of my first year at Tech, I wrote an article titled "Dissolving the Myths of the Show Choir," debunking the fictions of institutional monetary benefit, musical training, and career preparation that were routinely trotted out in defense of these groups. The article was published in the *Music Educators' Journal*, reprinted by two other education magazines the following year, then reviewed and summarized by the well-known scholar Alfred Mann in yet another.

The director of the New Virginians was not amused and immediately maneuvered his way onto my review committee. What a surprise when, the following fall, that committee decided not to renew my contract.

The nonrenewal was a moot point because I was departing in any event, having already been accepted to the Indiana University doctoral program. But I learned a valuable lesson from that predictable outcome, one that would resonate years later in Lake Forest and another, larger community that shall remain nameless: In the arts and academia, as in government and business, expect the entrenched and powerful to protect their turf at the expense of the common good.

My only significant singing during those two years was as the Evangelist in Bach's *St. John Passion*. The performance was planned before I was hired, to be conducted by James G., the school's violin instructor and conductor of the university's town-and-gown orchestra. I would have the task of preparing the chorus and, I assumed (as the only tenor on the faculty), singing the Evangelist.

This assumption was the first of two miscalculations. Little did I know that James had already offered the role to my predecessor.

I brought this uncomfortable situation to the attention of the department chairman, who agreed it was inappropriate for someone recently fired to be performing at the university. Strike one.

My other mistaken assumption was artistic, not political. Once James and I were over that first hump, we put our heads together to discuss details of the piece. At some point in the conversation, I referred to a certain line of text, and James stopped me midsentence.

"You do realize," he said, "we're performing the piece in English?"

I guffawed silently. From my perspective it was ridiculous. We were making the staggering effort of preparing this lengthy, difficult work, only to arrive at a performance in a clumsy English translation? I told him I wasn't interested in singing the Evangelist or preparing the choir in English, but digging in my heels was not the best choice. I was 27 and headstrong, and—with the show choir article still in my future—arguing about the text wasn't close to the stupidest thing I'd end up doing at Tech.

Neither of us would back down, so once again we found ourselves in the chairman's office. He didn't like the idea of Bach in English any better than I did, and the matter was settled. The other matter settled that day, unfortunately, was my relationship with James. Two strikes, and I was out.

Only two years out of school, I saw myself as hoisting a banner of righteousness, defending Bach against the rural Virginia heathen. Later I considered the idea that I was the newbie who should have kept his mouth shut. But more recently I've returned to the notion that, bullheaded and self-destructive though my behavior may have been, I was right the first time.

Summer Stock

After teaching one year at Virginia Tech, I found myself exactly where I'd been a year earlier. I needed summer employment, but this time I had no intention of spending two months on the plains of North Dakota.

A professional stock company in the Northeast posted a notice seeking actors, singers, and pianist/music directors for their twelve summer productions. Intrigued, I sent my resume and was instructed to present myself for an interview at the Bucks County Playhouse in New Hope, Pennsylvania, just northeast of Philadelphia.

The Bucks County Playhouse, a charming, old theater that had seen better days, was swarming with Broadway wannabes on that sunny, spring afternoon. Working my way around a line of headshot-doting beautiful people, I found a woman in the lobby who appeared to be in charge. Realizing instinctively that I was not there to audition as an actor—this was, I think, not a compliment—she sent me into the theater, telling me to find Norman.

Even amid the chaos of a cattle call audition, Norman was impossible to miss. He was somewhere north of six feet tall, perhaps two hundred forty pounds, with a tenor voice that echoed throughout the theater as he called out instructions (think Nathan Lane, but a foot taller and twice as loud).

I waited for a break in his bellowing and approached.

"Yes, David!" he roared, as I retreated a step to avoid hearing damage. "Go on up there."

I hesitated, responding, "Uh, no . . . I'm here for the music director job."

"I know, I know," he bellowed jovially (think gay Santa Claus). "He," indicating the man seated at the piano, "needs a break. You play for a while."

By "you play for a while" he meant I should sight-read audition songs for the next several singers. This was, it turned out, my audition. I must have played well enough, because an hour later I had a job. He shook my hand and told me to go back to the lobby where the woman with whom I'd spoken earlier would explain how everything worked.

Ralph Miller, a theatrical entrepreneur, owned three theaters: the Bucks County Playhouse (New Hope, Pennsylvania), the Pocono Playhouse (Mountainhome, Pennsylvania), and the Falmouth Playhouse (Cape Cod, Massachusetts). Three distinct performing companies rotated between the theaters in a three-week cycle, giving eight performances per week while simultaneously rehearsing their next show. All this was explained that afternoon, but hearing the words is different from living it.

I arrived at the Pocono Playhouse in late May, ready to begin rehearsing the first show on my schedule, *Hello, Dolly*. Norman, the loud-voiced supervising music director for Miller's conglomerate, greeted me effusively, made sure I'd found my lodging, and then explained a small wrinkle in their plans.

In short, he needed me to fill in as one of the disciples in *Jesus Christ, Superstar* for its final week of performances while, during the daytime, I got *Hello, Dolly* rehearsals underway. Seeing no way out, I reluctantly consented. This absurd request led to a nightly out-of-body experience during which I wandered the stage in terror, glued to another disciple like a lost puppy.

The morning after my arrival, we began rehearsals for *Hello, Dolly*, my first opportunity to meet the delightful, diverse group of performers who would be my colleagues for the next fourteen weeks. Many were seasoned B-level pros, the rest either talented up-and-comers or burned-out wannabes. After a week rehearsing in the Poconos, we moved to Bucks County for the final week of rehearsals and first week of performances.

I thought I was working long hours during those first two weeks, but it was not until we opened *Hello, Dolly* that I realized just how strenuous our schedule would become. We opened on a Tuesday night with a production still a bit unsteady on its feet. Anywhere else we would have picked up the following day with further *Hello, Dolly* rehearsals, but not at Ralph Miller Productions. Instead, at 10:00 a.m. Wednesday, we started rehearsing our next show, *Mame*, due to open in less than three weeks. We rehearsed for six hours during the day, with just enough time remaining to find something to eat and rush to the second performance of *Hello, Dolly*. Rehearse, eat, rehearse, performance, eat, sleep, repeat.

When we finished the final performance in Bucks County that Sunday night, we had ninety minutes to prepare for the six-hour bus ride to Falmouth. Instead of hiring buses to take each company from point to point on the isosceles triangle that described the geography of the three theaters, Miller saved money by arranging our transportation as a tag-team event. Our bus drove to a point in the middle of nowhere en route to Massachusetts, where, at 3:00 a.m., we met buses carrying another company coming south. There we transferred our belongings, as well as the luggage and other equipment beneath the bus, to the other company's vehicles. Then we headed to Falmouth while the southbound company took our buses back to Pennsylvania.

While the professional universes of theater and orchestral music may seem light-years apart, we have much in common. Running along parallel tracks are the issues of work hours, transportation, housing, and the general treatment of the artist/employees. While I may not agree with everything issuing from the AFM (the musicians' union) or Equity (the actors' union), the conditions under which we worked at Ralph Miller Productions make the need for oversight abundantly clear.

We arrived at Falmouth with the Monday sunrise. There we were fed and allowed to sleep until that afternoon's put-in rehearsal, a work-through of the current show to make it fit in a theater of different dimensions. Tuesday morning we were back at rehearsal for *Mame*, and Tuesday evening we opened *Hello, Dolly*'s Falmouth run.

Despite a baseline level of exhaustion, we were consistently reenergized by our talented colleagues and the joyous nature of the work. Passing all understanding, the actors and I found the energy to perform in the theater's bar following weekend performances. Miller encouraged us to do this (with compensation solely from the tip jar) because live entertainment brought an audience to the bar where he could make more money selling drinks.

The third show in our rotation was *Evita*. Though we had performers capable of all the major roles, I knew this production would be challenging because the chorus music is substantially more complicated than the average Broadway tune-fest. Adding to that hurdle was the fact that most of the chorus were primarily dancers, not singers, making complicated vocal music a steep climb. After just one rehearsal, I decided I wasn't beating that dead horse and, instead, created simplified chorus parts. I briefly considered staying the course for the sake of artistic integrity, but then observed the dark circles under my eyes in the dirty, cracked mirror in my dressing room and thought, *you must be kidding*.

Two casting surprises awaited us in *Evita*.

Though the director and I had identified the two women in the company who would play Eva Perón (the major roles were double cast to avoid exhaustion), at the last moment news descended from on high that Miller's wife would play the title role. This woman was some sort of socialite, amateur actress, and church choir singer. The quality of her performance, which was semi-adequate, was not the issue. It was the meddling hubris of our boss that raised our hackles.

In addition to heading off vocal and physical exhaustion, the major roles were double cast for the usual, more practical reason—having another actor ready should one become ill. Early in the final week of the *Evita* run, one of the actors in the leading role of Che caught a bug, so his counterpart was obligated to do all remaining performances. Unfortunately, the second actor quickly lost his voice under the strain of repeat performances. But tickets were sold, and Miller made it clear that cancelation was not an option. We were being paid, he commanded, to figure these things out.

The director and I put our heads together, sorting through the men in smaller roles to see if anyone could handle it. But there was no one else in the company with the required vocal range and stamina. And so my debut as Che in *Evita* was born. I played the role for two performances while my assistant led the musical end of things. With two days to rest and recuperate, both actors intended for the role resumed their duties later in the week, much to my delight.

The final production before I returned for my second year at Virginia Tech was *A Chorus Line*, a show I'd fallen in love with during high school but had never conducted. Rehearsals progressed well for two weeks—this time the fact that the chorus members were better dancers than singers was a plus—and then another message arrived from the mountaintop.

Miller had discovered, to his horror, that *A Chorus Line* has no intermission. This detail is important to the narrative, as the show takes place in real time during a Broadway dance audition and its creators probably reasoned that breaking for intermission would ruin the illusion. Never at a loss to place commerce ahead of art, Miller demanded we insert an intermission so he didn't lose the opportunity to sell drinks. This did real damage to the show and was also, I believe, a violation of copyright, though it was difficult to say which of those issues concerned him less. We appealed and were rebuffed. So an awkward intermission was inserted into *A Chorus Line*, and my summer was done.

Not every theatrical event is a multimillion-dollar Broadway production, as not every orchestra concert is performed by a major ensemble at the highest level. But every endeavor in which we involve ourselves should receive our full diligence as leaders and our utmost care as artists. Quality, integrity, and artistry are important at all levels, and Ralph Miller Productions, despite its challenges, was no exception. Under the most trying conditions, this band of brothers and sisters labored not just to survive from one performance to the next but also to make tiny blossoms grow in deeply infertile soil. Working conditions and genre should have no effect on our level of commitment, nor are they an excuse for sloth. We cannot suddenly learn to value our craft when the big gig arrives; we either live our principles every moment or we have lost our way.

Postscript: In 2006 the flooding Delaware River caused extensive damage to the Bucks County Playhouse, and in 2016 Ralph Miller was convicted in an insurance scam and money-laundering scheme connected to that event. He was sentenced to thirty months in federal prison. The Pocono Playhouse burned to the ground in 2009, and fire officials found the blaze to be of suspicious origins.[1]

[1] Howard Frank, "Pocono Playhouse Owner Pumped Up Insurance Six Months Before Fire," *Pocono Record*, November 2, 2009, https://www.poconorecord.com/story/news/disaster/2009/11/03/pocono-playhouse-owner-pumped-up/51813469007/; Robert Viagas, "Man Whose 3 Theatres Burned Is Convicted of Insurance Fraud," *Playbill*, June 3, 2015, https://playbill.com/article/man-whose-3-theatres-burned-is-convicted-of-insurance-fraud-com-350468.

Chapter 4

Indiana, Pakistan, and Leonard Bernstein

~~~~~ The City That Never Sleeps ~~~~~

After four years leading high school and college choirs, I decided I had sat on my hands long enough. It was time to see if I could make it in the world outside of academia. I had fallen into a decent career as a choral conductor, but it was a path that seemed to have chosen me rather than the other way around. I knew that, regardless of my ability, no one would give me a second glance as an orchestral conductor because on paper I looked like something very different.

Two years earlier I had been accepted to the doctoral program in orchestral conducting at Indiana University, but the allure of a salary at Virginia Tech was too tempting. So in early 1986 I applied a second time and was offered an assistantship. After receiving this news, I planned a spring break vacation in New York with my parents, intended as a celebration, of sorts, for the redirection of my career.

There are perhaps a dozen top-flight American schools of music. Several of these institutions are in New York City, where they have access to extraordinary faculty and sit at the heart of the performing arts universe. I had no intention of abandoning Indiana University, but I thought it might be fascinating to climb another of the Everests of music schools. I contacted the admissions office at one of these conservatories and discovered that the audition/testing period was within a few days of my planned visit. It seemed meant to be.

Conductors who were invited to audition were subjected to a three-day process. Day one was the ear-training test. If you survived, you conducted a chamber orchestra on day two, and those still standing on day three conducted the full orchestra.

My ear-training exam was one on one with a junior faculty member who played various intervals, harmonies, and modulations for me to identify. Next my inquisitor asked me to take his seat at the piano, placing before me the score of a Bach chorale. Glancing up, I saw the chorale was printed using the four original clefs rather than in modern notation—their way of quickly separating the haves from the have-nots.

To my surprise he asked me to sing each chord vertically, from the bottom voice upward. That is, one note from the bass, then the tenor note in the same chord, then the alto and soprano. With that accomplished I was to move on to the next chord, singing upward in the same manner. For nonmusicians this is like being given a passage of text in four different languages—one of which you speak fluently, two reasonably well, and one haltingly—each word alternating from one language to the next, with the instruction to read and translate fluidly and quickly.

As nerve-racking as it was, this was not out of bounds for applicants to a doctoral program in conducting. It was a trial by fire intended to evaluate our fortitude as much as our ears.

Those of us who survived the sight-singing exam moved on to conduct the chamber orchestra the following day in the presence of the current head of the program, Mr. X. I had been warned about the idiosyncrasies of both the man and the process, including his habit of placing wrong notes in the parts.

The assigned work was the thirteen-instrument version of Aaron Copland's *Appalachian Spring*, the ubiquitous graduate school audition piece. Well-substantiated buzz about the attitude of students in this school to the contrary, the musicians in the orchestra were attentive, pleasant, and responsive.

The first minute or two went well. Then it started—a wrong note here, a wrong note there. I stopped and corrected the first two or three, then picked up where we'd left off. Almost immediately another wrong note. I stopped and fixed, but I was growing annoyed.

Up to that point, Mr. X had never looked up, appearing more interested in whatever papers he had in front of him. I continued, nonetheless. More wrong notes, but this time I didn't stop. With each wrong note I cast an overacted surly conductor look at the offending individual and kept going. This went on for two or three minutes, at which point Maestro X stopped me.

"Didn't you hear all those wrong notes?" he asked in a condescending tone.

Too busy shuffling his papers, he obviously hadn't seen my surly conductor look. I answered, "Yes, I heard the preprogrammed wrong notes, but I'm tired of stopping every thirty seconds. The ear-training test was yesterday."

I glanced at the orchestra, the students' tight-lipped expressions displaying both mirth and terror.

Following a cavernous pause, he muttered, "All right, go on."

He allowed me to conduct the next few minutes uninterrupted.

Then, without looking up, he mumbled, "That will be all."

I thanked the players and headed for the door. But he wasn't finished. Just before I reached the exit, as though we'd been interrupted mid-conversation, he asked, "Two of the last movements of the nine Beethoven symphonies have the same metronome marking. Do you know which two?"

"No," I replied, "and if I want to know, I'll look it up—kind of like you did this morning."

Yes, I was inappropriately sassy. But this final exchange still deserves a moment's reflection.

Expecting an aspiring conductor to have broad knowledge of the repertoire is entirely reasonable. But his question was not designed to sincerely examine my expertise. When children stump their parents with a new fact they've learned in school, we find it adorable. By a sliver of superior knowledge, the child gets to feel important. But that does not explain why an adult was playing this trivia game.

And the circumstances in which the question was asked speak volumes. Maestro X didn't quiz me because he cared about what I knew. He simply wanted an audience for his one-upmanship. Just as the child asks Dad the trivia question in front of Mom, the game is no fun without spectators.

And there is the larger picture to consider. It was already clear he wasn't interested in me as a student, nor I him as a teacher, so the only reason to ask the question was as a display of conductorial machismo. This is the sort of playground-bully mentoring that disposes young conductors to act the same way when they acquire positions of authority. When conductors cannot win respect through their musical leadership, they sometimes resort to this behavior, attempting to bolster the myth that they are superior to their students or the musicians in the orchestra.

The following fall I began doctoral study at Indiana University. But it was not until late in my first year that this story found its final chapter. That spring (1987) I conducted my first Dvořák's Cello Concerto for the master's recital of a friend. During the postconcert party at his apartment, an attractive young woman about 22 years old, one of the violinists in the Dvořák, walked over to me.

Without a word of introduction, she demanded, "It's you, isn't it?"

I studied her face intently, racking my brain. It doesn't take much imagination to guess what my first thoughts might have been. Fortunately, I was way off.

"It was you at the conducting audition, wasn't it?" she queried again.

Still on my heels, I asked what she meant. She told me she was one of the players in the orchestra during the unpleasant exchange with Maestro X. I braced myself for a tongue-lashing.

But instead she said, "Nobody knows who you are, but at that place you're a hero."

Apparently, the students were in sync with my feelings about Maestro X's behavior. I'd felt badly about that scene, as I don't derive any pleasure from confrontation. But knowing that I had helped to voice some other musicians' frustrations made me feel a bit better.

The final footnote to this tale took place the following summer, fourteen months after the scene in New York. Through an odd series of coincidences, I found myself assigned to assist that same Maestro X for one concert at a summer festival. I had no choice about this assignment and anticipated an uncomfortable situation at the first rehearsal. But my concerns were groundless because—hardly surprising—he recognized neither my name nor face.

A few days later, at the performance of Mendelssohn's Symphony No. 3, the great man was so taken with his own dancing that he failed to conduct the last two measures of the second movement. The excellent orchestra finished without him, and he quickly flailed his way through the final bars, attempting to look like a leader rather than a follower. We are all mortal, and anyone can become distracted for a split-second. But I confess, I might have gazed heavenward to thank whoever is in charge for that moment of cosmic payback.

Adventures of Operatic Proportions

For graduate students in orchestral conducting at Indiana University, being offered the associate instructorship (AI) in opera was the coveted brass ring. This appointment granted not only tuition and a living stipend, but also, more importantly, the position of assistant conductor of the IU opera program.

In my first year, I was given a different assignment, while the opera AI went to a talented, incredibly arrogant French-Canadian third-year student. He carried himself with enviable confidence, tossing off the names of famous European conductors as though they were his drinking buddies. Coming off four years as a high school and university choral conductor, and feeling underprepared from the first day, I found him very intimidating. Also, he annoyed the hell out of me and never let the rest of us forget that *he* was the opera AI. He served his time and then went on his way, never achieving the ultimate goal of conducting an IU opera performance.

I acquired the position in my second year, looking forward to an enticing repertoire including *Madama Butterfly*, *Candide*, *Peter Grimes*, *Abduction from the Seraglio*, and *Beatrice and Benedict*.

After a glorious summer in Aspen studying with Paul Vermel, I adjusted to life back in Indiana, where intensive rehearsals for *Madama Butterfly* were yielding a stunning production. I stayed on top of my tasks as assistant conductor, but that did not keep me from occasionally feeling overwhelmed. The stage at the Musical Arts Center (MAC) has the same dimensions as the Metropolitan Opera, with substages of the same size left, right, and behind. It was the largest stage I had ever seen, with an orchestra pit to match. The graduate students singing leading roles were far more mature and experienced than I and seemed like professionals from where I was standing. I was back where I'd been thirteen years earlier conducting my first musical—feeling out of the loop and getting by mostly on attitude.

One of my principal mentors, Thomas Baldner, was conducting the production. At midweek following the penultimate performance, he suddenly turned to me in class and barked in his perpetually hoarse voice, "David—the *Butterfly* this Saturday—you do it!"

I assumed this was a joke at my expense. As far as anyone knew, no student had ever conducted an opera performance at IU except as the result of illness or disaster. But it wasn't a joke, a fact that should have been obvious because Mr. Baldner had no discernible sense of humor.

For the next eighty hours I did little other than prepare for this challenge. I'd conducted many hours with the singers in a rehearsal studio but had been in front of the orchestra for only fifteen minutes, several weeks earlier. For three thrilling, agonizing days I vacillated from intense concentration on the score, to picturing the walk into that gigantic orchestra pit, to feeling like I was about to lose my lunch.

Despite how it appeared on that Wednesday morning, I don't think Mr. Baldner's offer was unpremeditated. This was, I believe, a carefully planned final exam, an opportunity for each of us to assess whether I would sink or swim when thrown into the deep end.

The first notes of *Madama Butterfly* are feared by some conductors, even more if one has had no rehearsal with the orchestra. In truth, the passage is no more difficult than exercises I've taught in a beginning conducting course. But orchestras are so accustomed to panicked, technique-free maestri flailing about at this moment that they may be on edge and prone to nervous, uncharacteristic errors.

Once past the opening notes, the opera was over in ten minutes, or so it seemed to me. Moving in exquisite slow motion, time contracted, and we were suddenly in the final scene, where Cio-Cio-San says goodbye to her child, "Addio, piccolo amor," before taking her own life.

At the symphony with my grandmother, then in the Quonset hut in California, and through hundreds of experiences following, I thought I'd begun to understand what this music thing was all about, but I hadn't even started. Striking the shocking, sarcastic major chord that ends the opera, I realized my face and shirt were soaked with tears. It was nothing like rehearsal, where everything was about technique and putting things together. This seemed real. Butterfly was dead, and I was in pieces because, for one awful moment, I'd done what Grandma taught me: I'd let the music in.

As yin as *Madama Butterfly* was yang, the next production was Leonard Bernstein's *Candide*, conducted by Robert Porco, the director of choral studies. The overriding silliness of the story, not to mention the farcical nature of my onstage involvement, was a laughable contrast to the tragedy of Puccini's masterpiece. Through no desire of mine, I ended up on the stage during the performances, instead of waiting patiently backstage where an assistant conductor belongs.

Short of male extras, the stage director asked me to play two small nonsinging, nonspeaking roles. At one point I played an outrageous gay priest who purchases the title character out of servitude, after which Candide finds himself, we imagine, in an entirely different sort of bondage. I wasn't convinced the character should be played that way. But those were my instructions, so I swished uncomfortably around the stage to the best of my ability.

My other silent role was as a prisoner tied to a stake and beaten during the Inquisition. Occupied simultaneously with preliminary rehearsals for *Peter Grimes*, I did the *Candide* rehearsals in my street clothes, but at the final rehearsal I was required to don the costumes.

As the priest I wore a long, hooded robe with a rope belt, which seemed simple enough. On the adjacent hanger I found cotton peasant pants that had been cut short around the calf and shredded to the midthigh, simulating the beating my character had undergone. They were a bit revealing, but I figured it was a little late to complain. The rest of the costume was missing, so I sought out an assistant costumer and asked where I might find the shirt that completed my outfit.

"That's all there is," she replied, with a mocking, lecherous grin.

When the lights came up on the auto-da-fé scene that evening, the rehearsal nearly stopped. The conductor looked amused, a few singers lost their places, and I stared at my feet. There, tied to a stake, shirtless and barefoot, was the conducting student for whom many of these same singers had given their final performance of *Madama Butterfly* two weeks earlier. It was not my finest hour. But I recovered, and even gained a certain notoriety.

By the time *Candide* closed, we were in the final stretch of preparations for Benjamin Britten's *Peter Grimes*, with my other principal teacher, Brian Balkwill, conducting. Each evening for weeks, I conducted staging rehearsals with the singers. Around 7:30 Mr. Balkwill would step in to conduct for ten or fifteen minutes, just long enough to keep me in my place. Then he was off to dinner, leaving me to continue until 11:00 or later.

On the Thursday evening preceding production week, two unusual things happened. First, Mr. Balkwill failed to appear. Second, Charles Webb, Dean of the School of Music, was later seen peering through the window in the studio door.

Around midnight, as I struggled to keep my eyes open through some bit of required reading, the phone rang. I reached to pick it up, assuming my parents had forgotten the time difference. The voice on the other end of the line was the last one on earth I expected.

Dean Webb apologized for calling so late and quickly told me that Mr. Balkwill had been taken to Indianapolis by ambulance and was scheduled for retinal surgery the following morning. After the procedure he would have to remain nearly immobile for several weeks, so conducting *Peter Grimes* was out of the question.

My heart was in my throat. *Peter Grimes* is not just another opera. It's a huge, complicated work with disaster lurking on nearly every page for a conductor who doesn't know the score intimately. The dean asked if I knew the piece well enough to take it on alone, then paused, as if anxious to pick up any hesitation on my part.

But he would be disappointed. I knew the opera inside and out, I told him. And it was the truth—sort of.

I hung up the phone and dropped onto a chair, my legs a bit wobbly, pondering the scale of the commitment I had just made. I wasn't concerned about learning the remainder of the score in eight days. I was worried about learning it in fifteen hours, before the following day's orchestra rehearsal. It was 12:30 a.m., so I poured a half-consumed glass of wine down the sink and made coffee.

I was well-versed in the vocal material, though I had not studied the orchestration in detail. In addition, I needed to learn the five substantial orchestral passages (the "Sea Interludes" and the "Passacaglia"), at which, to my shame, I had hardly glanced. The next afternoon the dean explained the situation to the orchestra, quietly observed the first half hour of rehearsal, and slipped out. There I was again, feeling like an imposter, holding on by my fingernails, propelled by adrenaline, caffeine, and a modicum of panic. But as far as I could tell, no one was ever the wiser.

The next eight days were a blur of rehearsals, score study, and cat naps. Things went well at the opening performance. In fact, they went far better than any of us deserved. I had my first review in a major newspaper, the *Indianapolis News*, and had done what I came to Indiana to do.

Certain experiences shape and define us for the future. The opportunity to conduct this magnificent opera, particularly under those circumstances, changed me profoundly. There have been other performances that have driven me to a new level or provided unique perspectives, but none will ever have the force of this one.

In the process of absorbing this massive score and attempting to communicate its meaning to a student orchestra and cast, I discovered some important things. I learned it's not about talk but about being in the moment and doing. I learned it's about the music, not about the man. And, perhaps most important, I learned for the first time that I wasn't afraid to be myself.

Building on what I'd experienced during *Butterfly*, I knew I needed to control my emotional energy, channeling it to the performers and not allowing it to sneak up and overwhelm me. Focused on thousands of details in the rehearsal process, it was not until we began dress rehearsals, where the music truly becomes storytelling, that the personal nature of the work fully revealed itself.

Madama Butterfly has only a few characters, but its impact is larger than life, universal in its themes of sacrifice, suffering, and redemption. By contrast, *Peter Grimes* has a huge cast of diverse characters, including the sea itself, but its themes are personal and intimate. Peter is a misfit, shunned by others for his differentness, lacking belief in himself sufficient to create an honest, happy life. He is the stranger in our midst, the odd man out, the extra child.

I came away from *Peter Grimes* having learned much about myself and my relationship to music but also carrying with me a truth I'd have preferred to leave alone: we don't ever know anyone. The guy at work with whom we occasionally chat may be a pedophile. The next-door neighbor we greet in passing may be a Klansman. And the quiet grocery store clerk might be a terrified, closeted homosexual on the brink of suicide—what we assume Peter to be. His inner turmoil only stirred my own, and from that day forward I have looked at the world, and each person in it, quite differently. While the last moments of *Butterfly* are a tear-drenched emotional conflagration, *Peter Grimes* leaves us empty and dead inside, wondering if we'll ever smile again.

While our profession was never as pure as I'd like to imagine, in the past few decades things have changed, and not for the better. Being a successful conductor has become more about who you know than who you are; more about salesmanship than musicianship; more about pretense than character; more about the size of your ego than the content of your heart; more about your expertise in PR than your knowledge of Mahler, Sibelius, Beethoven, and Mozart.

Is it any wonder that when orchestra musicians confront this package on the podium, with its perfect clothes and hair, choreographed movements, and precisely timed brow mopping, they yawn and fuss? This conductor has only the feigned passion of an aging prostitute: all the sweating and gyrating with none of the substance—the show of intellect and emotion, but not its truth. Music demands so much more from us: *our* heart, *our* spirit, the pain and joy drawn from *our* life, not a show imitating the life of someone else.

Before *Butterfly* and *Peter Grimes*, I was not the vacuous showman just described. I was, perhaps, something worse: a technician perfecting the motions with no clear eye on the goal. Afterward, I was still a long way from the destination, but I'd glimpsed where the road might lead.

~~~~~ Desert Song ~~~~~

When I arrived at Indiana to begin doctoral study, my on-and-off life as a singer needed to fade into the background. But the harder I tried to hide my shady past the more people seemed to discover it. I decided to take lessons, just to keep in shape, registering to study with the Cuban-born tenor Carlos Montané. But one thing led to another, and soon I was offered a once-in-a-lifetime opportunity to sing in far-off, exotic locales.

During my second year, Carlos organized a concert tour of Pakistan and four Arab Gulf states (ironically billed the "Indiana University Goodwill Tour") spanning December to January, 1987–1988. Nine singers and a pianist were scheduled to perform twelve concerts in thirty days in eight cities. In a school full of outstanding singers, I was honored to be asked, but also wary.

Carlos insisted I sing extremely difficult repertoire, all of which contained high C's and D's. In addition, there was the stress of traveling and the uncertain condition of one's digestion in a place like Pakistan. There was also the ethnic issue. Jews were not allowed in some of the countries we'd be visiting, so I would have to lie on my visa applications—a criminal offense, if discovered.

And then there were the planes. I don't like flying, and we were scheduled to travel thirty hours each way, plus a dozen shorter flights within the region, all on airlines with questionable safety practices. And, lest we forget, the Iran-Iraq War was ongoing, and we would repeatedly fly over the Persian Gulf.

I changed my mind a hundred times. One day my biggest worry was cracking a high note in front of important diplomats, the next I was doubting whether the aircraft service manuals had been translated into Arabic and Urdu. Then I'd think, *What does that matter? We'll probably be shot down by a stinger missile anyway.* Finally, I'd pivot to, *Come on, have an adventure! What have you got to lose? They probably won't figure out you're Jewish.*

The Indiana University "Goodwill" Middle East tour program.

We left Bloomington by car on a snowy December morning, headed for Indianapolis. By the time we landed at JFK, following a hideously turbulent flight, I was ready to turn back. Once in New York, we discovered that the Pakistan International Airlines flight to Karachi was six hours behind schedule. After wandering aimlessly around JFK for nearly seven hours, we boarded the plane at 3:00 a.m. Fifteen hours into the trip and we still hadn't left the United States.

One plane took us from New York to Paris to Cairo to Karachi, and during those twenty-five hours, we ate and drank little. We'd been cautioned, correctly, that shortly into the flight the plane's restrooms would not be functioning.

Passing over Saudi Arabia at dawn (our second sunrise onboard), we decided it was safe to eat and drink. No first cup of coffee following a night of overindulgence has ever been so welcome. I was groggy and cranky, and the coffee was thick, black, and restorative.

Stepping through the cabin doorway, we were greeted by the piercing, but very welcome, desert sunshine. There was no jetway, and after descending the stairs onto the tarmac, we were directed to shuttle buses for the less than one-hundred-yard ride to the terminal. I was stiff after twenty-one hours in the air and made the mistake of trying to walk. Four soldiers responded to my choice by blocking my way and pointing their assault rifles at my chest. Welcome to Pakistan.

Chaos at airport immigration and a fender bender later, we arrived at our digs at the Karachi Holiday Inn. After eleven hours of sleep, I awoke to a sound I will never forget. The Muslim call to prayer, the azan, floated through the bone-dry air from the throats of a half dozen muezzins, chanting from minarets in every direction. Like opera singers at full throttle, each man seemed determined to outsing the others, creating an ensemble of voices both unified and combative. I stepped onto the balcony to absorb the breathtaking sounds floating through the still-dark sky, wondering if this could possibly be real.

From our unique perspective as artists and musical ambassadors, the experience to come would be an enlightening, terrifying shock to the senses—an emotional roller coaster taking us from the homes

Moments after arriving in Karachi, 1987. The author at far right.

of the wealthiest families in Pakistan, to city streets where people missing arms and legs begged for coins, to concert halls where we communed with Donizetti, Verdi, and Puccini.

Our travel costs were covered by the Bata shoe company, and a modest compensation for our concerts in Pakistan was underwritten by a wealthy, well-connected family. The family's heir apparent, a young man about my age, was faultlessly hospitable toward us in the same way a seventeenth-century nobleman might treat his servants on their day off. At every opportunity he made it clear that, as musicians, we were of a different class.

His family, we discovered, was an important cog in the Pakistani underworld. We'd heard this rumor but didn't believe it until we went to their home late in our visit and entered a palace surrounded by high walls, electrified fences, and a half dozen guys with machine guns at the perimeter. I haven't referred to the family by name because, having exited the country alive, I'd like to keep it that way.

Their home, where a small army of servants waited on them and their guests, was a disturbing contrast to the crushing poverty we saw elsewhere. Surrounded by this opulence, I could not help but wonder how long a system in which the nation's wealth is concentrated in the hands of so few could possibly last. Even in a totalitarian theocracy, I thought, someday there must be a reckoning. Eventually, the impoverished, unarmed have-nots will surely rise up and take back from the haves what is rightfully theirs.

Some of the superrich acquire their wealth through generations of hard work and ingenuity, respecting their society and honoring their civic and private commitments. When the rich have earned their way honestly, pay their taxes, and give back to their communities, why should they not enjoy the fruits of their labors? On the other hand, if the revolutionary bloodbath begins in the living room of thieves like the heir and his family, I am disturbed to admit that I probably won't mind all that much.

On our second day in Pakistan, this same family arranged a trip to their beach house on the shore of the Arabian Sea. On the drive, as camels and oxen trotted alongside us at intervals, we observed poverty far worse than what we'd seen in Karachi. In the countryside entire families lived in tiny grass shacks at the side of the road. When we asked how those huts held up in the weather, we were told not to worry since it hadn't rained in that part of the country in more than a year.

Following a lovely repast and camel rides on the beach, we discovered there were more surprises in store. Despite Carlos's best efforts, the heir would not be dissuaded from organizing the traditional cobra/mongoose fight for our entertainment. We were instructed to gather on the patio, where we encountered a shabbily dressed little man carrying a caged mongoose and a wiggling canvas bag. After a brief primer on this national pastime of Pakistan, the keeper deposited the two animals on the floor without a word of warning, and they immediately engaged in fierce battle. We watched, stunned, from perhaps ten feet away, with no barrier between us and the combatants.

As Westerners, knowing a bit about cobras but little about the mongoose, we assumed the cobra was the easy winner. But not so. The mongoose is equipped with tightly woven fur that protects it against this, its natural predator. But good genes weren't the only thing contributing to the mongoose's inevitable victory. On this day—as with most cobra/mongoose battles and many other things in Pakistan—the fix was in. The cobra had been de-venomed in advance. With no poison at its disposal, the snake's fangs were mere pinpricks against the mongoose's dense fur. Eventually, the mongoose got hold with its razor-sharp teeth and squeezed until the cobra bled out.

Following this gory display and the collection of his live mongoose and a cobra carcass, the animal's owner approached the heir for payment. They stepped out onto the beach, and we heard raised voices. Later, we learned that the heir had paid half the agreed-upon fee, and that amount only begrudgingly. But the heir's stiffing of the cobra man was only his warm-up act.

The stipend originally agreed upon between Carlos and the family was 230,000 Pakistani rupees, around $11,500, to be divided between the ten members of our group. Nine days and multiple negotiations later, Carlos collected 30,000 rupees from a family worth more than $500 million—$1,500 to be split ten ways as payment for two weeks of concerts.

Anticipating $150 each, we asked Carlos to give it back, our way of showing the heir our collective middle finger. But our leader, usually the least cautious and judicious of men, was adamant. The family, he told us, could cause us serious problems—like suddenly withdrawn visas or invented legal charges—if we showed disrespect.

Despite Carlos's detailed instructions and our best efforts, we all ended up with dysentery at one or more points on the journey. This detail may seem tasteless and irrelevant, but our varying states of intestinal health had a profound effect on our performances. Foreseeing this, Carlos arranged for two singers to know every part in every program. This plan worked, for the most part. But on concert days when nearly all of us were ill, we just did the best we could, taking turns running from the stage to the bathroom, often changing the program on the fly.

After Karachi we flew to Islamabad. This was our first encounter with outbound airport security in that part of the world and, having experienced it, I have not felt safe on a domestic US flight since. After our luggage was both X-rayed and searched, we were thoroughly frisked.

When I say "thoroughly," I mean the security people in Karachi knew more about us than the partner on a great third date.

Approaching Lahore, where we would change planes, I harkened back to my concerns about third-world airlines. In a cloudless sky, we circled the airport tower several times at low altitude—almost close enough to the controllers to see the whites of their eyes. Finally, the pilot informed us that the landing gear indicator light wouldn't illuminate. He assured us, however, that visual inspection from the tower confirmed the gear was down and they were "pretty sure" it was locked. Apparently, his colleagues on the ground didn't share his optimism, because as we approached landing, we looked out to see dozens of firetrucks and ambulances lining the runway.

That evening, as I nursed ailing intestines in my hotel room, the rest of the group headed to a dinner party organized by Indiana University alumni in Islamabad. With transportation plans worthy of a Chevy Chase movie, the two vehicles got separated and the van carrying the students wandered the dark Karachi streets for nearly three hours, chauffeured by a man who had lived in the city for four days and spoke no English. Eventually, my friends returned safely, having missed the party, suggesting that if this was not a metaphor for our entire journey, then nothing ever would be.

Arriving at the venue the following evening for our first concert in Islamabad, we found the piano tuner still hard at work despite an already half-full concert hall. The elderly tuner—who was nearly deaf and tuned by feeling sound vibrations through the piano's wooden frame—lived more than two hundred miles away, in Lahore. Despite his hearing handicap, he was the only competent tuner in the region and had been flown in early that morning against his objections—having no desire to hurtle through the air at hundreds of miles per hour. Confused upon arrival, he never connected with his ride and instead made his way to the local bus station, traveling nearly five hours back to Lahore. At length he was located, transported to the airport, and flown to the capital a second time. Thanks to this comedy, our concert began more than an hour late, but that was par for the course.

Our next stop, in Lahore, coincided with Christmas Eve, where we were invited for dinner at the home of the American consul. Wisely guessing that in addition to being ill we were tired of Pakistani food, our host provided a quintessentially American dinner of turkey, broccoli, and corn, accompanied by a white wine that probably would have sold for three dollars in an American grocery store. To us it was like dining in a Michelin star establishment, and we were very grateful.

Our reaction to this nice meal may seem overdramatic, but our entire relationship to food was, by this point, deeply dysfunctional. Food is an important element of appreciating a new culture, and we were looking forward to that part of the adventure. Unfortunately, between our fear of illness and, later, being ill, many of us were skittish about eating throughout the trip. In Pakistan, no dish outside of the consul's residence came without a liberal dose of ginger and chiles (even the "American hamburger" in our hotel was prepared this way), and we came to associate these tastes and aromas with illness. This connection was so strong that I have not been able to tolerate even the smell of ginger in the intervening thirty-five years.

The following day we were treated to a private visit at Lahore's two most important historic sites, the Badshahi Mosque and The Fort. The latter, a magnificent palace citadel, was the historic residence of various rulers and conquerors over the centuries. Here, my senses reeled with yet another sudden shift of perspective. For days we had seen nothing but the inside of airplanes and vans, our rooms at the Holiday Inn, and concert venues like those found nearly anywhere else in the world. But for the language barrier and the cuisine, we could have been in Omaha.

Then, suddenly, we stood before a dazzling three-hundred-year-old Mughal structure, finally experiencing what we'd come halfway around the world to see. Our communal bad attitude temporarily melted away because, bumps and all, the real adventure was finally underway.

By the midpoint of the journey, exhaustion, illness, and the ceaseless stream of commands from our leader were taking their toll.

Our jointly perceived lack of agency was poignantly expressed when our pianist, Richard Carsey, played "La donna e mobile" a half-tone too high, knowing full well that this would make the final note nearly impossible for Carlos. Following the aria's unsatisfying conclusion, Carlos stalked off the stage while Richard sat smirking at the piano and the rest of us ran for cover.

After two weeks in Pakistan, we began the second half of our journey, to four Arab Gulf states, beginning with Bahrain. At the Manama airport, we were detained a long time by customs officers who wanted to be bribed with free tickets to our sold-out New Year's Eve concert. They chose well, as the New Year's Eve event proved an affair of such drunken hilarity that it was difficult to tell which part of the evening was our performance and which the after-party.

Our next stop was Kuwait, but we arrived in Kuwait City two of our company shy. The other student tenor, Todd, had become so ill with his second bout of dysentery that he'd been hospitalized in Bahrain. Because he was not with us, I sang all my repertoire for the concerts and most of his, which pushed me to the limits of my vocal and intestinal stamina.

Next was Doha, Qatar. On our first day, we were granted an audience with the minister of culture in his ministry office, where few foreigners were allowed. Security was even tighter than the airports, but at last we were admitted. In the minister's lavish office, we sat in uncomfortable silence sipping authentic Turkish coffee while Carlos made awkward small talk.

Rising at last to depart, we were escorted through unfamiliar, increasingly narrow hallways and stairwells—clearly, not the way out. Finally, we entered a small television studio where Carlos, a sheepish grin suffusing his face, told us we were about to do an abridged version of our opera arias concert—on live television. There was no time to warm up and no opportunity to dress properly. But when the emir's brother-in-law says you're singing on live TV, you're singing on live TV.

Following our next, planned, concert in Qatar, we were invited to supper at the American ambassador's residence, where we met some of the town's diplomatic fat cats. Among them was the French ambassador, who took me aside to tell me he found my pronunciation in excerpts from *La Fille du Regiment* and *The Pearl Fishers* exemplary. I beamed and clinked glasses with l'ambassadeur.

The same evening, a police officer attending the party regaled us with disturbing information regarding our sightseeing jaunt earlier that day. Our driver had taken us by the emir's nearly completed new palace, where we stepped out of the van to gawk and snap pictures. Back in the vehicle, we alerted the driver that a guard with a machine gun was chasing us, waving his arms, and shouting. Rather than stop, the driver sped away. He'd done the right thing, the policeman at the party told us. Had we stopped, we'd have been taken to a station, interrogated regarding our illegal photos of the palace, and questioned about which subversive, anti-Arab agenda we represented.

Well into week four, our last stop was Dubai, United Arab Emirates. There we visited the gold Suk, window-shopped overpriced electronics, and marveled at a city that seemed to have birthed itself fully formed from the desert. The pendulum had swung to its opposite extreme, from the crushing poverty and despair of Pakistan to the gawdy opulence of Dubai. We had come, sung, seen, and been seen, and it was time to go home.

Unbeknownst to me at the time, I was destined for my first professional conducting post only seven months later, so our time in the Middle East was the beginning of the end for my years as a singer. Since then I have only dabbled at intervals, occasionally singing a duet in a pops concert and, most recently, sharing the mic with my dear friend Kristen Herzenberg (Christine in the Las Vegas cast of *Phantom of the Opera*) and my daughter, Stasia, in a concert of rock and roll standards. But although my years as one of "them" are in the past, all music becomes a part of who we are, and the essence of the once-and-future tenor lingers on.

Getting ready to rock out with Kristen Herzenberg in Abilene, 2021.

Toes in the Water

Not long after returning from the Middle East, the end of my second year of doctoral study was approaching. And despite the rewarding experiences I was afforded at Indiana, I found myself in a familiar predicament. In 1982, with my master's degree at Eastman nearly complete, I'd had no idea what to do next, and my position in 1988 felt similarly unsettling.

Before going to Indiana, I'd spent four years teaching, and now my conservative impulses took hold again, so I sought out another university position. I had already been offered a post in Pennsylvania, and there were rumblings in my direction from

Louisiana State, but even these attractive possibilities left me cold. I'd come to Indiana to redirect my career toward professional orchestral conducting, so accepting another professorship was a step in the wrong direction.

In January I applied to the Affiliate Artists Conductors Program and was invited to the audition along with one of my Indiana classmates. The other IU student, Akira Mori, was a tremendously talented Japanese conductor whom we all considered the most gifted person in the program.

The scale on which we evaluate our musical careers is relative. Akira, like many musicians I've known, deserved far more than the world delivered. (Conversely, I sometimes peer up the food chain, amazed at what I see.) By odd coincidence he accepted the orchestral conducting position at Louisiana State several years after I declined it. Later, he taught at Drake University, then returned to Japan. He now guest conducts in Europe and Asia, where I assume his considerable abilities are being put to better use.

The Affiliate Artists Conductors Program invited a dozen candidates to its audition each year. These lucky few conducted a professional orchestra for fifteen to twenty minutes and were then interviewed by the program's national director and the music director of the host orchestra. Two or three candidates were designated as finalists at the conclusion of the audition and were then eligible for positions with orchestras seeking an Affiliate Artists Assistant Conductor. Advancing to finalist status meant that you were, to some degree, on your way in the professional world. You had been distinguished from the crowd of thousands of aspiring conductors in their mid-20s who populated graduate programs all over the world.

We made the trip from Bloomington to Louisville by car, where Akira conducted on the first day and acquitted himself admirably. I conducted the following morning and felt reasonably satisfied with what I had done. Like many other Affiliate Artists hopefuls, I was conducting a full-time professional orchestra for the first time and tried desperately not to telegraph that I was a bit overwhelmed.

I had a brief shared history with Lawrence Leighton Smith, the man who was then music director of the Louisville Orchestra. We had met more than a decade earlier, though I had no expectation he would remember me. When I was in high school, regularly attending concerts with my grandmother, the conductor of the Oregon Symphony was the same Lawrence Leighton Smith. As a teenager I had watched him in awe week after week, trying to learn from afar about the craft of conducting and the art of making orchestral music.

My high school orchestra conductor, Mr. Kaza, was a violinist in the symphony and prevailed upon Maestro Smith to visit our school and conduct a rehearsal during my senior year. I reflect on that event frequently, as I have made dozens of similar visits to high school orchestras. I remember and attempt to emulate Maestro Smith's generosity of spirit whenever I'm asked to speak to, or work with, a group of students.

Maestro Smith's session with the Wilson High Orchestra opened the door of my understanding regarding how real conductors think about music, though only the first sliver of light penetrated my adolescent skull. Afterward, Mr. Kaza introduced a few of us who he thought would benefit from the opportunity. My one-on-one with Lawrence Leighton Smith that day lasted perhaps thirty seconds, but I clearly remembered his radiant intellect and quiet dignity.

At the Affiliate Artists interview following my session with the Louisville Orchestra, Mr. Smith began by saying he was positively impressed by what I had done on the podium. I thanked him but assumed he opened every interview with a similar remark. He must have read my mind, because as soon as I responded, he replied, "No, I don't mean it like that. You were really something special."

I was stunned by both the content and the directness of his response. Next, he offered detailed impressions of my conducting—both the positive and needs-improvement varieties—then asked about my background and career hopes. Mentioning where I grew up, I casually dropped the fact that we had met before.

Unflapped, he said, "Yes, I know. At Wilson High."

I can barely remember people I met last week, but he remembered me and the circumstances of our meeting after thirteen years.

A half hour later, as I stood to leave, he shook my hand and said, "I'm going to make this happen for you," and only days later I was informed that I had achieved finalist status. Perhaps it was an inappropriate confidence at that stage of the process, but I found his words refreshingly candid in a situation that usually suffers from an excess of secrecy and double-speak.

After Louisville Mr. Smith's career took some unusual turns, but I still consider him among the best and brightest America has produced. And whether the ups and downs of a career bear out that evaluation, he remains a shining example of a musician who became a conductor but remained a gentleman.

The Ballad of the Bayou

Due, in part, to the recognition I received for my performances of *Peter Grimes*, in March 1988 I was contacted by the Louisiana State University School of Music and asked to apply for the position of director of orchestral studies. This was an extraordinary possibility, the opportunity to conduct a fine university orchestra and teach conducting when I had not yet finished my doctoral degree. I'd hoped for an Affiliate Artists position, but no spots were coming open that season, so I was excited to have an opportunity at LSU.

I was given Richard Strauss's Horn Concerto No. 1 and Mozart's Piano Concerto No. 17 for my one-hour audition session with the LSU symphony. We started with Mozart, which allowed me an opportunity to discuss sound, style, ensemble, phrasing, and other important issues in this music.

On the page, Mozart appears simpler than the music of later composers, a quality that can lead student musicians to overlook its complexities. But Mozart's music is among the most demanding in our repertoire. Its simplicity and transparency—lacking the density and bombast of Brahms, Tchaikovsky, or late Beethoven—means that our specificity of phrasing, articulation, color, ensemble, and meaning must be of the highest sophistication. If the music of the late Romantics is like shooting fish with a shotgun, achieving success in Mozart is—as Mr. Scott of the Starship Enterprise would say—"like trying to hit a bullet with a smaller bullet, blindfolded, while riding a horse." It is either absolute perfection or abject failure. With only thirty minutes at my disposal, I attempted to bring this issue, and its specific applications, to the group's attention.

The horn soloist was a tall, handsome young man who played well but exercised a great deal of rhythmic freedom while paying little attention to the details in the score. At one point, when he took an awkward, self-indulgent liberty in direct conflict with the composer's instructions, I decided it was time to stop and teach.

"Can you help me understand why you're taking this tempo," I asked, "when it's the opposite of what the composer wrote?"

In a disdainful monotone, he replied, "Cause I wanna."

His response put me in a bind. Should I deal with his senseless response as I would under normal circumstances, or should I temper my reaction in consideration of the fact that *I* was the one auditioning? I found some gray area between the two strategies, getting my point across without being too aggressive.

And my response was tempered for reasons beyond self-preservation. Though annoyed and distracted by his behavior, I asked myself why a 22-year-old was approaching music making with a combative, self-important attitude. Despite his steely-eyed bluster, I saw fear in his expression and detected a slight tremor in his voice. Was he a decade-younger version of me, cloaking his insecurities in arrogance exactly as I'd done? This idea gave me pause, but the issue extends further than this one encounter.

I said something like, "Hey, orchestral music is a team sport, and we're all on the same team," but I wasn't getting through. In music schools his outlook is, too often, the norm. And it is this star attitude—fostered principally in the private teaching studios—that, intentional or not, has spawned successive generations of perpetually disgruntled orchestral musicians.

But his was not the only arrogance I experienced in connection with my brief stay in Louisiana.

Following the official part of my visit, the dean treated me to a dinner of Louisiana's ubiquitous crawfish. He ordered for us and explained the process, including the part where one sucks the goo out of the head. I found the entire affair messy and disgusting and couldn't figure out why anyone thought this was food for civilized people.

There was a great deal of Scotch on the menu, as well, though he did most of the imbibing, as I try to keep a clear head when I'm the interviewee. Over alcohol and shellfish brains, we found common ground in his dissatisfaction with their current opera conductor—the husband of a luminary on the voice faculty, appointed solely to please the diva. I expressed my desire to have opera as part of my portfolio if offered the job, and he said it was a match made in heaven—bottoms up.

Just before my visit to Baton Rouge, I was contacted by the Alabama Symphony with an invitation to audition for their associate conductor position, an indirect result of my success in the Affiliate Artists audition. But the day before I left for Birmingham, the dean of LSU called to offer me their job, placing me in an odd spot. I was suddenly catapulted back to age 17, trying to choose between a sure thing playing the drums in *Godspell* or taking my chances at the cast audition. But this decision had serious consequences and, though I'm not proud of my lack of daring, I wasn't rolling those dice. I accepted the LSU job, then telephoned my contact in Alabama. To my surprise they asked me to come despite my verbal commitment to LSU.

The audition in Alabama went well (my second time in front of a professional orchestra), and two days later I received a call from the executive director, asking if there was any wiggle room in my LSU situation. I told him I was flattered, but felt I had to honor my commitment. What I didn't divulge was that the recently delivered LSU contract was not what I'd expected. The document mentioned conducting their orchestra and teaching graduate students but not a word about opera.

Unable to reach the dean directly, I spoke with a senior administrator who said something I'll never forget: "Deans don't specify, they suggest." In other words, he's not writing this into your contract because then he'll have to keep his word.

I felt betrayed and little inclined to move to Louisiana. Then, as I deliberated over my nonexistent options, a bolt from the blue. The Alabama Symphony called again. This time the message was more emphatic: "You're the music director's and the orchestra's favorite. Isn't there some way to work this out?"

I don't believe in the hand of fate, but this was neither the first nor the last time a job has floated down from the heavens exactly when I needed it. I asked Alabama to hang on for twenty-four hours while I contacted the university again. I was told the dean was out of town, but that I could leave a message and someone would get back to me.

I said, "Okay, here's the message: Please do what you promised, and put it in writing, or I'm going to Birmingham."

The following morning I received a response. It was, and I paraphrase, "You're an ungrateful little shit who can go to hell."

Those words, the sweetest I'd ever heard, launched me into the professional orchestral world. Despite a near-miss in Louisiana, the improbable goal that had propelled me from Virginia Tech to Indiana University had been achieved. And Goethe was right: at the moment of commitment, the universe had conspired to assist me once again.

The Maestro

I met Leonard Bernstein only once. With a nearly forty-year career as a conductor behind me, one might assume this encounter was at a master class with the maestro, seeing him in concert and meeting him afterward, or something similar. However, none of that is the truth.

At the tail end of my time at Indiana, the IU Opera Theater mounted a production of Bernstein's *Mass*, to be performed in Bloomington that spring, and again in August at the Tanglewood Festival for the composer's 70th birthday celebration. *Mass* is an enormous work requiring singers, dancers, orchestra, costumes, rock band, and blues band, so the forces available at one of the nation's largest and finest schools of music were a perfect match.

The complexities and expense of producing the work, as well as its unusual structure, eclectic mix of musical styles, and message—many Catholics consider it sacrilegious, while people of other faiths often find it rambling and pointless—have relegated the piece to the ranks of the seldom performed. But Maestro Bernstein requested the piece for his birthday celebration, and so it had to be. Singing the part of the Celebrant was a recent IU alum, now a well-known master of the role, Douglas Webster. Robert Porco, IU's director of choral studies, conducted.

In addition to the Celebrant, choir, orchestra, and rock and blues bands, the work features a group of solo and ensemble performers called the Street Singers. These motley characters function as dramatic foils for the Celebrant and have significant solo roles as well.

Though I was neither a choral conductor nor a voice major at Indiana, Mr. Porco and I were acquainted because he had been the conductor of the *Candide* production that saw me shirtless and tied to a stake. Though our work together (in my role as opera assistant) was related to my conducting degree, Mr. Porco knew I had been a singer in earlier days. He had heard me sing, among other things, "Ah, mes amis," the aria with nine high C's from Donizetti's *Daughter of the Regiment*, at the send-off concert before the IU Middle East tour.

Strapped for a tenor with reliable high notes who looked like one of the street people (i.e., not like a typical operatic tenor), Mr. Porco asked me to sing the brief solo "I Believe in God." The short passage contains, not by coincidence, seven consecutive high C's. That treacherous high bit is often sung falsetto, or in a Broadway mix, but Professor Porco wanted it sung full out, in the manner I'd sung the Donizetti.

The piece was first presented in Bloomington in April, just before I departed for my new position as associate conductor of the Alabama Symphony. Settled into my apartment in Birmingham, with toes dipped into the new job, I traveled back to Bloomington in

Bernstein at 70! Tanglewood

Saturday, August 27, at 8:30

The Boston Symphony Orchestra is pleased to present

A production of the
OPERA THEATER of the
INDIANA UNIVERSITY SCHOOL OF MUSIC

BERNSTEIN — MASS, A Theatre Piece for Singers, Players, and Dancers

ROBERT PORCO .... Conductor
JACK EDDLEMAN .... Stage Director
STEPHANIE HALL .... Choreographer
C. DAVID HIGGINS .... Designer
MARY GOETZE .... Director, Children's Choir
ALLEN R. WHITE .... Lighting Designer
WAYNE JACKSON .... Sound Designer

Texts from the Roman Liturgy and by the composer, with additional texts by Stephen Schwartz

The role of the Celebrant is sung by Douglas Webster.

Please note that portions of this performance are being videotaped for future telecast and that pictures of the audience will be included.

Please be sure the electronic signal on your watch or pager is switched off during the performance.

MASS

I. DEVOTIONS BEFORE MASS
1. Antiphon: *Kyrie eleison*
2. Hymn and Psalm:
"A Simple Song" .... Celebrant
3. Responsory: *Alleluia*

II. FIRST INTROIT: Rondo
1. Prefatory Prayers
2. Thrice-Triple Canon: *Dominus vobiscum*

III. SECOND INTROIT
1. *In nomine patris*
2. Prayer for the Congregation
(Chorale: "Almighty Father")
3. Epiphany

24

IV. CONFESSION
1. *Confiteor*
2. Trope: "I Don't Know" .... Craig Curtis, Timothy McAdams, Charles Davidson
Descant .... Paul Augustine
3. Trope: "Easy" .... Thomas Barrett, Rita DiCarlo, Daniel Proctor

V. MEDITATION No. 1 (orchestra)

VI. GLORIA
1. *Gloria tibi* .... Celebrant
2. *Gloria in excelsis*
3. Trope: "Half of the People"
4. Trope: "Thank You" .... Melanie Sarakatsannis

VII. MEDITATION No. 2 (orchestra)

VIII. EPISTLE: "The Word of the Lord" .... Celebrant

IX. GOSPEL-SERMON: "God Said" .... Monte Stone, Preacher, with Paul Augustine, Patricia Dewey, Jane Dutton, Meera Popkin, Philip Zawisza

X. CREDO
1. *Credo in unum deum*
2. Trope: "Non credo" .... Daniel Proctor
3. Trope: "Hurry" .... Nancy Coulson
4. Trope: "World without End" .... Colleen McCarthy
5. Trope: "I Believe in God" .... David Itkin

XI. MEDITATION No. 3 (*De profundis*, part 1)

XII. OFFERTORY (*De profundis*, part 2)

XIII. THE LORD'S PRAYER
1. Our Father .... Celebrant
2. Trope: "I Go On" .... Celebrant

XIV. SANCTUS

XV. AGNUS DEI

XVI. FRACTION: "Things Get Broken" .... Celebrant

XVII. PAX: COMMUNION ("Secret Songs") .... Christopher Almond, boy soprano, Richard Carsey, Elvira Ponticelli, Charles Davidson, Melanie Sarakatsannis, Monte Stone, Celebrant

25

The program for *Mass*, Tanglewood 1987.

August, where *Mass* was re-rehearsed and a few new cast members put into place.

Arriving in Massachusetts the day before the performance, preparation activities— including fitting the production onto the Tanglewood stage—were a whirlwind. Curtain time arrived, and our unbearable anticipation mounted as one frustrating hold followed another.

The performance finally got underway around 8;45 p.m., a glorious success thanks to Robert Porco, Doug Webster, and the brilliant musicians, cast, and crew. Later, we learned that a preconcert dinner attended by Seiji Ozawa, Mr. Bernstein, and others, had run long. This explanation of the lengthy delay was, to some degree, the truth. We also learned, sadly, that Lenny was so far in his cups by the end of dinner that it was difficult to get him to the venue in a timely manner.

The elbow-rubbing portion of this story lasted around thirty seconds in a room backstage where the performers were given an opportunity to greet Maestro Bernstein. When I arrived at the small desk where he was seated, he looked up and graciously mumbled a few words about what a great performance I'd given—I was convinced he had no idea who I was in the show—and scrawled his initials on the back of my Tanglewood pass.

Later, I discovered that I had been a victim of mistaken identity. When my friend Richard Carsey (a Street Singer of roughly my height and build, who was also the pianist on the Middle East tour) approached Mr. Bernstein, the Maestro greeted him with, "Oh, you're the tenor with the crazy high C's!" Hearing that story years later, I was at least glad someone received credit for my efforts.

They say you should never meet your idols, and perhaps that's true. But thirty-eight years later, I still have that Tanglewood pass with "LB" scribbled on the back.

Chapter 5

Inspirations

We spent most of our conservatory years learning *how*, but rarely did anyone ask us to think about *why*. Why are we playing this music? What does it mean?

Once in a long while, one of my mentors would accidentally stray into the subject, like a confused motorist taking a wrong turn. But these conversations were unexpected, few and far between, strange and strained—as comfortable as the discussion of a recent divorce or impending colonoscopy. Punctuated by long, uncomfortable silences, they meant little because we were never encouraged to explore these questions for ourselves. When these ideas were presented without warning, it was difficult for young people to absorb or consider them meaningfully. Some sort of framework or consistency would have been helpful.

The subject usually evaporated as suddenly as it had appeared. After a tense moment or two, our professor would return to the important matters of sonata form, woodwind intonation, or independence of the left hand. The moment we all dreaded, when he would wander off into musing about how the music was related to Thomas Mann, Nietzsche, or the Buddha, had passed. We could all breathe again.

So why *didn't* we have those conversations? Why was so little time afforded to the questions "why?" and "what does it mean?" How could we have so badly misjudged what was important? How did we forget what brought us there in the first place?

Every day we berated ourselves, questioning why we could not play perfectly in tune, execute the difficult passage cleanly, or master every orchestral cue. But we often neglected to ask the most important question: What is the music demanding of us beyond the notes and rhythms, beyond the beauty of sound, beyond perfect execution?

As students we were to be somewhat forgiven for this shortsightedness, because getting the notes and the basic musical gestures correct was nearly all we had been taught. Our undergraduate auditions, then recitals and graduate school auditions all seemed to focus on little else. But when our teachers did break the silence—often in the awkward manner described above—why were we not more receptive?

We have all had professors who wander, annoyingly, into self-absorbed musings that concern the subject matter little or not at all. But when one of my conducting teachers delved momentarily into the Übermensch, emotional imagery, or schadenfreude, it was not irrelevant. Maybe we weren't ready, or the haphazard nature of the conversation made it difficult. Or, perhaps, we could have been less judgmental and opened our ears.

My students tire quickly of my often-repeated questions, "What is this about?" "What's happening in the drama here?" and "How do you feel about this?" I cannot read their minds, but it's not difficult to interpret their body language. Often, their unspoken reaction reads, "Professor, could you please just teach us conducting?" I wish, just once, some brave student would verbalize the question so I could respond, "I am."

But from the young musician's perspective, how much emotional or narrative importance can be placed on the two-measure diminuendo, linking an anxious-sounding rhythmically intense passage to a delicate, lyrical theme in the middle of a Schumann symphony? Perhaps a great deal, but we will never find the answer if we aren't looking.

Twenty minutes before a concert, I am sometimes overwhelmed by multiple responsibilities. I've just finished a preconcert lecture, I need to dress, and, hurrying down a hallway, I may be bombarded with questions and concerns by musicians and staff. As I approach my dressing room, I look toward the end of the passageway and see my wife, smiling, strolling nonchalantly toward me. My brain stops whirring as a smile suffuses my face, my shoulders relax, and the chaos fades. That's the feeling the two-measure diminuendo seeks to elicit. Great composers aren't just manipulating sound; they use music to write about life.

As conservatory students the answers may have been closer at hand than we realized, but because we were so far from satisfying our technical aspirations, we had trouble maintaining focus on the true goal. Somewhere in our passion for life, love, and music, we knew the truth all along. But many of us lost track of it in our drive for technical perfection and career advancement. Precisely when our emotions were tantalizingly close to the surface, we spent our time beating them down, grinding them away in the gristmill of our musical education and career preparations.

I spent my conservatory years, and well after, railing against performers (whether stars or peers) who sacrifice clarity, accuracy, and technique for the passion of the moment, and this is still a credo I hold dear. Emotion without discipline is adolescent nonsense. It took me longer to see the other side of the coin: discipline without risk, accuracy without emotional focus, and intellect without courage are roads to nowhere.

As students and young professionals who suffer the indignities of musical competitions and auditions, we are subtly encouraged to ask the wrong questions. And when we ask ourselves those incorrect questions twenty-four hours a day for a decade, we shouldn't be surprised when we keep coming up with the wrong answers.

We asked ourselves how to do it better, faster, louder, more perfectly. But each of us came to music asking why: Why does the music touch our souls, why are we brought to tears by a few notes?

These are the questions with which each of us began our musical journey, whether we knew it or not. And they are still the only ones that matter. Since few of my admired mentors seemed interested in dealing with these questions, I finally looked inward to discover *why*.

When I find I am savoring little in music or in life, it is because I know how but not why. I know how to make this collection of sounds technically perfect and exciting in a way that satisfies the audience, but at times might I forget that this music has the power to change my life and the lives of those who hear it? When we forget these things, the music has no such power. When we impose our mistaken priorities on the music, we rob it of its importance. And when we perform for our own aggrandizement, we transform the wide expanse of the musical universe into a thing as small as our ourselves.

Exploring the "why" means looking at those two undistinguished measures in the middle of a symphony and assigning to them human meaning that transcends the notes, then translating those ideas into technical choices and body language which communicate that meaning to the orchestra. But before any musician can begin this process, they must have an emotional and experiential framework from which to draw.

In my sophomore year in California, I found myself playing the piano for a friend's voice lesson with no idea I was about to get a lesson myself. The student was singing a piece from Schumann's *Frauenliebe und -leben* (A Woman's Love and Life), the first important song cycle in which a woman's emotional life is explored from the female perspective—albeit in a work with both text and music written by men. My friend's teacher didn't think her student was communicating the essence of the text and suggested that perhaps the reason was that she (the singer) was too innocent to fully understand what the protagonist was saying.

At the time I dismissed the remark as the snipe of a bitter old crone toward the pretty 19-year-old she wished she still was. But I was wrong. I was wrong, and the teacher—bitter old crone though she was—was right. Now, I often beat my head against the same wall, asking

20-something conductors to express joy, love, loss, and the entire gamut of human emotion and experience when they have lived little of it.

Following a rehearsal or conducting lesson, a student will occasionally point to a particular passage and ask how I came up with the idea to shape the phrase or orchestral color in a certain way. "Where does an idea like that come from?" is the question.

The answer I offer is simple, and, I imagine, frustrating: "Look at the music, play the music and sing the music over and over, think about the music your every waking moment, and ask yourself what it means and why it's there. Keep doing that until the image, idea, emotion, or memory appears to you."

"For every phrase, in every piece? That will take forever!" comes the common response.

When it does I breathe a grateful sigh, because it allows me to quote from my favorite film—another habit that irritates my students to no end.

Early in *Lawrence of Arabia*, the young Lawrence does a trick for a fellow soldier, extinguishing a match with his bare fingers but not so much as flinching. When his companion attempts it, his fingers singed, he exclaims, "It damn well hurts! What's the trick, then?"

"The trick," Lawrence explains, "is not minding that it hurts."

But advising, "Just do it," is often not enough.

Speaking to a student who had become frustrated with my repeated efforts to pry specific meaning and emotional content from her conducting, I asked, "Why do humans make art? Why do we paint, write, compose, play, and sing?"

The student stared, wide-eyed, perhaps hesitant to offer one of the obvious responses such as "fame," "money," or the banal "personal fulfillment."

"Here's a hint," I continued. "There are only two reasons human beings make art: one is the thing we desire most, and the other is the thing we most fear."

She tapped her sternum with one finger, and said, tentatively, "We want to be seen, heard, understood."

"You're almost there . . ."

The unusually perceptive student thought a moment, then offered, "Love. What we all desire is to be loved."

"Yes," I said, "and what else?"

"There is only one thing we all fear: death."

"Also correct."

There are four kinds of love. The first love we experience is between parent and child. The second, if we are fortunate, is the love between siblings. Both are irrevocable, regardless of the current state of the relationship. They are ties of blood and history that, family arguments and other dramas notwithstanding, cannot be undone.

The third love is the eternal friend. This is a person often encountered early in life with whom our bond was nearly instantaneous. As children we understood this instinctively, and no word about it ever needed to be spoken. This love remains throughout our lives despite time, distance, or lack of communication. And when contact is renewed, it is as though no time has passed and no previous misunderstandings are of any importance, so we pick up precisely where we left off. If we lose contact permanently, or our reencounter is awkward, then this was not the eternal friend.

The fourth type of love comes to us in adulthood, and most often arrives as a sudden, unexpected spark—a surprising connection of one soul to another for which we were utterly unprepared. This connection is not to be mistaken for the hormone-sparking exchange of glances in a rom-com. This meeting of souls may or may not have a romantic or sexual component, but whether it does or doesn't is irrelevant. Unlike an ordinary romantic couple, this unexpected connection cannot be, and does not need to be, justified by trivialities like similar backgrounds, age, or reading and movie preferences. It is a thunderbolt from heaven, a gift from a source unknown that we trivialize or ignore at our peril.

All these loves sustain us during our lifetime, while their absence brings us pain beyond measure. And it is in yearning toward, and gratitude for, these connections that through our art we are driven to speak.

The other reason we create is simpler: we are all going to die.

It has been said that humans are the only animals who have conscious knowledge of our own mortality. I'm not convinced that's true, but it doesn't matter. What matters is that we demonstrate this awareness by our endless efforts to leave something of ourselves behind after we are gone. We have children, we accumulate wealth, we acquire property and create empires, and we make art, all in an attempt to leave some mark on the world, some sign that we have passed this way.

But even if our efforts are pure vanity, without significance for the future, it is in the effort, in the act of creation itself, that we give meaning to a brief and finite existence. And combined with our yearning for love—and the joy, heartbreak, and Weltschmerz it brings—it is within this struggle to *be* that we find the kernels of inspiration that might guide us forward.

Between the Notes

As a student and young professional, I was often told I had unique gifts in the physical technique of conducting, and I considered it high praise. I still do. There is no sin in good technique and, contrary to popular belief, there is no inherent musical virtue in large, vague gestures.

Unfortunately, for several years I took the praise of my technical abilities and ran with it in entirely the wrong direction, draying orchestras endlessly on the minutiae of their execution while spending far too little time and energy on the music and its meaning. The technical confidence that could have liberated me, allowing me to focus on shape, sound, and the composer's intentions, led me, instead, to focus almost exclusively on technical matters. I erroneously equated the search for technical perfection (in myself and the orchestra) with the process of making great music. But one is a prerequisite for the other, not its substitute.

In literature there is much to be found between the lines of the text. We frequently discover an author's intentions by implication, nuance, or reference, not by what is directly stated. In the same way, an actor's performance guides us toward a more complete understanding of the playwright's meaning. The actor shows us what surrounds the words, and what is between them. For the orchestra, the conductor must be fellow actor, director, scenic designer, and more. If the conductor is only a stage manager, deftly ensuring everyone does their job at the right time but failing to coax mature pacing and nuance from the performers, then they are nothing.

In works of classical theater, we often hear young actors rush through long speeches as though the stage was on fire. They shout and spit and race through their lines in the hope of holding our attention through a lengthy, complex passage. The great acting teachers have offered contrary wisdom for generations: to find the meaning in the words, don't speed up, slow down. We sometimes observe the same phenomenon in young conductors. In place of thought, meaning, and shape, we are assaulted with faster and louder—the last refuges of the clueless.

Discovering what is between the notes, particularly what meaning is hidden in the composer's silences, is a never-ending quest. One often hears performances in which the silences are shortened or ignored. From a quarter rest in an adagio to a grand pause to the cavernous silences on the final page of Sibelius's fifth symphony, one regularly hears seasoned, accomplished musicians mishandle the silences. For many that vacuum is an unnerving, unbearable phantom. How can remaining silent, for what seems an eternity, be called performing? We feel the need to do something rather than nothing. It is an easy error to make, and the mysterious way time becomes compressed onstage only adds to the difficulty.

Without the silences the notes lose their meaning. And the notes acquire meaning, in part, by our understanding of what lies between them. As younger musicians we long for the big crescendo, the climax, the fast passage, the big, final chords, just as we live for the promotion, the raise, the reward. We fail, in both scenarios, to revel in the spaces in between.

But we do not always need to be doing something. When we choose to make the tempo of both our lives and our music so breathless that nothing new can surprise us by nesting in the empty spaces, then we have missed the point.

I used to think I would die regretting whatever important pieces I didn't get around to conducting, lamenting all the great orchestras that never invited me. When I'm ready to go I will regret, if anything, not having taken more time between the notes.

The Bowl of Fruit

Whether soloist, conductor, or orchestral player, a musician faces very different challenges than the painter, playwright, author, or composer. Five artists asked to paint the same bowl of fruit will produce five unique, individual works of art. They saw the same fruit, but each used their own vision and subjective judgment to re-create it on canvas. And it is these differences that make each painting a unique work of art, without reference to other paintings of fruit or the fruit itself.

Musicians who perform the standard repertoire are not presented with a generalization—a musical bowl of fruit—and asked to follow their muse. Our musical score is detailed, precise, and exacting. Re-creating a work of music from the printed page can feel less like an invitation to personal expression and more like an algebra equation with only one correct solution. One either plays all the notes or one doesn't. And if there is only one right answer to the equation, then must all other answers be wrong?

Early in my career, my mother asked, "When you conduct a certain piece, it's the same notes as when someone else conducts it, right?"

Naturally, I answered, "Yes."

"Then why does it matter who's conducting?" she puzzled. "Won't it sound the same?"

The answer, of course, is no. But explaining to a nonmusician how that comes about is challenging.

Our fundamental role as performers is not to create a new work of music each time we perform; it is to interpret an existing one. And yet, viewed another way, we are creating anew each time. Each moment of music, no matter how often repeated, should be as unique as a new day. Every morning the sun rises, we open our eyes, get out of bed, and brush our teeth. We did the same things yesterday, but that does not make this the *same* day. Today we will breathe, eat, and do a thousand other things identical to other days, but they will not have the same emotions, energy, or sensations about them. A kiss is a kiss; but does the first kiss feel the same as the thousandth, or the last?

Our role is like the actor who interprets the same text others have recited before. A great actor may speak the same words, but their unique personality, vocal instrument, and understanding of the character make the role new. The actor looks deeply into the text, the character, and themself to make the role unique. But they do not seek a unique performance by changing the essence of the original creation; they do not make the role their own by changing the words. The actor is not a playwright but a conduit for transforming the author's words into a living entity. Without strict adherence to the author's text, the play cannot stand, but without the actor's unique, personal input, it cannot live.

Similarly, we must be careful not to "fix" the work of the composer in our search for a unique performance. On the other hand, we are not musical actuaries for whom being right means we must arrive at the same answer each time we confront an identical musical equation. We are neither composers nor robots. We are actors on the stage of music.

Without the advantage of the actor's unique combination of voice, body, and temperament, what are instrumentalists and conductors to do? One soloist plays on an instrument virtually identical to another. Indeed, a pianist is likely to play the same instrument as those who come before and after in that concert hall. In general, the instruments utilized by one orchestra are no different from those in another. How, then, without taking unacceptable liberties, are musicians expected to make a work their own?

I suggested earlier that answers to these questions may have been closer to the surface when we were younger, less experienced, and less technically adept. The answers are not always found by searching outside ourselves. More often, they are instinctual.

As musicians whose art is in development—which is to say, all of us who are still breathing—we tend to vacillate from day to day, and from year to year, in our search for the perfect balance between technique and expression. One day it seems that the technical building blocks of our craft are the essence of what we do. The next day, or the next moment, those concerns are insignificant, and we let go of technical angst and allow the music to flow naturally through us.

In-depth study of musical detail and performance history is important, but it is not a substitute for personal exploration and discovery. Believing that score study and technique are the sole paths to unique music making is as foolish as the amateur actor who does no more than manipulate his voice or posture to bring his character to life. It is not until we free ourselves from both our technical paranoia and our fetish for musical detail that we begin to see the answers sitting right in front of us.

Finding personal meaning for the release of emotional tension in those two unremarkable measures of Schumann was never more complicated than identifying the specific image, moment, or idea that inspires a similar emotional and physical response. And with that accomplished, three seconds of music are accounted for. Next, we search for meaning in the other three million.

The solutions to important questions of music aren't in any books and they cannot be found online. They are either inside us or they are not.

Chapter 6

The Alabama Symphony and Other Adventures

The Alabama Symphony

Part 1: This Is No Way to Run an Orchestra

In January 1993 the Alabama Symphony Orchestra canceled two masterworks concerts—the result of a relatively minor dispute between musicians and management. But the disagreement dragged on. Two concerts became a week, then several weeks, and the organization filed for bankruptcy several months later. I had been associate conductor since 1988, and the orchestra's collapse came as no surprise to me or anyone else. If we were surprised, it was only because an organization in such disarray had survived for so long.

The orchestra struggled for years to make good on its monthly obligations to eighty-eight full-time employees. Every payday we heard rumors of insolvency, but there was always an emergency bail-out, a loan, or some other band-aid solution—all while I, in my first job in the professional orchestral world, wondered, "Is this how it's supposed to work?"

Immediately following the New Year's holiday 1993, another payday was at hand and, once again, the organization was short of funds. Management's solution was to ask the musicians to accept half the payment due, with the remainder guaranteed following that weekend's performances.

First, we must state the obvious: this should never have happened. Musicians who are already undercompensated should not be saddled with the additional indignity of having half their salary withheld. On the other hand, cash-flow problems do occur in nonprofit organizations and small businesses. When everyone is on the same team, people will usually try to be flexible for the common good. But when an organization is starkly divided between "us" and "them," there is no perception of a common good. The musicians of the Alabama Symphony rejected the request, and management responded by canceling concerts scheduled for that weekend.

The rampant perception that the shutdown was caused by the stubbornness of musicians was unfair. To say so is like believing that the spouse who files for divorce is to blame for the breakup of the marriage. When both parties are demonstrating irresponsible behavior and shortsightedness, the person who got fed up first is not necessarily the worst offender.

In a clumsy attempt to frighten the musicians back to work, the board suspended season ticket sales. Having failed to effectively frighten their employees, the leadership issued an ultimatum: the musicians would forego payment for all canceled concerts and make wage concessions applicable to the following season, or the sale of season tickets would be postponed indefinitely. Threat led to counter-threat, all of which led to the inevitable digging in of heels and, several months later, chapter 11.

In the months directly following the shutdown, I was asked countless times what went wrong and who was to blame. I have always given the same answer: just about everything that could go wrong did, and nearly everyone involved deserves some of the responsibility.

This was hardly how I imagined my entrée into the business, but learning what not to do has proved its worth time and again.

The Alabama Symphony had been performing since the 1960s, when it was called the Birmingham Symphony. At the outset it was a part-time, per-service orchestra where musicians rehearsed in the evening and were paid between $4,000 and $6,000 annually. Despite noteworthy financial and artistic growth during the next decade, the musicians' salaries were still far from a living wage—nor were they intended to be. Birmingham had the orchestra it wanted, conforming to the community's entertainment needs and fiscal resources.

In the early '70s, the earthquake that later spawned an institutional tsunami shook the orchestra's foundations, but the rumblings went unnoticed. What some undoubtedly believed a glorious step forward was, in fact, the beginning of the end.

In a well-intentioned but desperately callow move, the musicians proposed a change from nighttime/part-time status to full-time/daytime status for all seventy-four musicians. The response from the board—who clearly had no idea what they were agreeing to—was something like, "You want to rehearse during the day instead of at night? Why should we care?"

It's easy to see how responsibility for the eventual meltdown falls on both the musicians and the board. Someone on the board of a regional orchestra ought to have realized what the organization was undertaking. In the blink of an eye, they'd committed to providing a full-time salary for every musician.

The musicians' leadership also should have known better. Convincing the board to bless the move was not a magic bullet that guaranteed a living wage. Most of the orchestra's players were better off financially before the change, combining their part-time orchestra pay with other full-time income. During the first season of full-time status, the base pay was $11,000. Fifteen years later, that salary had grown to only $19,000, and by that time the organization was almost $1 million in debt.

The move to full-time status was no guarantee that the community would have the enthusiasm and resources to support the venture. What this decision did guarantee was nearly twenty years of bitter struggles, bad attitudes, mediocre music making, and increasing debt in a city inundated with more concerts than it wanted or could afford.

During the '80s and early '90s, the orchestra's budget and its accumulating debt grew without check. In 1988 (the year I arrived), the budget was $3.4 million (with a debt of $800,000), and by 1992 the budget had grown to $4.25 million (with a $2.5 million debt)—a 25 percent budget increase in four years that grew the debt 212 percent.

With each new contract negotiated with the musicians' union, weekly salaries rose and the number of weeks in the season increased. All those extra services (2.5-hour periods for rehearsals or concerts) meant more revenue creating opportunities were scheduled. But more concerts meant more staff, increased marketing costs, extra music to be purchased, and a second conductor. By the 1991–1992 season, the Alabama Symphony was playing nearly one hundred concerts per season, in a city with a population of 700,000, in a state with a largely blue collar, lower middle-class population.

It sounds as though the blame for an exploding budget should be placed squarely at the feet of the musicians, but that's not true. While the musicians' union did press for more services and higher pay, they didn't have much choice. Compensation needed to rise swiftly from its initial $11,000 if a full-time job in the Alabama Symphony was ever going to be more than a joke.

Faced with mounting debt and an uncertain future, the organization had two reasonably good options. Paralyzed by fear, they chose neither.

The board could have (1) lived up to the (albeit unwitting) commitment made in the early '70s, ensuring that musicians were paid a decent wage in a financially stable organization, or (2) approached the musicians when financial pressures began to mount, saying, "We admit it, we didn't know what we were getting into."

Had the board executed option 2 in the early '80s, there might have been an opportunity to put the orchestra back on a part-time basis. That option would not have been popular, but at least it would have been honest and sustainable.

In 1992, confronted with a grim financial picture, the management floated several ideas to reduce expenditures and balance the budget, none of which involved cutting musicians' salaries. Their first thought was to reduce the number of full-time musicians, mostly through attrition, saving $25,000 per year for each job eliminated. The proposal pleased no one. But it was classic emergency downsizing, and this was a classic emergency mess.

A more benign proposal would have allowed management to provide meals for the orchestra on tours, instead of making cash per diem payments. But every cost-cutting proposal was rejected. Like many other dilemmas in Birmingham, the proposals were not rejected because they were unreasonable. They were dismissed because they violated the cardinal rule that changing the union agreement in any way, for any reason, is a mortal sin. Apparently, allowing seventy-four musicians to become unemployed is not.

One obvious cost-cutting opportunity was noticeably absent from management's to-do list. In an organization $2 million in debt, where the full-time base pay of musicians was around $20,000, the combined annual salaries of the music director, executive director, and marketing director was $240,000. It's easy to blame the musicians for being inflexible, but how accommodating were they supposed to be when the music director, who conducted less than 50 percent of the season, was making $105,000? In their shoes, with no cuts in top salaries on the table, I'd have been pretty inflexible, too.

The Alabama Symphony resurfaced under new board leadership in the late '90s and has been playing successfully ever since. While their resurgence is only to be applauded, one item is worth noting. When the orchestra closed its doors in 1993, its full-time musicians were, as noted, compensated at around $20,000. That salary has a value of $43,832 in 2024. But the 2023–2024 audition advertisement for positions in the Alabama Symphony offers a salary of $38,700. In the thirty years since the shutdown, the musicians of the Alabama Symphony have taken an 11 percent pay cut.

Doc

Less than one month into my job as associate conductor, I was assigned to conduct a pops concert featuring the celebrated trumpeter, TV personality, and raconteur Carl Hilding "Doc" Severinsen. To say that I was starstruck—not to mention terrified—is putting it mildly, because I'd watched Doc and his band on the Tonight Show since I was a kid. But my fears were foolish. As anyone who knows him knows, Doc is a prince among men. We immediately bonded over our shared Oregon lineage, and he was supportive, kind, and generous at every turn.

For this, our first of many outings, he performed his standard fare of jazz and big band style arrangements, alternating with light classical virtuosic displays, thrilling the crowd with his playing while charming them with his wit. After each concert that weekend, we adjourned to the bar of his hotel, where I basked in his adorable presence and enjoyed his many, many stories.

While a pops concert may seem an unlikely catalyst for self-reflection, that weekend's concerts forced me to reconsider one element of our craft, pushing my thinking and work habits toward what, twenty years later, would become my first book, *Conducting Concerti.* Doc's virtuosic showpieces required considerable technical and aural skill from the conductor, and there were moments when I realized my execution and accompanying were less than perfect. My self-flagellation was amplified by a phone call from one of the musicians, offering her unsolicited assessment that my performance as Doc's musical partner merited a grade of D+.

While she may have been a bit harsh—I wasn't her favorite anyway—she had a point. None of my training, including two years in the doctoral program at Indiana, included focused work on the craft of accompanying, the unique elements of score study involved, or the conductor/soloist relationship. I determined, from that moment, to rethink my approach, creating new methods of study, rehearsal, and performance practice that have served me well in the intervening years.

Following Friday and Saturday evening performances, on Sunday afternoon we took the concert to Tuscaloosa, one hour from Birmingham. On our way (I felt like a star, riding with Doc in his limo), he told me he had a tight time frame to catch his flight, so he'd be walking directly from the stage into the car when we finished—no second bow and no long goodbyes. Knowing I wouldn't see him after the concert, I went to his dressing room at intermission to thank him for the opportunity to work with him.

While encountering a celebrity in real life may be a bit surreal, walking into Doc's dressing room and finding him in a lounge chair, feet up on the ottoman, wearing only his light blue jockey shorts was a step beyond. At the threshold I took a moment to collect myself, making certain not to stare at the sky-blue undies. Despite my traumatized state, I remember my first thought upon entering the room: I hope I'm in such good shape when I'm 60.

Over the next few years, we played concerts together with several different orchestras. On one of those occasions, our conversation turned to his new gig as principal pops conductor of the Milwaukee Symphony. Doc knew I'd been arranging and orchestrating for years and asked if I'd write an arrangement of "Ding Dong Merrily on High" for piccolo, trumpet, and orchestra, which I happily delivered. He played the piece many times during the next decade, and it has also been performed and recorded by the Houston Symphony, among others.

Doc was so delighted with the success of "Ding Dong Merrily on High" that he set me a larger task the following Christmas—a setting of the poem "A Visit from St. Nicholas" (a.k.a., "The Night Before Christmas") for choir and orchestra, which he conducted in Milwaukee and elsewhere.

In one of our conversations along the way, Doc mentioned that he'd never performed a classical trumpet concerto as a professional but still hoped to do so before it was "too late." So in 2002 I booked him to play the Hummel trumpet concerto with the Arkansas Symphony on a pair of masterworks concerts.

At the first rehearsal, Doc was a bit less than his usual, technically impeccable self. After playing a passage not to his liking, he leaned toward me, held out his borrowed E-flat trumpet, and whispered, "I'm still trying to get the hang of this damn thing!"

A lesser person might have either pretended he was perfect or found some way to blame the orchestra or me. But not Doc. And, not surprisingly, by the time the first performance arrived, he had all cylinders firing.

His appearance in the concerto spawned the last of our compositional collaborations. After his first Hummel performance, he found an empty seat in the house and listened to the orchestra play Rachmaninoff's Symphony No. 2.

Afterward, aglow in a post-Romantic stupor, he took me aside. "David," he began, "that was amazing. I'd forgotten how beautiful that slow movement is. I need to play that."

I didn't respond because I had no idea what he was talking about.

He then clarified, "Can you write an arrangement where I play that tune? Maybe slow at first, then something faster?"

"No" was not a word in my vocabulary when talking to Doc.

A few months later, I sent him a draft of "Rach for Doc." The piece begins with a nearly verbatim version of the opening of the Rachmaninoff slow movement, with the solo trumpet playing the theme he'd admired. What follows is an up-tempo, disco/rock version, replete with abundant opportunities for Doc to show off his high notes.

Orchestral musicians uniformly roll their eyes at the piece, and I don't blame them. But instead of calling it kitschy or cheesy, I prefer to think of "Rach for Doc" as the quintessential example of the genre known as "Trash-tastic."

108
meno forte
brass
Doc
brass
Doc
Tuba
Timp.
Doc
Fender Bass
Drums
Vln I
Vln II
Viola
Viola
'Celli
'Celli
Bass

"Rach for Doc."

The Alabama Symphony

Part 2: The Story of the Little Staff That Couldn't

The staff of a professional orchestra is often a mixed bag. This is particularly true at the regional level and below, where salaries and geography often limit the organization's ability to attract quality applicants. Nonetheless, there are many talented and dedicated people working in this part of our industry. These individuals give their all for too little money, working too many hours, and receiving too little credit.

Unfortunately, the nonprofit world also attracts individuals who come here to hide. They seem to believe that because the business is nonprofit, it doesn't matter how thoroughly, creatively, or diligently they do their job. Their collective attitude seems to be, "The place isn't supposed to make money anyway, and I'm not getting paid enough to sweat the details."

I have had occasion to express an opinion that some find objectionable, and it applies as much to our staff employees as is does to musicians and conductors: If you don't like the salary, don't take the job; but if you take the job, you've committed to giving your best. I've conducted many engagements where I was underpaid, overworked, or otherwise poorly treated, but it stays off the stage. That's another thing my father taught me: when the lights go on, it's only about the work.

The Alabama Symphony staff was a heterogeneous stew of the dedicated and able mixed with the lazy and clueless. The number of employees fluctuated unpredictably between twelve and fifteen, the result of sudden resignations and unexplained disappearances. More than a dozen staff is a lot of salaries at this level, but more disturbing was the fact that, even with all those people on the payroll, important tasks were left undone. This is a difficult subject because some of these people were my dear friends. On the other hand, some of those friends were part of the problem, and the truth is the truth.

During my time with the organization, the position of executive director was filled by two different men. The first, Ed W., resigned under pressure in 1990 and was replaced by Mark W.—no relation. Both men worked tirelessly for the organization and were called upon to make difficult and sometimes controversial decisions. Though very different in temperament, they shared one thing: both were intensely disliked by most of the musicians.

That enmity was utterly unfair. It was also par for the course in an organization in trouble. Mark had the unwished-for distinction of being the orchestra's last executive director (before its resurrection years later) and became a lightning rod for the anger of musicians and the community.

Four different people held the position of executive assistant during this five-year period, none of whom would have been employable in the for-profit world due to their checkered employment histories and dubious work ethic. But the larger contributor to their failures was that no one seemed to know what the job entailed. The executive assistant's portfolio was a catch-all of details overlooked by operations, administration, marketing, touring, and fundraising. Mostly, it was someone to blame when things went wrong, which probably explains why they kept getting fired.

The executive secretary was an extremely competent, organized woman with a fierce personality who took no bull from anyone and dispensed attitude by the truckload. Inexplicably, none of the other dozen-plus staff had clerical work in their job descriptions, so there was no one else who would, or could, so much as type a letter. This was a constant disturbance to operations and a frequent embarrassment.

The marketing department was a dizzying revolving door, where a parade of semicompetent individuals rarely stayed long enough to get up to speed. More on that subject in "Part 3: Confused Priorities."

Deciding how to structure the development staff is often a damned-if-you-do / damned-if-you-don't proposition. If the executive director puts proper resources into fundraising, they're "wasting money"; if not, they're "not taking development seriously." The Alabama

Symphony's development staff was in no way remarkable, consisting of two individuals with limited experience. Perhaps they raised funds equal to their salaries and benefits, but I doubt it.

Our ticketing personnel—L, B, and A—were a study in contrasts.

L, the ticketing manager, was a friendly, capable woman who neither understood nor cared to understand anything about the orchestra, its music, or its mission. She answered the phone, attempted to tell patrons what was being played on a given concert, and attended to the box office window. If there was anything going on *inside* the concert hall, she seemed blissfully unaware.

B, the ticketing assistant, was a troubling case. She came and went as she pleased, was regularly dismissive with patrons, and treated those above her in the administration as though they didn't exist. And even though she came to work only when she got around to it, no one ever seemed to get around to firing her.

Neither L nor B were bad people. They simply personified the difficulty of hiring qualified, committed staff even in a regional orchestra of substantial size.

The third member of the ticketing staff, A, was Ann Robinson. But her story, what little I can tell of it, belongs in a place far removed from this chaos.

Keeping the perpetually discontented musicians in line was not an easy task, but the personnel manager, who was also the principal trumpet, managed it with a steady hand. Though he had a bit of a blind spot when it came to disciplining his fellow brass players, he was by no means to blame for the orchestra's discipline problems. The music director sets the tone, and the personnel manager cannot be expected to enforce principles of discipline and professional behavior that, for all practical purposes, do not exist.

Our operations manager came to the orchestra the same year I did. We learned the ropes together and often commiserated regarding the general chaos. He was a former tuba player and his wife, a violinist, had recently won a job in the orchestra. Following the collapse they moved to Florida, where he took up driving an eighteen-wheeler.

Finally, there was the director of regional development, a position created from whole cloth when yet another well-groomed young man failed first as executive assistant and then as marketing director. How could they fire someone so popular, so slick, so corporate? Instead, they created a thoroughly redundant position, director of regional development. They paid him a good salary (around 200 percent of musician base pay), leased him a car, and spent a fortune on hotels and meals so he could set up concert dates in cities where the orchestra had toured every year as a matter of course.

The Dutch Dilemma

In the spring of 1989, one year into my life in Alabama, I was one of thirty-three conductors from around the world invited to participate in the Kiril Kondrashin conducting competition in Hilversum, the Netherlands. Thrilled to be included, I quickly set to work on the daunting stack of scores I needed to learn.

Each of the four rounds of competition had its own repertoire of two to five works, requiring the preparation of more than fifteen works in total. By the time I left the United States, I had committed two months of study and $2,000 (nearly 10 percent of my annual take-home pay) to the endeavor.

I arrived several days before the competition began, wanting to acclimate to the time change and settle into the town. As instructed, I reported to the competition's headquarters to receive registration materials, but I had another important errand at the same location.

Each conductor selected two works for the first round from a list determined by the competition. I chose Beethoven's *Egmont* Overture and Mozart's Symphony No. 39, but the official copy mailed to me showed the Beethoven and two Mozart symphonies, the 39th and the 40th. By telephone I expressed my concern to the competition director—only two works could be chosen in the first round—but he assured me that a corrected document would appear in the printed material when I arrived in Hilversum.

When I picked up my registration materials, however, the same list of three works appeared. Upon meeting the competition director, I expressed my continuing confusion, but he seemed to have no memory of our telephone conversation. When I asked him, again, to make the changes, he appeared annoyed and seemed to imply that the whole thing was my fault. Anticipating complications, I produced the form I had faxed weeks earlier, but he didn't seem interested.

To my request for a corrected document, he replied, "It's okay. If you don't want to conduct both Mozart symphonies, then don't."

His reply made no sense. The judges are free to request a performance of any work on the contestant's list, and saying, "I don't want to do that," is not an option. Clearly eager to move on, he brusquely told me the information would be changed on the document given to the judges. Then, he turned and walked away.

The jury asked first for the *Egmont* Overture, and I took the orchestra through the piece. *Egmont* is a simple work, made more complicated on this day by the orchestra's habit of playing extremely far behind the beat. Nonetheless, it was a decent playing, and I felt I had demonstrated both the craft and the art as I knew them.

Then, like watching a slow-motion car crash, the chairman of the jury asked for the work I had not chosen. In hindsight, I know the smart move was to conduct Mozart's Symphony No. 40, which I knew well, and shut up. But I was so aggravated I couldn't let it go.

I told the chairman that the piece was not part of my selected repertoire, and he replied by waving the paper in his hand, saying, "It's on the list. You cannot change it!"

By this time the competition director was out of his seat and standing next to me. I produced a copy of my original application and turned to him, expecting confirmation. Instead, he shrugged his shoulders as though he had no idea what I was raving about. The same man with whom I had spoken on the telephone two weeks earlier, who had assured me in person that the problem would be corrected, now acted as though this was all news to him.

Not wishing to delay the proceedings further, the chairman threw down the paper and said, "Fine, do the 39th, then."

I conducted the first two minutes of the symphony, until the clock reached the minimum time each candidate was allotted. Then, I was excused. It was clear I had been disqualified for changing the repertoire.

Two days later, after the first cut was announced, I had a chance encounter with three other conductors. We were two Americans, a Russian, and an Irishman in a bar. This sounds a bit like the beginning of a joke, and, in a certain light, it is. The joke began with an alcohol-lubricated admission from the Irish conductor, whose story sticks with me and has continued to color my opinion of conducting competitions.

The thirty-three invited conductors had been prescreened from several hundred applicants through résumés and letters of recommendation. In his impaired state, the Irish conductor, the only one at the table who had advanced to the second round, admitted that his résumé was almost entirely fiction. He was a drummer in a rock band in Dublin and had never stood in front of a real orchestra until the first round of competition. In fact, he confided, he only vaguely comprehended the conductor's score, and had learned the competition repertoire mostly by listening to recordings and imitating the gestures of famous conductors.

If I was not already put off by the idea of judging conductors in a fifteen-minute beauty contest, that information sealed the deal. I have always contended that a reading session is no way to evaluate a conductor's skills. What we do is a far more nuanced affair, the lion's share of which is apparent only in rehearsal. Almost anyone can learn to beat good-looking time, and my unknown Irish friend proved that even a novice can fool expert judges when the skills being tested are so shallow.

But all was not lost. My bargain airline ticket limited me to a flight home six days later, so I sought diversions outside the competition. On each of my remaining days, I borrowed a bicycle and took off into the countryside. Cycling for less than ten minutes, I was out of the city and wandering the narrow roads from farm to farm and from town to town.

After pedaling an hour or more, I'd passed through many small towns whose names all looked alike, and in the pre-GPS era it was challenging to keep track of where I'd gone and how I would find my way back. I'd come to Hilversum believing I had one purpose. But instead, there I was, wandering contentedly.

When I started college, I also thought I knew my goal, having little understanding that, for some of us, the path is not the straight line we'd imagined. The feeling of being lost—or nearly so—temporarily having no responsibilities, with no one knowing or caring where I was, brought a clarity and calm I had not experienced in years.

Much of our repertoire is narrative, a musical story that moves logically from point to point. But some composers have broken this mold, allowing the music to exist for its own sake—to flow forward, seemingly without goal, like a runner's high. In Sibelius's symphonies, for example, we often find ourselves swirling in directionless eddies of sound, buffeted by currents that seem to lead nowhere. When confronted with this music, many of us labor to impose direction on the directionless, function on that which is, by its very nature, narratively functionless. When we attempt to do so, both we and the music suffer.

J. R. R. Tolkien to the contrary, I'd always hated the saying "Not all those who wander are lost," believing it an excuse for not engaging with the real world. And though I still cling to my electronic calendar and find security in knowing what hotel I'm staying at during a gig eighteen months in the future, I no longer fear being lost. Of course, I was disappointed not to move forward in the competition. Like everyone there I had arrived with dreams of instant adulation and success. But instead of a big check and an armful of guest conducting engagements, I came home with the first glimpse of what it means to let the music take me on a wander.

But not all wanderings pull us toward the light, and not every journey is a road to revelation. All too often we find ourselves traversing dark pathways, lost in our quest to find the "why" in our music or ourselves. At these moments the innocent joy of Dutch cycling seems remote, as does the likelihood of finding our path home.

Mr. Ryder, the fictional renowned pianist of Kazuo Ishiguro's *The Unconsoled*, wanders in frustration among the streets and personalities of a nameless European city. He is searching for the time and place of his scheduled recital but, in reality, he seeks the source of his lifelong confusion and alienation. This is the quest we all share. The only question is whether music is the source of the problem or the answer. Those few who know me well understand that I wrestle with these demons daily. And although I seldom emerge as the victor, I still believe there is a pathway toward the light.

The Alabama Symphony
Part 3: Confused Priorities

The difficulties facing the orchestra's marketing department were plentiful. Management often behaved as though advertising was semi-essential, distributed bipolar swings in salaries, and made no effort to deal with the fundamental problem that marketers can't sell a product the public doesn't want.

Every orchestra wrestles with the same conundrums: attracting a younger audience, compensating for subscription losses with increased single ticket sales, and overcoming the Gen Z, Gen X, and Millennials' lack of interest in this music. So the fact that marketing is sometimes given short shrift speaks more to a sense of hopelessness than to any lack of business sense.

The issue of staff salaries in regional orchestras is particularly thorny as it relates to marketing and development, where genuine expertise and experience are vital. When I came to the Alabama organization, the marketing staff of two had a combined age of 45, accumulated years of experience amounting to three, and salaries totaling $35,000.

None of that means they didn't work their collective butts off and occasionally pull a rabbit out of their hat. What it does mean is that this wasn't an appropriate marketing wing for an organization risking more than $3 million annually.

From late 1988 to mid-1990, the organization was fortunate to have a bright young woman, Adelia, heading the marketing department. She had been hired in the subordinate position, but a few months after her arrival, yet another marketing director departed, and Adelia was given the top spot. Was promoting from within a lazy choice? Perhaps. But Adelia was a clever, creative woman with real potential to grow into the job, and the salary was never going to bring experienced marketing gurus out of the woodwork. As with development hiring, the executive director was damned if he did and damned if he didn't.

In 1990, about the same time Adelia left the organization, the executive director departed, and Mark W. took over that role. One of his first moves was to hire a marketing director from outside the organization. The new hire was an outstanding young man with energy, ideas, and experience in the business. Less productive was the schizophrenic change in philosophy regarding compensation in that department.

To some of us, it seemed a bit out of line for the new marketing director to be paid more than $60,000—300 percent of musician base pay, the equivalent of $144,00 in 2024. This meant the total compensation for that department had risen from $35,000 to more than $85,000 in less than one year. Yes, marketing salaries needed to rise to attract qualified people, and marketing needed to be placed higher on the organization's list of priorities. But this exponential increase in financial outlay for marketing staff was not nearly matched by new ticket income. It would have made more sense to hire Adelia back, give her a $10,000 raise, and spend the other $40,000 *on marketing*. Throwing money at that big salary didn't serve the organization. The orchestra needed to put dollars where they would sell tickets.

Having mercilessly beaten up on the marketing staff and the decisions surrounding them, I must now come to their defense. The reality was that no marketing director could succeed when the marketplace was oversaturated and the product was virtually unsellable due to the music director's odd leadership philosophy and quirky programming and the orchestra's resulting mediocrity.

The Oak Ridge Boys

Near the midpoint of my tenure, we booked the country-rock band the Oak Ridge Boys for our pops series. The band's management was placing renewed emphasis on symphony bookings and had commissioned new orchestra arrangements for their show. Two weeks prior to the performances, I inquired regarding the whereabouts of the music and was told it hadn't yet arrived.

A week later my phone rang. Our operations manager said he'd heard from the band's agent, who'd asked if anyone on the symphony staff did professional-level arranging and orchestrating.

I remember thinking, *this can't be what it sounds like*, and asked suspiciously, "Why?"

The band had hired an arranger in the Netherlands to create their new show, but after months of haranguing, they discovered he hadn't written a note. Now desperate, they wondered if someone at the Alabama Symphony could write orchestrations for them.

The obvious question was why the band had hired someone in the Netherlands when there are dozens of great arrangers virtually next door in Nashville. But that rumination wasn't getting me any closer to solving the problem at hand. After a few minutes of panicked consideration, I agreed to orchestrate ten songs—a task for which I was given less than one week.

I relayed a message to the band saying I would need two things immediately: lead sheets of their songs (the vocal line and guitar chords that would form the outline for my orchestration) and recordings of the songs exactly as they play them in their live shows. A couple hours later, I was told the band was heading into a studio that afternoon to record performance tracks of the songs, which would be FedExed to me the following morning. But regarding my other request, they were sorry to tell me that there were no lead sheets because no one in the band read music. This meant I had to create lead sheets from their recordings before beginning the orchestrating process. This is not difficult—basically a freshman music theory exercise—but it would take time, a commodity in short supply.

With all the back and forth, we had failed to discuss a price for my work. I had no idea what to propose, having never done an arranging project for a high-profile client in a similar time crunch, so I contacted a friend who had arranged for Stevie Wonder.

His response was simple, "The going rate is $500 a minute, but this is an emergency so you should ask for more."

At $500 per minute of finished musical product, a typical pop song would net between $1,500 and $2,000. They were sending ten songs, which landed us somewhere north of $15,000 for a week's work. That was close to half my annual salary, so I didn't feel the need to be a jerk and add the emergency penalty.

The cassette arrived punctually the following morning and, having cleared my schedule, I tore open the package and set to work. Though tedious, the task of taking dictation from the recordings went smoothly, and I estimated I could have all the lead sheets written by the end of the day.

Then I hit a snag. Those who remember cassette tapes may recall that those machines were produced in a variety of qualities. On some devices, if the motor drove the spindles marginally too fast or too slow, the pitch heard in playback was slightly higher or lower than the original recording. For most applications this didn't matter, because the difference would have been so slight as to be meaningless. However, in creating the lead sheets by listening and playing the piano by ear, I had to be certain I was transcribing each song in the correct key. There was a slight difference between the recording and my piano—most likely the fault of my equipment rather than theirs—but the apparent conflicts were easily resolved by intuition.

As fatigue set in, I came to the last song, a lovely ballad called "Make My Life with You." After starting the tape and beginning my experimentations at the piano, I panicked. The song appeared to be in the key of G-flat major, and few popular songs are in such an odd key. The song had to be in one of the adjacent, more obvious keys, F major or G major, but the sound on the tape was dead center between them. I was uncertain how to proceed, but a greater concern began to take shape. Did this anomaly call into question the work I had already done? Was every lead sheet I'd written in the wrong key? I couldn't continue until the question was answered, and by that point it was late in the evening.

First thing the following morning I relayed my question to the band. To my surprise and relief, the reply was simple, "Yes, 'Make My Life with You' is in G-flat major." With a sigh I put my nose to the grindstone, finishing the project as the band's bus pulled up to the concert hall five days later.

The Oak Ridge Boys were friendly, fun, and grateful for my quick work. Still, I was nervous as the rehearsal began, wondering if they would like the orchestrations and harboring lingering concerns about my cassette deck and everyone playing in the same key. The rehearsal went off like clockwork, as did the two performances, and the Oak Ridge Boys took my arrangements on the road for the next several years.

I suppose it was gratitude for my work, or just that we'd had a good time together, because during the following couple of years they flew me to other locations to conduct their show. We had fun playing with the Pacific Symphony, the Fort Worth Symphony (decades before I moved to Texas), and several others. It was as close to being a rock star as I would ever get.

The Alabama Symphony

Part 4: I Can Get It for You Wholesale

When an organization is in trouble, it's tempting to grasp at any straw. It's also easy to make the problems worse by repeatedly, if inadvertently, devaluing the product. Both mistakes plagued the Alabama Symphony.

The orchestra's survival strategies between 1990 and 1993 can be summarized in both its disastrous efforts to garner direct support from the state legislature and its groveling dependence on city funds for the Pops in the Park series.

In 1990 the organization began a statewide lobbying campaign. In a nutshell the goal was to remove the orchestra's funding from the state arts council, putting it directly into the hands of lawmakers. So a bill to add a $1 million annual appropriation was introduced in the Alabama legislature. The theory was that once the organization had a line item in the state budget, the orchestra's funding would be less volatile because it would not be subject to the whims of local or state arts administrators.

After nearly a year of deliberate, exacting work on the part of the executive director, board members, and sympathetic politicians, the legislature passed the line item. The organization would receive more than $900,000 annually and, in return, the orchestra would undertake a new, rural touring schedule—full orchestra concerts and in-school visits in cities that could not afford to pay the orchestra's regular touring fee.

The orchestra's budget was more than two-thirds fixed costs (salaries and benefits for musicians and staff, concert hall and office rent, etc.), so the organization would be using prepaid labor when performing these rural concerts. The orchestra would utilize unused musician services, spend around $100,000 on direct touring costs, and receive upward of $900,000 in return. In a perfect world, it was a great plan.

Unfortunately, the people who devised and fought for the symphony's line item miscalculated on several fronts. They didn't understand the anger that the appropriation would inspire in the arts community, they didn't adequately appreciate that a line item can be cut as easily as it was enacted, they didn't grasp the perilous nature of having all one's financial eggs in the same unstable basket, and, last, they didn't foresee proration.

During the first year to which the new funding applied, the orchestra dutifully inaugurated its rural touring schedule. All other problems notwithstanding, the idea of rural touring was inspired. During that year we felt like missionaries, exposing thousands of uninitiated adults and children to the experience of great music. The orchestra was not exactly flush with funds, but things were substantially improved.

And it was too good to last.

With its new line item in the state budget, the Alabama Symphony was effectively cut off from the traditional public funding pipeline. It was removed from the granting process with the state arts council, and the orchestra also lost favor at the city and county levels, where bureaucrats now saw the organization as "uppity." Encouraged by other arts organizations, those in charge of city and county funding now viewed the symphony as "taken care of" by the state. At the same time, the state of Alabama experienced significant revenue shortfalls, and legislators began to reconsider the current year's budget, reducing or eliminating unnecessary expenditures.

For reasons more political than fiscal, the budget trimming effort was amplified by the desire of some legislators to eliminate pork appropriations. But in the long run, political machinations were irrelevant, because the state's financial woes forced a 50 percent proration of nonessential budget items. More than $400,000 of the orchestra's current year appropriation vanished in a heartbeat.

Our rural touring schedule was fully planned and partially implemented, and the symphony's board felt that the best course was to proceed despite the state having reneged on its promise. So the organization continued to spend large unreimbursed sums for per diem, small ensembles, transportation, and hotels.

The logic behind the board's decision was sound, from a certain point of view. Once the state got its house in order, they reasoned, the symphony could go back to the legislature with clean hands. Unfortunately, expecting Alabama politicians to be grateful that the orchestra had kept its part of the bargain was a bit naïve. After the initial cut, another several percentage points disappeared in a second round of proration, followed by further attempts to eliminate the line item altogether. But before anyone could sort it out, the issue was moot. The orchestra had ceased operations.

The lesson, if there is one, is that it's not smart to count on people you don't know to doggedly support something expensive and politically unpopular, especially when it's a thing they neither understand nor believe in. Good advice anywhere, but particularly in Alabama.

The other half of this wholesale approach to orchestra funding is expressed in the philosophy "If people won't pay for it, give it away." This is essentially the same strategy used by drug dealers: give it away until people are hooked, then start charging for it. Great music can be an overwhelming experience, intoxicating and even a bit addictive, but it's not heroin. Consequently, a similar marketing strategy might not be appropriate. Instead of getting hooked on great music, what our audience learned from an abundance of free concerts is that music is, and should be, free. And if it's often free, why would they ever pay for it?

The practice of giving away what you can't sell was at the root of many projects initiated by the organization. If you can't sell enough runouts to make ends meet, tour to smaller cities and get the state to pay for it. If you can't figure out profitable ways to use the time between the end of the main season and the beginning of the summer season, get the city's outdoor music festival to sponsor admission-free performances. If you can't attract enough paying customers to outdoor concerts during the summer, get the city to pay for free concerts in public parks.

Despite how it sounds, I am not opposed to free, outdoor concerts. Quite the opposite, because these events can serve as an important introduction between the orchestra and the community. But when an orchestra plays twenty or thirty free concerts every season, and comps to the remaining performances flow freely, the community learns an important lesson: professional music making is so cheap to produce and so unimportant that it is given away. In other words, the price of a ticket to hear our orchestra is exactly what we think it's worth: zero.

Though unintentionally, the Alabama Symphony taught this lesson to the Birmingham public for years. Again and again people stopped me in the supermarket or on the street, raving about how much they loved coming to hear us. They told me endlessly how lucky we all were in Alabama to have such a resource. In that they were correct. But nine times out of ten these people had only attended free events. It would never have crossed their minds, it seemed, to pay for a ticket when there was always a freebie just around the corner.

The Alabama Symphony couldn't find the corporate, philanthropic, or marketplace support to underpin its budget, so the leadership wandered down the dead-end path of giving away what they couldn't sell. And at the eleventh hour, these same leaders wondered why the community didn't value the orchestra enough to save it.

A Brief Excursion into Jewish Catholicism

My first wife was raised in a strict Catholic family, so I knew there would be a significant Catholic component in our wedding ceremony. At the time I was not certain how much of the pressure in that direction came from my fiancée and how much from above. (By "above" I refer to her mother, not God.)

We had hardly begun preparations for our blended Catholic/Jewish ceremony when I learned that, even though the ceremony was taking place in a nondenominational chapel with a Rabbi co-officiating, we were required to take the church's premarriage class. We chose a weekend class in Birmingham, and a few months before the wedding she came to Alabama, where we spent the weekend with two priests, two lay leaders, and five other engaged couples.

The group remained cloistered the entire weekend, housed and fed in the same church building where the classes took place. Though we were less than twenty minutes from my apartment, this sequestration was required so we would "stay focused" on the experience. We all suspected, however, that the unspoken motive was to preclude inappropriate premarital activities for the duration of the class.

My worries about being the odd man out were unfounded. The other couples held a wide variety of beliefs, and several contained one non-Catholic partner, though I was the only non-Christian. I'd harbored concerns about being the outcast, but my fiancée and I were by no means the black sheep. Of the five other couples, three were living together and two were pregnant. This information, learned on the first evening, set me at ease: the Jewish guy would not be the constant object of attention.

Confronted with the distinctly un-Catholic behavior of several of the couples, the priests and lay leaders found themselves in a predicament that they handled with grace and tact. None of the couples who lived together and/or were pregnant were castigated for their behavior, but it was made clear that by allowing them to be married "in the church" their church was not condoning their choices.

Despite everyone's good intentions and the welcoming attitude of our leaders, it was a weekend filled with ironic, stark contradictions. I consider myself tolerant of any religious beliefs when those feelings are sincere and don't infringe on the rights of others, but the growing doublespeak got under my skin.

The first contradiction was subtle. There we were, receiving sincere (if tedious and somewhat infantile) advice on sex, fidelity, and chastity while it was clear that most of the couples had already made up their minds. And it was equally apparent that their decisions bore little resemblance to the teachings of their church. The moment when the cohabitating couples exchanged a chaste goodnight kiss before separating to their respective dormitories was too silly for words.

So whose hypocrisy was bothering me? I suppose it was everyone's, because no one seemed interested in addressing the disconnect between appearance and reality. When our leaders opened a subject on which I found their position particularly untenable, I decided the time had arrived.

A discussion on the evils of birth control was inevitable. But clearly the horses were out of that barn. The leaders' presentation focused on the idea that humans should not interfere in God's plans for creating children. It followed, then, that modern methods of birth control are unacceptable because they have the precise purpose of interfering with God's will.

But church leaders, as we heard, are not completely out of touch with reality. They are aware that expecting modern women to let nature take its course is unrealistic. Clearly, the church understood that most couples find the limited choices of many babies or abstinence unpalatable. Which brought us, predictably, to the rhythm method.

I was in high school when I first became aware of this term, but at that time the details were vague. Like many things in adolescence, we were just supposed to know. I assumed, as a teenager and a musician, it had something to do with exactly how you did it—that is, the rhythm employed in the act itself. This was the only meaning that, unaided, I was able to extrapolate from the term, but it never looked to me like that was going to work. Dating a Catholic girl a few years later provided me with a more detailed explanation, but she was from a family of six children, so it still didn't seem like a very good idea.

Long before my experience at the premarriage weekend, I'd been puzzled by the church's position on this issue: utilizing the rhythm method is acceptable while others are not. But never before that weekend had I been presented with the opportunity to receive a clear explanation. I wanted to hear how this doctrine made sense, directly from someone who should know.

When the leaders finished their presentation and asked for questions, I raised my hand. My fiancée went pale, wondering (wisely) if I was about to embarrass her. It was not my intention, but things may have turned out that way.

I asked our leaders why avoiding pregnancy in one way was acceptable while preventing it in another was not. Wasn't a person's motivation the real issue? Isn't the sin in the *attempt* to frustrate God's will? I couldn't see how the method made any difference.

The answer surprised me. When a married couple utilizes the rhythm method, they said, it is still possible to become pregnant. Therefore, since God can circumvent those efforts and make a child, God's will still controls the situation.

I was stunned. From their answer, what were we to understand? It is not the attempt to frustrate God's will but only *succeeding* that is a sin? I couldn't make sense of this, but there was another layer to my concern. It was the suggestion that God can circumvent one type of birth control but not others. I didn't imply it, they did.

I asked how God could be sufficiently potent to frustrate the rhythm method but not powerful enough to make a hole in a condom. Wrinkling her 30-year-old brow, as though the "c" word made a bitter taste in her mouth, one of the leaders assured me that God is plenty capable of making a hole in a condom, if that is His desire.

In response I offered the obvious question: If God can overcome modern techniques as easily as the rhythm method, why is one thing acceptable and the others are not?

Their answer was a theological nightmare. Without saying it in precise terms, one of the leaders suggested that by using the rhythm method instead of latex or a pharmaceutical, we were making God's job of creating a baby a bit easier.

Incredulous, I asked, "Easier? Some things are easy for God, and others are more difficult?" Did that mean, I wondered aloud, there are things God cannot do at all?

Our discussion came to an abrupt conclusion, but I still found this idea very troubling. I may be an agnostic, but on my believer days I'm all in.

And lest anyone think I am singling out the Catholic Church, it's only fair to mention that all faiths have their blind spots. A strict reading of the Koran (Surah 9:15) instructs followers to "kill the disbelievers," and the Old Testament (Deuteronomy 21:21) commands that our response to a rebellious child is to "stone him to death." When compared with instructions to kill our neighbors or children, a little fudging of the facts on how babies get made doesn't seem like such a big deal.

~~~~~ Under Water ~~~~~

Some marriages are, for whatever reasons, brief. Then there are experiments that, regardless of duration, cannot truly be called marriage. The latter describes my life from February 1991 to May 1993.

These two years, my last in Alabama, taxed every spiritual reserve I had and caused me to question nearly everything I believed. I considered abandoning music, frequently thought of suicide, and, uncharacteristically, started attending an early-morning synagogue service several days each week. While I remain skeptical of talk therapy and the modern tendency to label every personal problem a disease, during this difficult stretch—and in another episode many years later—I learned firsthand that the personal and family consequences of depression, bipolar disorder, and obsessive-compulsive disorder are very real.

There's no question about it; I should have known better. I was nearly ten years older than she, and if anyone is to blame for the mess that was our marriage, it is, to a large degree, me. The warning signs of a doomed relationship were crying out to be seen long before we were married, but I wasn't willing to look. I also should have noticed the obvious indications of her illness. But after twenty-three years, her own family hadn't picked up on the signs, so I suppose I am absolved to some degree.

Throughout her life, and particularly as a young adult, her family thought of her as "quirky" and "eccentric." In hindsight, her mother—who spoke those very words—also wished she'd seen it coming. But in her defense, who wants to believe their child is ill just because she's quirky and eccentric? And let's not ignore the obvious: she was an artist, and we artists need some extra latitude before anyone starts medicating us.

My bride had been exhibiting subtle symptoms of obsessive-compulsive disorder for years, but no one put the pieces together. She had kept the indicators reasonably in check until running up against a trio of emotional upheavals: leaving graduate school for grown-up life, getting married, and moving to an unfamiliar city.

Our honeymoon was a disaster. We were still at the airport, on our way to Florida, when our jointly crafted, unspoken myths—that both she and our relationship were fine—started to unravel. We kept it together as best we could, taking allegedly romantic walks—only after sundown—and scrupulously avoiding the trio of 800-pound gorillas in the room: her increasingly odd behavior, our relationship, and sex.

For the next several weeks we adjusted to life together, achieving a manageable, if rather dysfunctional, détente. Many couples who have not previously cohabited go through a tricky breaking-in period, learning to get along in the same space without driving one another crazy. But we found it easy. Though it was very little like being newlyweds, we were compatible roommates, and I continued to hope for the best, believing her odd behaviors would subside when the concurrent shocks wore off.

But they weren't subsiding; they were getting worse. Realizing that she, and our fledgling marriage, were in a dangerous place, I tried to help. This was a big mistake—the same error made by many people with loved ones suffering from similar problems. Predictably, the result of my ham-fisted attempts to help was that I became the bad guy. Now, and through no fault of hers, instead of battling her few remaining clearheaded instincts, she fought with me.

During this time I spoke often with family, friends, and my rabbi. Everyone sympathized with her situation, but they uniformly advised me to get out of the marriage as quickly and painlessly as possible. It was not, they all seemed to agree, as though it had ever been a real marriage. I would like to say that my best self always won out and I never considered following their advice. But I did, many times.

Just before our first anniversary, she came to realize that the problem wasn't going to solve itself, and during the following months things began to move in the right direction. Then, in April 1993, twenty-six months into our marriage, I got the call we were hoping for, offering me the position of music director of the Arkansas Symphony in Little Rock. We were reasonably certain this call was imminent and had discussed our potential move in detail. With her health slowly improving, it seemed a godsend; just as she was able to have a normal life again, we would move and get a fresh start.

When I got off the phone with the Arkansas Symphony and told her the good news, she had some news of her own: she wasn't moving to Little Rock, and we were getting divorced. Her new therapist—a woman I'd never met—had determined that the entire fiasco was my fault. How they reached this conclusion was never adequately explained to me, but I think it was a bit like the claims of weapons of mass destruction in Iraq: if you say something enough times, with enough conviction, it becomes the truth.

This was neither what I'd planned nor what I wanted. I was crushed, and though I spent several days trying to talk her around, I didn't blame her. We were a mismatch from the start but had clung tightly to this relationship for four years, perhaps feeling that any life ring in the choppy seas of young adulthood was better than none. But despite good intentions on both sides, those life rings were made of lead, dragging us both down when we'd hoped they'd buoy us up.

In hindsight, nothing better could have happened. Picking up the pieces, I would soon leave Birmingham and begin a new life unencumbered by a wife who didn't love me and who blamed me for difficulties with which she'd struggled since adolescence.

At the time it seemed like the right choice for all the wrong reasons, and I escaped to Little Rock foolishly eager for romantic adventures—as men tend to do. It would take many years, however, as well as a half dozen relationships and another failed marriage, for me to understand that our time together had left me nearly incapable of forming trusting, meaningful attachments.

But the familiar sensation that undeserved good fortune had altered my course visited me again twenty-one years later, when a beautiful, no-nonsense Chinese doctor would change all that had come before.

~~~~~ One Last Try ~~~~~

By spring 1992, more than a year after our wedding and well into my fourth season in Birmingham, every day felt like an opportunity for another wrong turn. From the outside I looked like a guy who had it all: up-and-coming professional conductor with a great first job, my first music director post in the bag (the Kingsport, Tennessee, Symphony), and a charming new wife. But from my perspective things looked very different.

My bride's health was improving, but she, and we, were far from out of the woods. And although I'd collected a few nice guest conducting engagements in the preceding several seasons, my career felt stalled, and the Alabama Symphony's problems only seemed to grow worse. Everywhere I looked there was a fire to extinguish, and despite my best efforts, the flames only rose higher.

Looking for a way out, I began to wonder—not for the first time—if I had chosen the wrong path. I had always thought about the road not taken, what might have happened if I'd not abandoned my hopes to be a singer. Now, combined with an intense desire to be anywhere else, the idea called to me again.

With help from an Indiana classmate who was establishing a fine career in Europe as a pianist, coach, and opera conductor, I corresponded with several singers' agents in Germany and Austria. Encouraged by their responses, I carved out ten days from my Alabama duties, spent several months retooling my skills, and set off.

The first of three stops was Berlin. I'd been on German time less than eighteen hours when I took an ice-cold shower in a coin-operated stall in the hallway of my two-star hotel and headed for the agency where I'd scheduled a morning audition. In a low-ceilinged meeting room, I struggled to keep my eyes open while singing "Ah, mes ami"—the aria with nine high C's from *La Fille du Regiment* I'd sung on the Middle East tour. The senior agent and his colleagues also seemed to have trouble staying awake and were utterly unimpressed.

On the train to Salzburg, I began to assess the foolishness of the entire enterprise. This was not because my first time at bat had been a humiliating strikeout. I'd expected some of that. It was foolish because the time frame I'd established for the venture could only lead to failure.

The initial exploration of a European singing career is usually measured in months, not days. A successful audition tour involves visits to agents in multiples cities followed by, one hopes, an agent expressing interest and sending the singer to audition at opera houses. Even for a singer who is instantly attractive to agents, the process takes far longer than the eight days I'd allotted. And in an imaginary universe where I was offered a contract, how did I imagine I'd respond? Would I really leave my fragile wife and quit my job to wander around Europe singing in C-level opera houses? As the train rattled into Austria, I resisted the urge to abandon the entire enterprise. Despite the dreary long-term prospects, I was having too much fun to go home.

Salzburg's unique charm got under my skin from the moment I stepped off the train. The adorable couple who ran the small hotel where I stayed were straight out of *The Sound of Music*, and I even started to appreciate Wiener schnitzel, something I would never have dreamed possible.

The following day I auditioned in a rehearsal hall at the legendary Salzburg Festspielhaus, singing for a musical entrepreneur who had invited me based on a friend-of-a-friend contact. After I'd sung two arias, my gruff, 60-year-old, German audience of one rose slowly and approached me, his face scrunched into a concentrated scowl. I braced myself for another "sorry about this" speech, but instead he asked if I knew the aria from *La Boheme*. I hadn't sung the piece in ages, and never in public. But even though this man had apparently skipped Madame Flora's lecture on Fach—I was not a *Boheme* tenor—we do not decline any request during an audition. The pianist opened a score stashed next to him on the bench, and I performed "Che gelida manina" for the first—and last—time.

Moments later I was offered a ten-week contract to sing Rodolfo in *La Boheme* on a tour of smaller cities throughout Germany, Austria, and eastern Europe. So there I was, precisely where I'd imagined myself while musing on the train. I'd achieved a modest success but had no way to follow through due to my shortsightedness. I told my kind listener that I needed to think about it, but accepting a ten-week gig would have meant giving up everything I'd worked for as a conductor. I was torn, imagining myself taking up my grandmother's fallen mantle, singing Puccini on European stages, but it was impossible.

The last planned stop was Munich, where I stayed with a colleague of my new father-in-law. I was surprised to discover that my hosts were closer to my age than my wife's father's, a detail that would prove significant later in my visit.

Next morning I made my way to yet another agent's office, where I waited a long time in a cramped outer room with more than a dozen other singers. Admitted at last to the inner sanctum, I greeted the senior agent—a tiny, middle-aged woman flanked by a half dozen young, attractive men who surrounded her like a fawning harem. Following perfunctory politenesses, I again sang the arias from *La Fille du Regiment* and *Le Postillon de Lonjumeau*.

When I finished, Frau whatever-her-name-was addressed me in a voice still etched on my eardrums for its thin, pinched nasality, projecting from the small woman at an astonishing volume.

"I like you," she began, in English, "but your voice is somehow bizarre. It is almost castratisch."

This unkind remark, a reference to the male singers of old who were castrated to make their voices sound like women, must be understood in context. In the German singing world, nearly every Fach is a notch heavier than in the more Italian-influenced American musical community. A voice we consider heavy in the United States is average in Germany, and a leggiero voice in America is *castratisch* to the Germans.

With no appropriate response at the ready, I smiled sheepishly, thanked her and her minions for their time, and headed for the exit.

As I reached for the doorknob, she barked, "Wait," and I turned to see her in tête-à-tête conference with the flunky in chief.

Turning to face me, she said, "There is something for you, I think. With that voice you are perfect for it. Leave your number and someone will call you in a day or two."

Feeling more mystified than victorious, I returned to my billet ready to wait out the unspecified interval. Though basically strangers, my hosts were delighted for me and asked if there was anything I wanted to do or see in Munich while I waited.

I told them I wanted to visit the concentration camp at Dachau, located in a nearby suburb, and they were mystified. Why, they wondered, did I want to go to such a place? I explained that since we were so close, I wanted to see the camp and honor the six million, an important pilgrimage to our people. I saw they were still baffled, and then it hit me: they were both born in Munich in the early 1950s and had never visited Dachau.

"Really?" I asked. "How is that possible?"

We had reached the crossroads of two cultures with diametrically opposing perspectives.

Among American Jews of my generation, the Holocaust is the elephant in the room, the subject covered in every grade of Sunday school our entire childhood. It was the reason we were told to avoid intermarriage and, to some degree, the new raison d'être of the Jewish people. But to non-Jewish Germans born after World War II, it was ancient history. The Holocaust was a thorn in the national side, and they were sick of hearing about it.

"Why would we go there?" she asked, incredulous, "Have you been to Wounded Knee?"

I had to admit being impressed that a 30-something German could pull Wounded Knee out of her head at a moment's notice. But her analogy was way off.

"Several hundred people died at Wounded Knee, more than a century ago," I answered, "and it's a thousand miles from where I live. Several million died in the Holocaust less than ten years before you were born, and Dachau is thirty minutes away."

I could understand why baby-boom Germans were tired of the subject and exhausted by the collective guilt heaped on them by the rest of the world. But not wishing to be blamed for something that happened before you were born is not the same as turning a blind eye. We were coming from very different starting points, and though we would never agree on the subject, we would later part as friends.

The following afternoon I visited the camp, where I was immediately appalled by the whitewashing (both literal and figurative) of history. The grounds were bare, all the barracks razed but for one that had been reconstructed and given a pristine coat of white paint, inside and out.

In the visitors' center, carefully selected photos were captioned in German, English, and Russian, but the stories told in the various languages were not identical. The English text gave the facts as the world-at-large understands them—that six million Jews, Catholics, homosexuals, Romani, and others were systematically exterminated in the death camps. In German, however, the reader learned that "hundreds of thousands" of prisoners died from "disease and malnutrition." Apparently, Holocaust denial is a slippery slope.

Near closing time, the sun was dipping low when I walked through an open gate at the far end of the compound into the area that housed the crematoria. I found perhaps a dozen other visitors there, all of us silent as we took in the sight of the infamous ovens. Fifteen or twenty minutes later, as though summoned by the same inaudible signal, we all rounded the corner of a small building as we made our way back to the gate leading to the main grounds. I was at the rear of the group, lost in my own thoughts, so it took me a moment to notice that the others had stopped suddenly. I stepped sideways to peer around the clustered forms in front of me and understood: the gate was padlocked; it was past closing time, and we were trapped inside the camp.

It was dusk and the temperature was falling. I started to shiver violently, but not from the cold. People started shouting in three or four different languages, hoping to attract the attention of any remaining staff, though we could see no one in the football-field-sized space beyond the fence. It was only about ten minutes before an older man came trotting toward us from the distant visitors center, but it seemed a lifetime. Until that moment the Holocaust was just something we talked about in Sunday school. Hurrying across the grounds toward the exit, clutching my coat around me, comprehension arrived like a punch to my gut: Never Again.

Forty-eight hours after my initial audition, the agent called as promised. I needed to get on a train as quickly as possible, she told me, so I could sing an audition for the title role in the Hamburg company of *Phantom of the Opera* the following morning. A limited number of singers had been invited, she crowed, and she had gotten me in. I needed to get to Hamburg that night and call her at 9:00 a.m. the next day for additional instructions.

A hasty goodbye to my new friends and I was off, arriving just after midnight in the same city that had witnessed my paternal grandfather's departure for America ninety years earlier. Leaving the train station, I found myself alone on dark, nearly deserted streets, and entered the first hotel that satisfied my two demanding criteria: lights on and no hookers standing in the doorway.

I awoke early to be sure I was properly warmed up for a potentially life-changing audition that was perhaps only minutes away. At the appointed hour, I called the agent's office and was put on hold for what seemed an eternity. Finally, the screechy voice, more subdued than when I'd last heard it, came on the line.

"Herr Itkin," she began, "there has been a mix up, I'm afraid."

It was only 9:00, so I couldn't have missed it. What kind of mix up was she talking about?

"I'm afraid my assistant misunderstood," she continued. "The final audition was yesterday. He has already telephoned this morning, but they say they are finished and will not see you today."

"Yesterday?" I stammered, my adrenaline high deflating in an instant.

"Ja. I'm sorry, Herr Itkin, and good luck to you."

I managed, "Danke," and hung up.

Was I crestfallen or relieved? Perhaps some of each. I'd been thrilled by the idea of changing my life in an instant, doing *Phantom* in Hamburg. But even if I'd arrived on the correct day, that was no guarantee I'd have gotten the role. And if I had been offered, what then? Even for a potentially long-term gig, would I have had the courage—or madness—to drop everything and go? In some secret place, I was relieved that the decision had been taken out of my hands—and that was me to a T. Not far below the surface, I was still the high school kid who couldn't summon the courage to tell his guidance counselor he planned to be a musician. As usual, I'd unbuttoned the blouse but had no intention of going all the way.

Is There Opera in Alabama?

Sitting on the board of a professional arts organization can be a precarious balancing act. If a board member participates fully, showing interest in the workings of the organization and offering advice, someone is likely to suggest they're butting into the business of the professionals. But when a board member does little or nothing, they are criticized for lack of participation. One thing is certain, however: the primary job of a board member is to support the financial health and artistic growth of the organization. Anything less is certain dereliction of duty.

But what happens when a board doesn't want that growth and vitality, even when it is within their grasp? What happens when the apparent goals of many board members conflict with the stated mission of the organization? And what happens when a board hires artistic professionals despite knowing they will be at odds with the direction taken by those they've hired? This is the story of the Birmingham Opera Theater.

During my first several years in Birmingham, 1988 to 1990, I was only dimly aware of the existence of the BOT, which was experiencing one of its periodic dormant phases (i.e., they had not produced an opera in three years). They functioned under the leadership of a local college voice teacher, and their activities were confined to small events with local singers at libraries and churches. Even in their dormant periods, however, they continued to sponsor a vocal competition each year. In addition to fundraising for the competition, the organization pursued other activities aimed at paying off their accumulated debt.

In 1990 the reins were handed to a theatrical director whose recent attempt to start a profession theater in Birmingham had gone belly-up in matter of months. Confirming that no one in leadership had a grip on reality, he got together with the music director of the soon-to-be-defunct Alabama Symphony, and they mounted a production of *Tosca* costing more than $100,000. The production's one performance attracted fewer than five hundred paying customers but was a qualified artistic success.

One hundred thousand dollars is a modest budget for a regional opera production. But it was more than the BOT could afford, and far more than they could make back in ticket sales and sponsorships. When the diva threw herself off the Castel Sant'Angelo, the BOT was drowning in a sea of red ink. By the time I became involved, the board was still paralyzed by their *Tosca* experience and seemed to have adopted the motto "The only good opera is no opera."

In late 1992 an enterprising young singer convinced the virtually nonfunctional organization to allow him to take over as business manager and artistic coordinator. I had known Greg for some time and was aware that his reach often exceeded his grasp. But that quality was his strength as well as his weakness. He believed the company could produce high-quality, tight-budget productions, and he was going to prove it.

His time at the helm was turbulent, but not due to any lack of leadership. He proved it was possible for the BOT to mount two fully staged productions each year with artistic integrity, drawing a respectable audience and breaking even. What caused friction between Greg and the board was that he was right, and they couldn't handle it.

Greg's first move was to locate the most competent, cheapest opera conductor he could find. Between April 1993 and November 1994, we produced *The Barber of Seville*, *Don Pasquale*, *La Traviata*, and *Cosi Fan Tutte*. These productions, mounted through Greg's ingenuity and the kindness of our singers for an average of $60,000, boasted artists like Diana Heldman (Rosina in *Barber of Seville* and Despina in *Cosi Fan Tutte*), Lincoln Clark (director for *Barber of Seville* and *Don Pasquale*), John Davies (as Don Pasquale), Patricia Johnson (Violetta in *La Traviata*, her first), Carroll Freeman (director for *La Traviata*), Paul Rowe (director of, and Guglielmo in, *Cosi Fan Tutte*), Christine Donahue (Fiordiligi in *Cosi Fan Tutte*), and Chip Huddleston (Germont in *La Traviata*). The collaboration of these artists with the talents of the musicians in the pit (those who remained from the Alabama Symphony) produced beautiful results even on our anorexic budgets.

But during this period of institutional renaissance and relative financial stability, all we heard from the board was whining. Why did we hire so many out-of-town artists when we had church choirs full of great singers? Why did we need so many professional orchestra players (an average of thirty, approximately half the number genuinely required) when a student group could do the job? Did we really need sets and costumes?

The stunning irony of the board's paralysis was that, at precisely that moment, the Alabama Symphony was nonfunctional, and $2 million in arts philanthropy was up for grabs annually in Birmingham. The moment should have been a financial bonanza for the BOT, but instead the board's malaise only deepened. What many of them wanted was the civic visibility of serving on the opera board without the connected responsibilities and stresses.

I have always believed that an arts organization belongs to the board and the community, not the artistic leadership. Therefore, the board had every right to determine that they wanted a church basement opera company. What we needed was for them to decide. For two years we'd heard mountains of lip service about wanting a high-quality, professional product. But nearly all their actions said something different.

By the time the second of our four productions was in the can, Greg was on his way out, having resigned over the daily frustrations. Dealing with it in person only four weeks each year, I managed to hang on for two more productions before the aggravation got the better of me, too.

In the long run, the Birmingham Opera Theater (now Opera Birmingham) has remained the mostly amateur, God-forbid-we-should-produce-an-opera organization they always desired. And if this is what they wanted, they really should have been more careful what they wished for.

Chapter 7

In the Trenches: The Arkansas Symphony and Elsewhere, Part 1

~~~~~ An Arkansas Traveler ~~~~~

Some tenures are musically pleasant and/or financially beneficial, and that's about all. But other posts become part of who you are, allowing your musicianship to blossom and establishing relationships that last a lifetime. I don't consider myself a person with extraordinary good luck, but the objective facts say something different. I have already mentioned several occasions when an opportunity seemed to fall from the sky at precisely the right moment. The beginning of my relationship with the Arkansas Symphony was yet another, and by far the most significant.

In fall 1992, as the Alabama Symphony teetered on the brink, the Birmingham arts council asked me to appear as narrator for children's concerts to be performed by Neil Rutman, then an up-and-coming artist on the piano faculty at the University of Central Arkansas. Neil and I hit it off immediately and had a great time performing *Babar, the Elephant* together.

On our second or third day of performances, he mentioned that the Arkansas Symphony was searching for a new music director, and because he'd heard good things about me around town, he suggested I apply. Somewhat frustrated at the mention of this subject, I told him I'd sent my materials weeks earlier and assumed the finalists had already been chosen.

But the orchestra was following an unusual procedure, he enlightened me, slotting candidates throughout the year as more applications flowed in. And there was one concert still unassigned. He promised to mention me to "some people" when he returned home but advised that if I wanted serious consideration, I needed to "make some noise" in a hurry.

Inspired to action, I contacted every musician of note I knew at the time—which was not many—asking them to call Arkansas and talk me up. Unbelievably, it worked. Two weeks later I was offered the final candidacy concert, scheduled for March 1993.

At the start of the new year, I geared up for a program of Barber's Overture to *The School for Scandal*, Schumann's Piano Concerto in A Minor, and Tchaikovsky's Symphony No. 6. It would be my first time conducting the Schumann and the Tchaikovsky, but I never mentioned that detail. I prepared with particular diligence because the Alabama Symphony had ceased operations in January, and now I really needed a job.

Little Rock was giddy following Bill Clinton's victory and inauguration. Though not yet an adopted Arkansan, I was swept up in the excitement, housed in the historic Capital Hotel where the staff regaled me with charming stories about the Gore family, who had resided there from November to January.

My audition experience was a lovefest from beginning to end, with great work from the orchestra and wonderful responses from the audience, board, and media. A couple weeks later I received a call offering me the position, precisely coordinated with the crashing and burning of marriage number one. Collecting the shards of my personal life and my relatively few belongings, I moved to Little Rock, rented a beautifully restored Victorian home, bought a swanky sports car—these two extravagances made me appear more in character of the dashing, young maestro, I thought—and got down to work.

The first of the three executive directors during my seventeen years in Little Rock was JoAnn Greene, a woman of imposing personality approximately my mother's age. She had initially been a fund development consultant for the orchestra and was hired as executive director eight years before I arrived.

JoAnn was, above all things, a penny pincher, which, in a nonprofit arts organization, is not necessarily a bad thing. But there are pennies and there are pennies. During my first season, after observing uninspiring audience numbers, I initiated a conversation about our marketing strategy. But "strategy" might be overstating the case, as one could hardly call a few thirty-second radio spots and a one-by-two-inch ad in the Friday newspaper a strategy. That, I learned, was the sum of our marketing for each concert, exactly as she had done it since her first day on the job.

My attempts to bring our marketing practices forward a few decades were relatively unsuccessful. But JoAnn was not stubborn for stubbornness' sake. She simply had a management philosophy in which she genuinely believed. Contradicting the common wisdom "You have to spend money to make money," she told me, "Every dollar we don't spend is a dollar we won't lose."

Allowing this bizarre philosophy to sink in, I suggested we close our doors immediately, because that's where this idea was inevitably leading. She scoffed, but I continued. If we didn't advertise effectively, I asked, how would we sustain and increase our audience?

She then ended the conversation with another maxim I will never forget: "We don't need to find new ticket buyers. Anyone who wants to hear the symphony will find *us*."

I was certain I had never heard anything so ridiculous—and I'd just spent five years at the Alabama Symphony, so that was saying something.

During my third year in Little Rock, JoAnn announced her retirement. Our differences of opinion were always respectful, and I don't believe her decision had anything to do with me. She was deservedly lauded for her excellent record of keeping the institution on the tracks in good times and bad, and off she went.

Profile article in *Soirée* magazine, 2002.

~~~~~ Suddenly Seoul ~~~~~

In March 1994 I neared the end of my first season in Arkansas. During the preceding eight months, I also commuted to Kingsport, Tennessee (where I had been music director since 1992), and Birmingham, Alabama (working with the Birmingham Opera Theater). Apart from the December holidays, there was only one week between September 1993 and May 1994 during which I was not conducting one of these three organizations or guest conducting elsewhere. After judging a competition in Atlanta the preceding weekend, I planned to spend my one week of freedom in New York, visiting friends from earlier chapters of my life.

In Atlanta I met George Zach, the conductor of the Lexington Symphony and one of the competition judges. On the penultimate day of competition, he surprised me by asking if I was busy the following week. I mentioned my plans for New York, and he continued, saying he'd had a call from an old friend who was currently the conductor of the Seoul Philharmonic. A French guest conductor had canceled for the following week and the Seoul music director had inquired whether George was available, which he was not.

Then, a surprising question: Was I? Shrugging, I said, "Sure," assuming nothing would come of it. There had to be competent conductors less than seven thousand miles from South Korea. Thirty hours later, with the situation still up in the air, George suggested I call Seoul before boarding a plane to New York.

A quick call from Hartsfield International confirmed that the problem had been solved. I was disappointed but also relieved. I desperately needed a break, and now I would not have to cram a new program in two days. Settled in at the Upper West Side apartment of my friends Bernadette and Eric, I mentioned over a glass of wine the near preempting of my visit. Now that I was on Seoul's radar, I thought aloud, perhaps I would get another chance sometime in the future. But the future was coming sooner than we thought.

The following morning, I strolled the neighborhood, wandering in aimless bliss. I had promised myself there would be neither score study nor excessive message checking while in New York, and this solitary springtime walk was proof of my self-discipline. Bernadette and I met for a late lunch near Lincoln Center, and after we ordered I excused myself to the men's room. On my way back to the table, I noticed a pay phone and my workaholic instincts took control.

From the restaurant's basement hallway, I called my answering machine in Little Rock and found that a Mr. Oh of the Seoul Philharmonic had left a message to the effect that their solution had fallen through. He gave his home number, requesting a call back no matter the hour. At 2:00 p.m. in New York, it was the middle of the night in Korea, but I followed his instructions nonetheless. After a quick chat with Delta, I called Seoul a second time and we concluded the arrangements.

He was in no position for a lengthy negotiation, and the sum I would be owed, including air and hotel reimbursement, was considerable. The concertmaster would manage the first rehearsal, and Mr. Oh would arrange for a work visa.

On the point of hanging up, I realized we had overlooked an important detail.

"Mr. Oh, what is the program?"

"Ah," he acknowledged the oversight, "an all-Berlioz program, *Harold in Italy* and *Symphonie Fantastique*. Okay?"

My knowledge of these two big works was limited, having studied one (a bit) and having heard the other (once). But fortune favors the bold, and, despite my misgivings, my first opportunity to conduct a top orchestra overseas was too enticing to pass up.

Twenty minutes after descending to the men's room, I returned to the table. Our lunch had arrived, and, as I sat down, Bernadette's expression seemed to ask, "Did you fall in?"

Undoubtedly looking like a deer in headlights, I sat, and said, "Eat fast."

Eight hours later I was at home in Little Rock with just enough time to locate the Berlioz scores, find my passport, and sleep for a couple of hours. The following morning I met my parents in the Portland airport, having called the night before to let them know I'd be changing planes in my hometown. My mother's anxiety gave voice to my own: "No visa? No contract? How will you ever learn the music in time?"

A few minutes after takeoff I resumed studying, trying not to attract the attention of people around me. Opening an orchestra score on a plane is like a red flag to a bull, eliciting interest and questions from flight attendants and fellow passengers. I have always hated this. Perhaps it's my dislike of making small talk with strangers, or maybe I'm fundamentally unfriendly. But on that day I was uniquely not in the mood, and had no time for chitchat.

The first several hours flew by, but as night came, I started to fade. I desperately wanted a break but was afraid if I "rested my eyes" (as my father used to say in synagogue) I would wake up in Korea with the remainder of the program unlearned. Soon the lights were dimmed, and the cabin was silent but for the whine of jet engines and the flurry of caffeine-fueled Berlioz swirling in my head. As the other passengers slept, the only light in the cavernous coach cabin was the pinpoint of illumination streaming down onto my lap like a spotlight.

My claustrophobia spiking, I peered out into the unnerving blackness. Surrounded by hundreds of limp bodies, lifeless as the clients in an opium den, I realized I was in the perfect environment to consider *Symphonie Fantastique*. Berlioz's five-movement, hour-long odyssey through the nightmares of a substance-abusing artist was a watershed work in the mid-nineteenth century, and nearly two hundred years later his genius shines through in every note.

I started to feel like *I* was the one doing drugs, but as the hours of darkness dragged on, I plunged from *Symphonie Fantastique* into *Harold in Italy*.

My previous exposure to the work was fleeting, and I quickly remembered why the piece enjoys a spotty reputation. Short flashes of genuine inspiration punctuate lengthy stretches during which we wonder about the composer's intentions and direction. Berlioz was consistently criticized by the French musical establishment for writing works they considered too long, too difficult, and too "modern." But their assessments of music produced by a superior talent were, for the most part, self-serving and shortsighted. Regarding *Harold in Italy*, however, someone close to the composer should have looked at the score and said, "Keep the good bits and rewrite the rest."

Faster than you can say, "opium-induced nightmare," daylight crept through the windows. We were nine hours into the thirteen-hour flight, and most of the analysis work was finished. But being prepared to rehearse a new work requires far more than this, and the longer I labored, the further from the goal I seemed to be. I was slogging diligently through the technical work but had hardly begun to figure out what the music would say through me the following morning.

It was too much to fully process in the time remaining, and a smarter person would have would have taken shortcuts. As when I first heard *La Boheme* years earlier, I recognized that greatness looked up at me from the pages, but I was no longer a passive observer sitting safely in a music library. Each phrase, each nuance and emotion demanded processing through my mind and experience to then be revealed to the orchestra through my conducting.

But how that would happen with eighteen hours remaining until rehearsal was still something of a mystery.

We touched down in Seoul at dusk, still light enough to see the craggy hills surrounding the city, allowing me to appreciate the accuracy of the California-filmed opening credits of MASH. Finding no one to greet me as I deplaned, I followed the crowd to the foreign nationals' receiving area and said nothing when the officer stamped my passport with a five-day tourist visa.

As I walked toward baggage claim, I glanced over my shoulder, certain I had heard someone say my name. A few steps later it happened again, but when I turned, no one appeared to be looking in my direction. More steps, and I felt a hand on my back.

I turned to see an armed officer who asked, "David Itkin?"

Amazed, I said I was, and he led me away from baggage claim, back in the direction from which I had come. Seating me in a small, windowless office, he took my passport and disappeared.

From the first time I went overseas, what did my travel agent mother tell me? Don't let anyone take your passport—ever. I felt helpless, defenseless, naked, imagining myself in a spy novel. In my sleep-deprived fiction, a soldier bursts in and demands my passport while I explain that the other officer just took it. He snarls, "You're lying!" and takes me away to be questioned.

Instead, the officer who had located me in the concourse returned with a superior. In difficult-to-understand English, he explained that I had obtained an illegal visa by allowing my passport to be stamped as a tourist.

He kept saying, "This visa no good, no good! Illegal!"

At that point I was certain the United States ambassador would need to intervene to secure my release from prison. But the officer's next sentence contained a familiar name.

"All arranged by Mr. Oh. Wait, please."

They had not retrieved me from the public area to berate or threaten me, but to let me know that things were under control. I still didn't understand why Mr. Oh wasn't in the room with us, but I no longer cared once I learned that Korean prison was not a part of my future.

About ten minutes later my passport was returned, and they pointed me toward baggage claim. The stamp made at passport control, the illegal visa, had been scratched out. On the same page appeared some brief lines of Korean handwriting, but nothing that looked remotely official. This was, apparently, my new, legal work visa.

As I passed a low partition leading out of the security area, I heard another voice. "Mr. Itkin?"

I turned and, to my great relief, saw Mr. Oh.

As our long drive into the city center neared its end, Mr. Oh pointed out an enormous structure covering several square blocks, adorned with towering columns in front. This was the cultural center, he told me, where the orchestra rehearsed and performed. Had I been paying attention to where we were and where we were headed, I could have saved myself considerable grief. Moments later, he dropped me in the Hilton's semicircular entrance drive, briefly reviewed my schedule, and bid me good night.

I bolted upright at the 5:00 a.m. wake-up call, having dozed only fitfully during the night. Though groggy, my body thought it was almost dinnertime, so I rose and showered, feeling surprisingly refreshed.

A restorative coffee in hand, I opened the score to *Harold in Italy* and was immediately chagrined. The handwritten notes were mine, and my usual methods of analyzing harmony, phrase, orchestration, and form were clearly present, but none of the music looked familiar. After another hour, reminding myself I just needed to wake up, both *Harold in Italy* and *Symphonie Fantastique* were feeling like old friends. Suddenly it was 9:15, so I finished dressing and descended to the lobby. I was neither tanned nor rested, but I was ready.

It was a breezy, sunny morning in Seoul, and the cool, smoggy air brought me better into sync with the time zone. I stood in front of the hotel, sipped my third cup of coffee, and wondered why Mr. Oh was ten minutes late—fifteen minutes—twenty minutes. At 9:50, with only ten minutes remaining until the start of rehearsal, I became seriously worried.

I like to arrive at rehearsal early when guest conducting in a new place. On the first day I want to get my bearings, feel the acoustic, and absorb any quirks in the orchestra's set-up. At 9:50 those plans were moot. In the best-case scenario, I was already late.

At one minute before 10:00, it was time for action. But what action, exactly? I didn't know where the cultural center was located, or even if that was the correct name of the building. To make matters worse, there were three professional orchestras in Seoul, so explaining my destination to a taxi driver with whom I shared no common language was going to be difficult.

When the clock struck 10:00, I was deep in conversation with a driver. "The Seoul Philharmonic," I said repeatedly, each time louder, like an ugly American. "The Cultural Center."

I didn't have much faith that my message was getting through and was not excited about jumping into the cab and letting him improvise. As my indecision approached critical mass, I heard my name on the loudspeaker overhead. I turned toward the towering glass doors, but a clerk intercepted me.

Mr. Oh, she told me politely, was stuck in the ubiquitous Seoul traffic and had called from his car instructing me to take a cab. Why he waited until nearly 10:00 to make this call is a mystery I have yet to unravel. At any rate, the clerk handed written instructions to the driver, and we were off.

In less than five minutes, we arrived at the Sejong Cultural Center, where a junior administrator, speed-walking as though we were in the Olympics, escorted me through a maze of corridors and elevators. Finally we entered an enormous rehearsal hall filled to bursting with 107 musicians. Alerted that the arrogant American conductor who couldn't come to rehearsal on time had finally arrived, the orchestra was tuning as I crept around the edge of the room.

By the time I reached my place, the hall was silent. I gazed around the room, my head reeling from jet lag, an overdose of caffeine, and our roller coaster ride through Seoul traffic. Then, suddenly, as if by magic, it was game on.

With my first step onto the podium, I remembered a story that Thomas Baldner had told me about his first international engagement going catastrophically wrong in just the first few minutes. Why my subconscious chose to dredge up that anecdote at that moment probably says a lot about my state of mind, my maestro-like posturing notwithstanding. I took in the huge assemblage—a sea of humanity staring expectantly as though from the pews of a cathedral—and began to wonder if the preacher would remember his sermon.

But these thoughts passed in an instant. The baton descended delicately, inviting the first tentative notes of *Symphonie Fantastique*. Somewhat detached, I watched my right hand elicit sound from the orchestra, the baton held by novice and master simultaneously.

The orchestra demonstrated high-level skills as individuals, though they seemed a bit lacking in their common understanding of important ensemble and sonic issues. Though they played with excellent technical precision, we did not lack for things to do in rehearsal.

Always outwardly polite, their furtive glances suggested surprise when I asked them to play a single pizzicato chord repeatedly until it was perfectly together. They were also nonplussed when I insisted that passages marked pianissimo should not be played at whatever volume happened to be convenient.

These ideas, and other matters they deemed unnecessarily picky, seemed strange to them, but we got along well. Best of all, they didn't seem to realize that the music was brand new to me. It felt like the fake job of a lifetime. But perhaps "fake job" is a bit unfair. As rehearsals proceeded, I found, to my relief, that both my knowledge of the scores and the specificity of my musical intentions went deeper than I'd realized. My trans-Pacific efforts to find connections between the notes on the page and the protagonist's mania seemed to be paying off.

Following the second rehearsal, I went to Ewha Women's University to meet with a faculty member who would be our viola soloist. She was a fine player, and we enjoyed working together, though we later ran aground of the unavoidable difficulty inherent in *Harold in Italy*. During a substantial portion of the piece, the orchestration is so heavy that the solo viola cannot easily be heard. But, in the view of many, it is not necessary that she be heard, as the solo line is often playing in unison with the orchestral strings. And it is this lack of soloist focus that caused Paganini, for whom the work was written, to refuse it. Paganini was not alone in his consternation, and the issue has frustrated violists and conductors ever since.

Our only rehearsal in the concert hall took place the morning of the performance. Seating nearly four thousand, the hall is a chasm that seems to go on forever, dwarfing those onstage by its dimensions. I was surprised to see television trucks outside the stage door as I came in that evening. Apparently, someone had forgotten to mention that the concert was being televised live and filmed for later broadcast to other parts of Asia. There, at the eleventh hour, attempting to focus my jet-lagged brain on the performance, there was nothing I could do but shrug *whatever.*

Following the concert Mr. Oh came to my dressing room and, after thanking me, pulled a sheet of paper from his jacket and asked me to sign the payment receipt. From the same pocket, he then retrieved a plain, white envelope with Korean handwriting on the outside. Both hands extended, he offered the envelope with a bow and was gone.

It was too thick to be a check, but what was I going to do with wads of Korean bills in Arkansas? I tore it open and found $9,000 in brand-new $100 bills. It felt more like a drug deal than payment for conducting Berlioz. As it turned out, I wasn't the only one who'd have that impression.

In the '60s and early '70s, when my brother, Hank, was a hippie, he told me that the amount of time you spent going through US customs was directly related to the look of your clothes and the length of your hair. He tended, in those days, to be a little paranoid about such things, so I never put much stock in his analysis. On the other hand, when my brother made that pronouncement, he had long hair and I didn't. When I went to Korea, he didn't and I did.

At passport control in the Portland airport, the agent was not pleased to note my lack of a Korean entry visa. After I pointed to the scrawl in the corner of one page and explained the circumstances of my arrival, she rolled her eyes, stamped my passport, and passed me to the next step.

When I arrived at the customs station, an agent about 25 years old looked me up and down and asked me to open my luggage. My brother was right. If the second agent received a signal from the first, I didn't see it. The search of my luggage appeared to be based on nothing more than my bedraggled, unshaven, long-haired appearance.

I removed everything from my suitcase, but the agent appeared displeased. Whatever he'd hoped to find wasn't there. As though reading my mind, he asked me to empty my pockets, going straight to the inside of my wallet and removing the envelope. He fanned the ninety crisp $100 bills, once again taking in my appearance.

When he noticed my odd-looking visa, he asked, "Tell me, again, what you were doing in Seoul?"

"Conducting the Seoul Philharmonic," I said, though it sounded like a lie even to me.

He fanned the money again, stuffed it back into the envelope and tossed it carelessly onto the suitcase, but gave no indication that our interview was finished.

"I know what you're thinking," I quipped, seriously misjudging my audience, "but the drugs go that way," I pointed in the direction of the main concourse, "and the money goes that way," gesturing vaguely toward the parked planes.

Stone-faced, he motioned for the next person in line.

~~~~~ New Blood ~~~~~

Following JoAnn Greene's retirement, I was asked to serve on the search committee to locate a new executive director for the Arkansas Symphony. The orchestra was growing rapidly in the mid-'90s, and this selection would be of paramount importance to our future.

Thumbing through a stack of resumes, I came across a familiar name: William Vickery. It couldn't be the same person, I thought, because the man I knew with that name had been vice president of the Aspen Music Festival when I was a fellowship conductor in 1987. That guy was a significant player in the industry, and there was no way he was applying for the job in Little Rock. To my surprise, there was.

After leaving the Aspen Festival for a high-profile position, fate slapped his hand when he was blamed for failing to salvage an orchestra that was foundering before he arrived. Interviewing in Arkansas, he was as energetic and charismatic as I remembered.

Bill's experience and confidence brought a new sizzle to everything we did for the next decade. Together we planned, innovated, brought big stars, broadened the touring schedule, expanded our roster of full-time musicians, and created a chamber music series, all on an ever-growing, balanced budget. Little Rock had never experienced the likes of that decade, and perhaps never will again. In just those few years, we worked with Itzhak Perlman, Yo-Yo Ma, Joshua Bell, Janos Starker, Misha Dichter, Kiri Te Kanawa, Alicia de Larrocha, Christopher Parkening, Sarah Chang, Marilyn Horne, Midori, Nadja Salerno-Sonnenberg, Ray Charles, Bernadette Peters, Aretha Franklin, Maya Angelou, President Clinton, Kenny Loggins, and many others.

After Haydn and Dvorak concerti with Yo-Yo Ma, Little Rock, 2003.

After the Beethóven violin concerto with Itzhak Perlman, Little Rock, 2002.

After a dream-come-true concert with Marilyn Horne, Little Rock, c. 1997.

After the Brahms violin concerto with Joshua Bell, Little Rock, 2008.

~~~~~ That's the Chicago Way ~~~~~

During my third season with the Arkansas Symphony (1995–1996), my (former) agent contacted me about a last-minute guest conducting date in suburban Chicago. A great group, he said, whose conductor had departed suddenly (i.e., was fired), leaving gaps in the season. If it went well, he said, I was a shoo-in to be one of the finalists invited the following season.

Uncharacteristically, everything he said was accurate. The orchestra was excellent, made up of experienced Chicagoland freelancers, and Lake Forest is a charming, affluent suburb on the northbound train line. On that first visit, and throughout my tenure, I was housed at the Deerpath Inn, a lovely boutique hotel where the staff always knew my name, what I ate for breakfast, and probably my shoe size.

I guest conducted for the second time, now as a candidate, during the 1996–1997 season. When I'd conducted the previous year, there had been an executive director heading the staff, but by my second visit he was gone, replaced "temporarily" by the board chairman, Jean Beck. The executive director, I discovered, had been swept away in a purge not dissimilar to the one that had taken the music director one year earlier—an institutional proclivity that should have given me pause.

To allay my obvious concerns, Jean assured me that her place as executive director was short-term. To no one's surprise, her position was not temporary, but that wasn't really the issue. If Jean wanted to manage the day-to-day affairs as an unpaid executive director, that would have been between her and her peers on the board. The problem was that she wanted to help with programming and artist selection when she knew very little about either.

Before I could begin drafting my first season's repertoire and guest artists, she told me she had already signed guests for the entire season. In fairness, it's not unusual for a new music director to be presented with their first season's guest artists and/or programming as a fait accompli, because the institution needed to make plans before a conductor appointment was finalized.

But she didn't stop with season one. Throughout my tenure Jean insisted on reengaging the same soloists, despite some having appeared with the orchestra in multiple consecutive seasons. She knew what she knew (about ten soloists and twenty pieces of music) and was afraid of everyone and everything else. When I detailed the pedigree of soloists I wanted to invite, musicians who were higher profile and less expensive than those on her never-changing list, she told me I didn't understand the community and, besides, she was the board president.

I loved the orchestra's musicians, a stunning array of talented individuals of diverse experiences and backgrounds. We did, however, have our moments, nearly all of which involved our differing views on rhythm and ensemble.

Every large musical community has its own unique personality. This personality, and the musical practices associated with it, often flows from the largest musical institution in town. In this case that institution was the venerable Chicago Symphony, where many of my LFSO players frequently substituted. And those who did not directly interact with the CSO played in orchestras with those who did, unconsciously picking up Chicago Symphony norms, as in any ecosystem.

One of the hallmarks of the CSO's playing—beyond its well-known excellence and artistry—was its tradition of playing well after the conductor's beat in the manner of the great European orchestras. This habit was codified during the tenure of Georg Solti, and successive music directors have either allowed or encouraged it. I, on the other hand, adhere to a conducting method that encourages the orchestra to play on my beat. Neither the Lake Forest musicians nor I meant any disrespect to the other, but if I had a dollar for every time I asked them to play on the beat, I would currently own my dream villa in Tuscany.

In their defense, it is not easy to change gears at a moment's notice, especially after years of doing things a certain way. Each time I visited, they adjusted their playing incrementally until, by the time concerts arrived, they were very close to where I wanted them. Then several weeks passed before I saw them again, and during these intervals they all played with either the Chicago Symphony or other suburban orchestras. Consequently, when I returned to Lake Forest we were back to square one. Our rhythmic struggles notwithstanding, we admired and respected one another and made some great music together.

By my third year, the administrative situation was becoming more difficult. The board had repeatedly promised to hire an executive director, but no search ever materialized. Jean's tenure was in stone, and I began to consider a departure. At nearly the same time, two other events occurred that either galvanized my resolve or made my decision moot, depending on one's perspective.

In late 1998, two years into marriage number two, my daughter, Stasia Belle, was born. Every time I left home my heart was broken for missing the little girl who bore her great-grandmother's name. By fall 1999 she was one year old and way too much fun to leave behind. I started to think about my priorities, and with each visit to Lake Forest the path became clearer.

But little did I know that my ruminations were meaningless. Despite the orchestra's generally acknowledged artistic growth, validated more than once in the *Chicago Tribune*, Jean had been working behind the scenes to remove the thorn from her side. I was about to receive my first lesson in what becomes of the truth when wealthy cronies get together behind closed doors—and it wouldn't be my last.

Just after the millennial new year, I was asked to join several board members for lunch in the dining room of my hotel. The invitation came from Charles Fry, a retired executive, former CIA operative, and a guy I considered a close friend, so it never occurred to me that I was being summoned to the principal's office.

We hadn't even ordered when someone broke the ice. "Clearly, things aren't working out" with Jean.

I agreed, suggesting they hire someone who understood our business and the role of the executive director, as they had promised. No, they said, Jean was a community fixture and a major donor.

And though they had mixed feelings, considering how the orchestra played under my leadership, I was the one who was leaving.

Even taking my own plans into consideration, this was a sucker punch. I instinctively drew breath to argue, then wondered why. They were obviously committed to this path, and I felt as though a great weight had been removed from around my neck. Was I really going to argue because they said it first? Wasn't this a win for me, passive-aggressive though its execution may have been?

I would miss my orchestra colleagues, but I didn't lament the departure from Lake Forest. What I did feel was betrayed by people I considered friends. In hindsight, that assessment was desperately naïve. Sadly, there is almost no circumstance in which money doesn't trump doing the right thing.

After I left they hired a local choral conductor to lead the orchestra—someone Jean knew, and knew she could control, a guy so grateful for the gig that he would go with the flow no matter what. The next two decades brought several changes of conductor, Jean's death, and the coming and going of various executive directors. The Lake Forest Symphony closed its doors in early 2020, just before the onset of the COVID-19 pandemic.

~~~~~ Shanghai Song ~~~~~

From a limited, Western-centric viewpoint, I imagined my first time conducting in China would be somewhat like my experience in Korea, but I could not have been more wrong.

In Korea I was paid quite well, whereas in China I was paid almost nothing. In Korea I stayed at the Hilton, and in China I was billeted in an ancient, isolated guest house. In Korea I was nearly ignored by my host orchestra, whereas in China I was showered with attention like a visiting dignitary. In Korea the orchestra compared easily with the best regional orchestras in the United States, but in China I worked with a group that barely stood its ground with an American youth orchestra. I returned from Korea financially better off yet feeling I had missed a meaningful experience, whereas I left China financially drained but personally enriched.

I was invited to conduct the Shanghai Broadcast Philharmonic via the overtures of several Chinese musicians, some of whom were prominent in that country and some transplants to the United States. I quickly discovered through Lin Chang (Arkansas Symphony violist and our trans-Pacific go-between) that hard currency for items like air tickets and artist fees was in short supply, so I offered to provide the ticket using my airline miles. This turned out to be a no-good-deed-goes-unpunished moment, because the free ticket cost me $1,000, involving four flights (each way) and an overnight stay at the Tokyo airport.

Having acquired my costly free ticket, I used this magnanimous gesture as a wedge to revisit an earlier discussion.

"The orchestra is providing the hotel?" I asked Lin.

"Absolutely."

"And it will be a first-class, Western hotel?"

"Absolutely."

I suggested a few names I'd researched. "Perhaps the Hilton or the Garden Hotel?"

"The Garden Hotel? No problem."

With instructions to craft a "loud and tuneful" program, we settled on the *Peer Gynt* Suite No. 1, the Shulman Variations for viola and orchestra (with Lin as soloist), and Tchaikovsky Symphony No. 5. The music seemed too simple for a professional orchestra, but if that was what they wanted, it was all right with me.

I'd made multiple requests for details before I finally received the name of a hotel that neither my travel agent nor the official Chinese travel agency in San Francisco could identify. By the rarest coincidence, Stewart Beck, son of Jean Beck (executive director and board president of the Lake Forest Symphony), lived in Shanghai. He reconnoitered on my behalf and reported that the hotel was "not awful" but was far from what I was promised.

Three days before departure, I received information on a different hotel that, again, no reputable travel agent could locate. This time Stewart offered only that it was "a big improvement." Running out of time, I decided the trip was meant to be an adventure, and I had better resign myself to it. So, the Hotel Xing Guo it was.

I touched down in Shanghai at 8:00 p.m. local time, was efficiently met by Lin Chang and Xu Wei Guang, the orchestra's public relations director, and found the hotel Xing Guo to be delightfully uneventful.

The only real surprise was the hotel's overall construction—six low buildings occupying more than a city block enclosed by a high concrete wall, as if originally conceived as a minimum-security prison. Balancing its spartan appearance, Lin informed me that Chairman Mao always stayed at this guest house when visiting Shanghai, and I was duly impressed. I was only allowed to drop my luggage in the room because sleep, my priority at that moment, was being postponed in favor of a three-hour dinner party commencing at 10:00 p.m.

Following the protracted dinner and a delicious sleep, another extended meal was on the docket. At lunch the next day we were joined by the orchestra's concertmaster and Professor Lin, the flute instructor at the Shanghai Conservatory.

Professor Lin's company, which I had the pleasure of sharing several more times that week, was one of the highlights of my visit. He spoke English very well, so we were able to converse easily and in some depth. He owed his language expertise to music-related travel in the United States and to the good fortune—in his words—to have been educated before the cultural revolution.

I don't recall how we wandered onto the subject of religion, though it may have had something to do with me passing a pork dish without partaking. Professor Lin was fascinated by the fact that I am Jewish, saying he had never conversed with a Jew before but had read much about the faith and the people. In the United States, it is nearly impossible to discuss Western religion with someone who has no personal stake, and as he waxed eloquent on the subject, I listened with interest.

His first remark, "Ah, a very brilliant people, the Jewish," brought a sly grin to my face.

This was followed by insightful, if politically incorrect, thoughts about the Middle East and its three religions. He found it amazing that the Jews had become a "literate, scholarly people," while our cousins, the Muslims, became a "savage people." (His words, not mine.) He even insisted I teach him some Hebrew, and together we recited the blessing for bread. But there was no bread on the table, so we blessed the rice and called it close enough.

Before leaving the United States, I had remarked to Lin Chang that six rehearsals for such a simple program seemed like overkill, but he told me not to concern myself. Less than five minutes into my first rehearsal, I understood.

Unlike the Seoul Philharmonic, a group of very talented musicians in need of musical leadership, the Shanghai Broadcast Philharmonic played like an American high school orchestra. Rhythmic coherence between the sections was poor, and some individuals, several of them principals, played like amateurs. Nonetheless, that morning's unproductive beginnings were followed by hints of technical and musical progress.

After rehearsal we ate lunch with several local musicians, including Mr. Wong, the orchestra's regular conductor. That meal was my first encounter with food brought to the table alive. This is common with shellfish, I was told, because it guarantees the food's freshness. Fresh is good, but when I named each shrimp—Steve, Julie, Bob—no one seemed amused.

After lunch Lin and I headed to a museum, but we never arrived. A cab dropped us off about a block from our destination in a drenching rain where we took refuge under an awning. But the rain intensified until, after nearly an hour, the water rose over the curb and lapped at our feet. I grew up in Portland, where we calculate time by when it *isn't* raining, and spent a year in Atlanta enduring thunderstorms of indescribable ferocity. But a deluge in a coastal, zero-elevation city is a completely different experience. Soaked by the horizontal rain, we abandoned our museum quest, traversing several yards of calf-deep, ice-cold water to reach a taxi.

With each day in China, my sense of purpose continued to evolve. Exchanging views with Professor Lin, naming shrimp in a vain attempt to spare their lives, experiencing the torrential weather firsthand, and events still to come were, I realized, the reason I was there. I would, of course, continue to do my best with the orchestra. But unlike in Seoul, where the limited goal was making music at the highest possible level, I felt I was in Shanghai to experience and absorb, to see and to feel—to take every impression and fold it into all later music making.

After our second rehearsal, Lin and I spent some time looking over the Shulman Variations. While in the United States, I had seen only a piano reduction and was assured I would receive the conductor's score in Shanghai. They couldn't find (i.e., could not afford) the printed parts, so a music theory professor at the Shanghai Conservatory transcribed it as best he could, using the piano score and a recording as his guides. Unfortunately, his penciled score was littered with mistakes, and those errors were copied verbatim into the orchestra parts.

After Tuesday's rehearsal I cut short the planned sightseeing and headed for the hotel. I spent the entire evening combing through the parts, correcting mistakes and blowing my nose, the first sign of the illness about to overtake me. I was a little put out at having to spend my time doing librarian work, but my only other diversion was CNN International, and there was only so much chaos and catastrophe I could stand.

I awoke Wednesday with a throat so inflamed I couldn't speak. I'd been advised to carry a supply of common Western remedies but, naturally, I didn't listen. Compounding my woes, all those hours in bed had made my neck and back very stiff. I headed to round three with the orchestra walking slowly and coughing vigorously, looking like a 90-year-old consumptive. Despite my worsening condition, I was unable to beg off lunch and dinner events during which I politely avoided both salted, congealed chicken blood and choosing my entrée from a case of live snakes.

Following the fourth rehearsal, during which the orchestra began to play Tchaikovsky with a modicum of expertise and style, I set off on a sacred mission at the request of Lee Ronnel, an older friend from Little Rock. Born in Shanghai, Lee was half Russian Jew and half Chinese. He had come to America after his father—an orchestra conductor named Itkis, by bizarre coincidence—passed away. He used his stepfather's surname, so I'd had no idea his last name at birth was nearly identical to mine.

When Lee learned of my trip, he asked me to locate his father's grave. The Jewish cemetery where the man was laid to rest had been destroyed, but Lee remembered—not entirely accurately—that it was in the Honk-yoo district.

Lin and the orchestra's Mr. Xu graciously agreed to accompany me, but first we needed to locate the cemetery. To those of us who don't speak Chinese, the difference between what Lee wrote, "Honk-yoo," and the name of the district, "Hong-koo," may seem minor. But to native speakers it was a matter of considerable confusion.

Though we located the neighborhood easily, the cemetery itself proved elusive, and locals could only tell us it was "right around here somewhere." Eventually, an octogenarian showed us that the cemetery was only steps from where we were standing.

We entered and saw what remained—essentially nothing. The cemetery is now a small walled-in park with a memorial tablet describing the fate of the Jews in Shanghai. The gravestones and all other traces of the departed were destroyed shortly after the Communists took over. Unfortunately, the only news I took home for Lee was that a marker in English, Hebrew, and Chinese stood on the site, and that an old man from the neighborhood believed the remains themselves were untouched. Considering my initial goal, to bring back a photo of his father's headstone, it felt like precious little.

After aiding us in this modest success, our accidental guide mentioned that what remained of the old synagogue was just a few blocks away. Like the cemetery, it was not easy to find. The ground floor was a bookstore, and what remained upstairs was a two-room gallery of photos and memorabilia documenting the history of the Jews in Shanghai.

The museum was dutifully watched over by Wang Fa Liang, the museum's "storyteller" and "narrator." Mr. Wang's job, it seemed, was to wait around in case someone happened to show up wanting to hear the story of the Jews in Shanghai. He started talking when we hit the top of the stairs and didn't take a breath for an hour. His narrative began in the 1840s, when many European and Russian Jews emigrated to China, and continued through both world wars, the arrival of more Jews fleeing the Holocaust, and, later, when some of the same families fled Shanghai to escape the Communists.

Though our excursion was exhilarating, I returned to my hotel feeling wretched. My cold had worsened and moved into my chest, but I had made dinner plans with Stewart Beck—the savior of my hotel situation—and I couldn't stand him up.

I had attempted to do the when-in-Rome thing by allowing the orchestra's physician to treat my ailment, but the Chinese cough syrup he'd given me had the efficacy of a breath mint, and I declined his offer of snake blood. Hearing of my condition, Stewart promised to help me locate some Western medicine on our outing.

By the time he picked me up, I was in bad shape, and I'm sure I looked it. However, there is an ancient Chinese saying that roughly translates as, "There is nothing on earth that cannot be cured by rigatoni, red wine, and some serious pharmaceuticals." We ate, imbibed, found a drug store, then went to the hotel where Stewart moonlighted as a bartender. I took my first dose of whatever remedy I'd purchased, washed it down with a beer, and was soon feeling like a new man.

The Chinese language, with its enormous pallet of sounds, tones, and symbols, is so complex that the word "fluent" cannot be used as it is in the West. The tones are so subtle that two words sounding identical to the unschooled may have very different meanings. On the way back to my hotel, I learned that the language is difficult even for the Chinese.

There are two Shanghai hotels with names sounding quite alike: the Shing Guo (a very nice, Western style hotel), and mine, the Xing Guo. After leaving Stewart to a night of bartending, I gave the man at the cab stand a card with my hotel's name and address written in Chinese. He read it and repeated the information to the driver.

Shanghai is a huge, complicated city where I had been for only a few days, but I knew enough to be concerned that the driver's route was not correct. Unfortunately, I had no way to communicate this, since he spoke no English, and none of the Chinese I'd picked up applied to the situation. At length he pulled into the circular drive of the Shing Guo Hotel. Showing him the card (which I probably should have done sooner), I managed to communicate that we were in the wrong place. I never figured out if the man at the cab stand didn't read Chinese very well or if the cab driver was hard of hearing.

Friday morning's rehearsal was fruitful—I think. With all the drugs coursing through my veins, I felt like someone else was conducting. Though I am adamant about maintaining a sober musical workplace, I enjoyed abandoning myself to the music and found it easier to tune them out when they weren't playing well.

That evening we dined at the Blue Heaven, a revolving restaurant on the forty-second floor of a hotel. In contrast with the usual family style, dinner at the Blue Heaven was a buffet. This was a great relief because it allowed me to stick to safer choices without repeatedly explaining why I was not eating this or that.

Having heard from Lin Chang that I enjoy a glass of wine now and again, our hosts ordered a Chinese red wine called Dynasty, which many others in the restaurant were also drinking. It tasted like Carlo Rossi Burgundy you'd left sitting open on your kitchen counter for several days—in August. But the gesture was appreciated.

Once again, dinner lasted more than three hours. And, as usual, more than two hours elapsed between the time I finished eating and the moment everyone else was done. Much to his credit, Lin restrained himself, telling me to "eat more" only about ten times. When dinner was over, we exchanged gifts, as this would be our last evening together.

Rehearsal the following morning took place in the theater, our first and only in the venue. To my delight I found that the hall was quite beautiful and resonant, seating about eleven hundred and masking some of the orchestra's inaccuracies. The final rehearsal went well, apart from a few terrifying mistakes during the Shulman Variations, the result of meter changes that continued to perplex some of the players.

The previous day I had asked Lin if we could find Western food for my last meal before the concert. Eschewing suggestions I'd acquired from Stewart, Lin insisted on Hartz's Chicken Buffet, which he described as the Chinese equivalent of Shoney's.

His description was quite accurate, and the food was not bad considering it was a convoluted attempt to make a Western style restaurant palatable to Chinese tastes. But all I cared about was the salad bar, iceberg lettuce accompanied by a strange variation on Thousand Island dressing and a few containers of other veggies. Surveying the salad bar, it struck me that if one is especially thrilled by the sight of cold corn on the cob, it's probably time to go home.

Navigating to the concert hall required some ingenuity. Due to the intense traffic in Shanghai, only certain vehicles were allowed in certain districts on certain days—a system that makes New York's alternate-side-of-the-street parking look like child's play. Before 7:00 p.m. on Saturdays, the symphony's car was not allowed in the district where the concert hall is located. Fortunately, the driver had a card stating that she worked for the China television network—which she did not—and she blew by a policeman at the checkpoint with a wave and a smile.

Arriving at the theater, we found the stage door locked. After some searching we located the backstage attendant and entered, and my question from earlier in the day was answered. That morning, seeing the stage crew dismantling the orchestra set-up after rehearsal, I had asked Lin for an explanation. But he'd muttered something about Communists and said no more.

Entering through the stage door, we were greeted with energetic "Shh!" gestures from the attendant. Proceeding quietly into the pitch-black backstage, we were surprised to hear loud noises and music.

Walking further, we found ourselves behind a movie screen, with a film in progress. About ten minutes later, the movie ended, the audience departed, and the crew reset the stage for the concert.

The performance went smoothly, relatively speaking. To their great credit, the orchestra played well, and I would hardly have known them as the same musicians I'd met the previous Monday. Though the concert was a significant step forward from where we'd begun, I was surprised when, after the Tchaikovsky symphony, I was recalled to the stage six times. After the second bow, I was sure we were finished and was all but undressing. But the applause continued, so the orchestra and I took one more bow—four more times.

Afterward, a handful of musicians offered to take me to a special spot, and as we ate and drank, they explained why this otherwise undistinguished establishment held particular meaning for them. This out-of-the-way hotpot joint was where they had taken Isaac Stern after his performance with the orchestra, and it was his favorite place in the city. I was honored to end my time in Shanghai at the legendary violinist's favorite haunt.

Little could I have known at that time the outsized role that China would come to play in my life. In 1997 Mei (my third-time's-the-charm wife) was a 22-year-old medical resident in a Shanghai hospital. She has often wondered aloud if perhaps we passed one another on the street, our eyes meeting for an instant, never imagining that our lives would come together seventeen years later and seven thousand miles away.

Mei and David, Payette Lake, McCall, Idaho, 2018.

~~~~~ The Poet ~~~~~

During most of my tenure as music director, the Arkansas Symphony presented a concert each February to celebrate Black History Month. This program always featured a prominent African American guest artist, usually a luminary in music, film, or government.

In February 1998 we were honored to host poet, author, and activist Maya Angelou. In that performance Dr. Angelou narrated Joseph Schwantner's *New Morning for the World*, an exquisite blending of orchestral music with words from the speeches of Dr. Martin Luther King Jr.

Our guest had been sent the text and a brief explanation of how the words and music interact, but a meeting before the first and only rehearsal was required to discuss the finer details. She was conveyed from her hotel and ensconced in the star dressing room at Robinson Auditorium (the "star" designation makes her digs sound swankier than they were), where she awaited me and my assistant. I have met many famous individuals on this journey; some are exactly as you'd expect, some nicer, some quirkier, and then there was Maya Angelou. Kind, charming, intelligent, witty, and radiant are all inadequate. Language simply fails us.

At the time of her visit, I was 40 years old, though I looked a bit younger, and my assistant was a woman in her late 20s. We knocked, received a musical "Come in," and opened the door.

She remained seated as we entered, and greeted us, smiling, teacup in hand, "Well, aren't you two just as young as morning?"

The rest of our meeting is something of a blur, like being sucked into a poetic vortex from which you hope never to be expelled. But released we were after an all-too-brief twenty minutes. Rehearsal with the orchestra followed, where she charmed the musicians with her grace and humility. The audience that evening would have walked on coals for her, as would we all. From the back row of the hall, they hung on her every word and intonation. Some people don't have to do anything to accomplish that. It's simply who they are.

God of the Cello

I spent the better part of two years within a few dozen feet of one of the greatest cellists in history, but we never met. At Indiana University in the 1980s, a few members of the faculty occupied a rarified, deity-like space. Chief among these godlike personages were violinist Joseph Gingold, mezzo-soprano Margaret Harshaw, saxophonist Eugene Rousseau, and cellist Janos Starker. Mr. Gingold and Miss Harshaw were somewhat illusive, but I passed Mr. Starker in the halls of IU many times, always averting my eyes in respect and fear.

Not long after Bill Vickery arrived as executive director of the Arkansas Symphony, he suggested Janos Starker as a guest for the following season. It goes without saying that I'd thought of Mr. Starker earlier, but I always assumed that the combined effects of his schedule and the ASO's budget would prove prohibitive. Fortunately, Bill's earlier connections with many distinguished artists allowed us to more easily navigate the issues of fees and scheduling.

The first of my several musical adventures with Janos took place in 1998. While this encounter was notable for his extraordinary Dvořák concerto, I remember it most vividly in terms of my learning curve regarding his charming eccentricities.

Our first face-to-face was in his dressing room, a quick chat over Dvořák before his rehearsal with the orchestra. But before I made it as far as the artist's dressing room, the stage door guard stopped me, saying we had "a problem."

Not long after Janos had entered his room, the guard smelled smoke. He had knocked and found the great man nonchalantly puffing on a cigarette in a nonsmoking, city-owned building. When the befuddled guard called this to Janos's attention—"Sir, I'm sorry, but you can't smoke here"—the response was something like, "Sure I can."

I asked the guard what he expected me to do. Viewing me as the ultimate authority in the building, he naturally suggested, "Tell him he can't smoke in there."

Meaning no disrespect to our loyal guard, I chuckled and shook my head, saying, "Yeah, right."

A few minutes before going on stage to conduct the first performance, I checked in on Janos. I found him practicing diligently, though not on Dvořák, a silver flask and a half-full glass of amber liquid within arm's reach. I asked if everything was okay, told him I'd see him in about an hour, and withdrew. Naturally, I was surprised to find my soloist drinking scotch before a performance. But I wasn't concerned, because I figured a tipsy Janos Starker still played the cello about a hundred times better than just about anyone else on earth.

Following intermission, we stood in the darkened backstage as the orchestra tuned, moments from stepping through the door and into the light. When the stage was quiet and the crew chief had given me the nod, I asked the question I put to every soloist at that moment, "Ready?"—meaning, "Let's go."

But Janos's feet didn't budge. He looked over his shoulder and barked, "No."

I thought, *Oh, God, he's ill or something. And he's really old, so who knows?*

But before I could process his "No," he stepped briskly onto the stage, muttering just loud enough for me to hear, "—but I'm not getting any readier."

He was just messing with me, and I fell for it.

Janos graciously invited us to join him for dinner after that first performance. I assumed we would meet in the dining room of the Capital Hotel, where he was staying, but as he left the hall, he told me we should join him in his room after I had changed. A few minutes later, he greeted us warmly, a tumbler of scotch in hand, and ushered us into the nicest suite in the hotel. He had ordered a lavish dinner from room service, which arrived moments later, elegantly arranged on the large dining table.

I can hold my own with most people in the scotch drinking department, but Janos was not most people. By the time we left, I'd had two fingers two or three times, and was sure I wouldn't be driving home. Janos had filled the tumbler at least that many times, not counting what he'd had in his dressing room, and he was steady as a rock.

We all know smoking and drinking have deleterious effects on our health and are likely to shorten one's life. How Janos's liver and lungs survived to the age of 88 is a mystery, but we are all the better for it.

They Made Me an Offer I Couldn't Refuse

I visited Sicily for two weeks in July 1998, representing the Sister Cities Commission of Little Rock. Our destination was Ragusa-Ibla, Little Rock's sister city near the southern tip of the island. To this remote outpost we were sent as jurors for the Ibla Grand Prize, an international competition for pianists and singers. When my official invitation arrived, we realized their dates conflicted with my previous commitments, so Bill Vickery, the Arkansas Symphony's executive director, agreed to take my place.

A few weeks later, the competition's dates suddenly changed. I told Bill I wouldn't deprive him of two weeks in Italy, but he would not hear of it. I am almost certain he did not intentionally send me into the situation I am about to describe. But, on the other hand, he gave up two weeks in Italy far too easily.

Regardless of the cosmetic differences, certain basics apply to every reputable competition. These fundamental similarities center around basic fairness and creating a level playing field in terms of repertoire, performance time, adjudication procedures, and jury qualifications. Unfortunately, none of these items were under control during the Ibla Grand Prize in 1998. Far from being an unbiased event governed by generally understood rules, the Ibla Grand Prize was the private fiefdom of its director, president, impresario, and jury chairman, a singular Sicilian character we will call Z.

I arrived at the closest airport, in Catania, already thirteen hours, three planes, and an hour-long bus ride into the journey, with a harrowing two-hour car trip still ahead of me. Following that travel and its accompanying jetlag, I was, not surprisingly, a bit disoriented at the first session. Little did I know that I was more alert on day one than I would be at any point during my stay.

When competition began the jury was composed of approximately a dozen members. This would change throughout the fortnight as various jurors arrived or departed midstream. And, to our disbelief, the Johnnies-come-lately were allowed to deliberate and vote as though they had been present throughout.

Some large competition juries contain one or two members who are appointed for reasons of politics or fundraising. Those jurors may not be artistically qualified, but they usually form a small percentage of the votes and are sufficiently self-aware to stay out of the fray in deliberations. But at the Ibla Grand Prize of 1998, the final jury contained more than twenty persons, barely half of whom were qualified to judge a musical competition. The dilettantes would score a fine pianist poorly for one obvious missed note, while giving a terrible singer high marks because she sang very loud or flaunted other assets.

We worked on Italian time, rarely beginning before noon or quitting before midnight, with lunch and dinner breaks accounting for at least four hours of our day. Near the close of one of these extended lunches, Z casually distributed the composition entries to the jurors still present. He asked us to glance at them but assured us they were all "garbage" and deserved a "last place." When he casually dismissed the work of these young composers—or gave no thought to performers who'd spent months preparing only to be tossed aside without a fair hearing—I couldn't help reflecting on my experience in the Netherlands, seeing myself in their shoes.

My favorite local character in Ragusa was the Assessore di Cultura, the man charged with overseeing the city's cultural affairs. He had roughly the same importance as the chairman of the arts council of Hayes, Kansas, but this character worthy of Charles Dickens carried himself as though he were Vittorio Emanuele reborn. With his hand extended in greeting—palm down, as if expecting his ring to be kissed—the locals referred to him as Il Signore (The Lord), but it was difficult for an outsider to assess the sincerity of this moniker.

Competition began bright and early, anywhere between noon and 4:00 p.m., depending on various whims and the World Cup schedule. At the end of each day, the jury was asked to give preliminary votes while impressions were still fresh in our minds. And it was during one of these early voting sessions that we had our first glimpse of the relationship between our votes and the final results.

After the jury voted a certain pianist as our current favorite, we were told that the woman was out of the running because she'd balked when asked to play in the piazza the previous evening. She'd had the temerity to object to performing poorly amplified, on an out-of-tune piano, in a public square bombarded by noise from motor scooters and automobiles. In the kingdom of Ibla, those still in contention for a prize did not refuse to perform in the piazza—their nightly ritual of obedience.

"I cannot possibly work with such a prima donna," Z told us.

I refrained from pointing out the obvious—the pot was calling the kettle black—because nothing I said would change the fact that she was history.

Street noise and out-of-tune pianos weren't the only problems with the piazza concerts. The competitors assumed, quite logically, that being selected to perform was an expression of the jury's favor. For the most part, this was correct. Unfortunately, some competitors were merely in the right place at the right time. If the competition's assistant director was short of performers for that evening's concert, any competitor hanging around the hall might get the nod. What that musician assumed to be a stamp of approval was no more than happenstance.

In the small, overheated, stone-lined recital hall where the competition was held, the jury was confined to consecutive seats in the first row where the decibel level of banging Rachmaninoff wannabes and screaming would-be divas was nearly unbearable. One afternoon, overwhelmed by the volume and accumulated body heat, a few of us spread out, only to be greeted by a very public tirade commanding us to return to our seats "immediately" because following instructions was our "job."

The jury was exhausted, and competitors were either assigned ridiculous performance times (e.g., beginning a fifty-minute performance at 11:45 p.m.), arrived at the theater to discover the process was several hours behind schedule, or occasionally both. Repeated pleas from the jury to begin the day earlier and tighten the schedule fell on deaf ears. Musicians who were lucky enough to play in the first few hours of the day made high scores, while those scheduled well into the evening, when the jury was sleepy and somewhat intoxicated, fared poorly.

With no applicant screening or age limitations, many of these competitors had no business in an international competition. Worse, pianists in the artist category were allowed to play an initial program of up to fifty minutes. So the jury was confined hour after hour with no possibility of parole.

But all was not darkness. Occasionally, a real artist stepped onto the stage, and our joy was palpable. The room seemed to lighten, and our dazed postures came to life in appreciation of a truly interesting young musician.

The jury's most colorful character was the former first lady of a southeast Asian nation. In public she was referred to as La Principessa—though this was uttered most often in sarcasm. Her money had bought an honorary title of some sort, and she was allowed to vote even though she arrived three days before the end of competition and understood nothing about what she'd witnessed.

She was dressed to the nines every waking moment and spent most of that time denigrating the Italians. On her first night in Ragusa, holding court in the bar of our hotel after competition was complete, she told a group of jurors in a loud voice that she had flown on Delta instead of Alitalia to avoid flying with "those noisy, smelly Italians." A few days later, during a supper party at a villa outside town, she inspected a piece of homemade ciabatta and loudly asked why the Italians couldn't make any decent bread. After all, she continued, with our hostess not ten feet away, she could get better Italian bread in New York.

But the last straw fell on the final day, during jury deliberations, as we considered an extraordinarily talented 15-year-old Armenian girl who had played the Goldberg Variations. She was short and slight, looking even younger than her age, and I was mesmerized by her elegant, subtle, expressive, and astonishingly mature performance of Bach's massive keyboard work. She was a ray of sunshine during an otherwise soul-sucking experience, and we loved her for it.

As the jury discussed the merits of her playing and deliberated her prize level, the Principessa interrupted. She announced that this girl could not possibly play concerts representing the competition because she was "so incredibly ugly," saying, "When she grows up, she will look like a horse. It's tragic." As the Principessa spewed her bile, I recalled the girl's performance, thinking I had never seen anything so beautiful.

On the final day, jury deliberations yielded yet another drama. After a slate of four vocal winners was proposed, the period for discussion began. I raised my hand, offering that one of the four had sung terribly out of tune in both of her performances.

The response was, "If you don't want one singer with your orchestra, don't take her. That's all. The rest is not your business."

Stunned by this assault, I watched my colleagues stare at their shoes in embarrassment. Before arriving in Ragusa, my Sister Cities contact and fellow juror warned me that the process for awarding prizes was "unique," and that when jury votes didn't concur with certain predeterminations, those ballots magically disappeared. This turned out to be true, as we learned to our chagrin on the last day.

Despite my objection, the jury voted for the slate of four vocal winners, three Eastern European dramatic sopranos and one Chinese coloratura, the last of these being the only reasonably cultured singer of the group. That evening we stood on stage as the vocal winners were announced, but there were only three—the Chinese coloratura had been left out. We exchanged furtive glances, but no substantive communication was possible under the audience's gaze.

Several hours later in the hotel bar, we were treated to a convoluted story about how the competition had been forced to cancel the coloratura's prize because she had chosen her repertoire for the gala concert badly. Judging from the available evidence, it appeared that Z and the Principessa had removed the Chinese singer despite the jury's vote. Was this jealousy on the part of the Principessa—the Chinese singer *was* very attractive—or perhaps had the singer not behaved with appropriate deference? We would never know.

Further details of vote manipulation came to my attention several hours later, at 5:30 a.m. in the Catania airport. In the lounge a Russian juror and I chatted about the odd phenomenon that so many capable people agreed to serve on the jury under these bizarre conditions. I had come as service to my city and my organization, but I couldn't understand why these other well-credentialed people were involved.

The Russian juror had traveled from Moscow with several piano competitors in tow and had only agreed to judge because there were "additional motivations." When I asked what that meant, she told me that an agreement had been made, in advance, that all pianists she brought to Sicily would be included in the group touring the United

States the following year. In other words, the competition had guaranteed they would all be winners.

I have never been a fan of musical competitions because I don't think music making can be fairly evaluated in that environment, though there are many excellent competitions that strive to maintain the highest levels of integrity. Having admitted I don't approve of the whole idea, it may appear hypocritical that I agreed to participate. It seems that way to me too. But I had two good reasons for accepting.

First, after being asked by our Sister Cities Commission to represent the Little Rock artistic community, it would have been difficult and disrespectful to refuse. Second, I had hoped to exert a positive influence on a situation that badly needed it.

But there were two things I didn't understand. First, the situation had more problems than I, or anyone else, could possibly solve. Second, those in charge in Ragusa didn't want change because they didn't perceive anything was amiss. They were perfectly at ease with a competition featuring an uneven playing field, an inattentive jury made up largely of nonmusicians, no adjudication rules to speak of, and voting procedures that would make a Third World dictator blush.

Though the Ibla Grand Prize is an affair of little consequence in the larger scheme of things, the experience forced me to revisit my never-ending quest to understand why many worthy artists never achieve their goals while mediocre talents frequently fall into sustainable solo careers. Part of that phenomenon is the age-old who-you-know issue. But artistic careers often succeed or fail early on over the flimsiest of circumstances. While being named a winner in the Ibla Grand Prize may be worth nothing on its own, it is entirely possible that this distinction could be leveraged toward an entree into the next level. On the other hand, the superior young artist who wore the wrong tie or doesn't look like a runway model is saddled with a career trajectory in the opposite direction.

I am pleased to report that a recent conversation with my Sister Cities compatriot—twenty years after my visit—revealed that Z has "mellowed," the event has been shortened to one week, the Principessa no longer serves on the jury, and the judging process is closer to expected norms. This is very good news, indeed, but an awfully long time coming.

Darth Vader Likes Kids?

In 1999 the Arkansas Symphony hosted James Earl Jones. To say that I was excited to work with this distinguished actor is understating the case. From the first moment, he was down to earth, friendly, and fatherly, and his performance of Copland's *Lincoln Portrait* was thrilling.

A reception for Mr. Jones followed the concert, to which my second wife brought her son for a brief period. It was later than an 11-year-old should be out at a party for adults, but we couldn't deny him the opportunity to meet Darth Vader. I remained at the gathering after they headed home, finally walking our guest as far as the lobby of his hotel.

We said our goodbyes and headed in opposite directions, he toward the elevators and I out the hotel's front door. As I stepped outside, my phone rang, and I immediately picked up. An odd moment for a call from home, I thought, when they should have been nearly in bed. Her son was in quite a state, she told me, because he had forgotten to ask for the great man's autograph. Was I still near Mr. Jones, she asked, and could I manage it?

Glancing back inside, I saw him at the elevator being chatted up by a fan. Not wanting to shout, but determined to catch him, I sprinted the length of the lobby, catching his eye just before he stepped into the elevator. He moved toward me, asking if everything was all right—I was, after all, running full-tilt through a hotel lobby dressed in white tie and tails. When I explained the situation, a huge grin blossomed on his face. He stepped to the front desk, requested paper and a pen, and, asking the boy's name, wrote, "Dear Christopher, May the force be with you. James Earl Jones."

Mission accomplished.

Chapter 8

Within the Silence

Silence is everything. Without silence there is no music, because empty air is the canvas upon which music is made. And when that canvas is overwhelmed, when the noise is ever present, there is no space in which to create something new.

There are many kinds of silence. There is silence that opens the door to inspiration and human connection, like the moment of breathless wonder before the tentative opening notes of Debussy's *Prélude à l'après-midi d'un faune*. There is the paralyzing silence of loneliness and alienation. And there is the final, suffocating silence of death.

To make music we must find stillness in ourselves, quieting the din between our ears. But there is more to stilling the noise than simply taking a moment to collect ourselves before stepping onto the stage. We must create a renewable, ever-present well of silence that is always within reach, because this deep, dark, welcoming place is essential to begin the process of making music. Finding this silence, and making it a permanent part of ourselves, is an ongoing, often difficult task.

I've spent too many of my sixty-plus years allowing the noise inside my head to consume each moment. Periodically, I ask myself why so many things that should bring satisfaction and fulfillment leave me empty. Over time I began to understand that silence is also essential to the joy of everyday living. The simple delight found in everything from petting the dog to hearing a few notes of Mozart is immeasurably enhanced when experienced without a storm of constant, distracting, often negative thought.

I am, of course, not the one who discovered this. I am merely looking for its place in my life. Some great people (and some great animals) have tried to show me the way as I grope through the darkness.

In recent years I find I am more observant of, and increasingly appalled by, what passes for human interaction. At a typical family gathering, you're likely to see a dozen people who came together to be with loved ones, yet each is sequestered amid their private noise. They text, navigate social media, or wander YouTube, glancing up just long enough to giggle before retreating to their virtual environments. This is a gathering in body but not in spirit; a confluence of travel plans but not of hearts; a sharing of space but not love. They cannot not part with their various sources of noise for even a few moments. And, thus, it is a moment lost for want of redeeming silence.

There are a few special individuals among us, those who seem to shine from within, whose inner silence and gentle wisdom, uncluttered by ego, radiate to everyone around them. Few of us are like this. I certainly am not. If we encounter even one such person in our lifetime, we count ourselves unspeakably blessed.

Animals, I believe, are more fortunate and possess this inner light more uniformly. Though their lives have changed a great deal as humanity continues to dominate and pollute the earth, they have not changed fundamentally. Animals have adapted to the trials through which we put them but are still the same patient creatures they have always been. Is this their superior soul manifesting itself? Perhaps that's a question worth exploring.

Years ago a friend and I wandered into an abstract spiritual discussion, and I proposed, offhandedly, the question of whether animals have souls. I was taken aback when she expressed her absolute certainty they do not. Only humans were given a soul, she told me.

My difficulty with her response was not in the specifics. I don't know if animals have souls. For that matter, I'm not sure *I* have one. What disturbed me was the arrogance her answer demonstrated.

Animals, who, despite our interference, live in peace and reasonable harmony with the planet and one another, have no souls. Humans, on the other hand, who have slaughtered each other for centuries over nothing more important than what God looks like—we, who have elevated human suffering and the destruction of our planet to an art form—are the ones uniquely endowed with a spiritual essence?

But even as I utter that blasphemous question, I reflect on the fact that your cocker spaniel could not have conceived a creation like the slow movement of Beethoven's Ninth Symphony. On the other hand, do we know whether the beloved animal is moved to canine tears by this music? We do not.

So I must question why we would deny a soul to companions whose capacity for loyalty, patience, forgiveness, and selfless love is far beyond that of any human. Their storehouse of these virtues may, in fact, be boundless. No matter their outward circumstances, they live in the glow of their essential goodness, and when the ultimate silence approaches, they bear it with equal tranquility. They do not ask why there wasn't more time but instead revel in love and years shared, setting an example we follow only poorly.

The joy derived from sharing our brief time on earth with those we love is balanced by the eventual grief of loss, and this is only natural. But a perversion of this balance also exists. For some, moments of joy are experienced as though gazing into a distorted mirror in which we view not the present time but the darkest of possible futures. Watching our toddler at play we see neither their delight and innocence nor their bright possibilities, but only inevitable alienation and parting. Holding a new puppy, we cannot abandon ourselves to ecstatic joy and laughter but look instead to a far horizon and that final tear-filled embrace.

This is the weight some of us bear, and perhaps it is part of the reason we became performing artists in the first place. Musical compositions, works of theater, paintings, sculptures, and the like, are forever, living far beyond their creator's mortality. But a performance ceases to exist the moment it is concluded. Like life itself, our works as performers are gone in an instant.

But whether we acknowledge the approaching darkness or not, it comes for us all. And modern psychology has, I believe, a strange perspective on this loss. After we rage and grieve, we are told to find acceptance and closure. But what if we don't want closure because the pain is all we have? My strength and consolation from the loss of my parents—both unexpected and so close together—and the loss of many friends, colleagues, and beloved creatures comes not from the promise that closure is at hand, but quite the opposite.

In the unique agony of the finale of Tchaikovsky's Sixth Symphony, and any number of other musical moments, I find myself closer to lost loved ones than at any therapy session or religious ceremony. In that moment, pain and silence exist side by side, each filling its place in the natural order of things. And though I attempt to conceal the moment from my colleagues with a gnawed lower lip, if the feelings overwhelm me—if they become the music—then so be it.

Pain, as much as joy and silence, is an essential part of the wellspring from which our creativity is born. We desire closure because we fear the pain. Instead, we must embrace the reality that pain never ends, that closure is a myth, and that these facts form the core of our humanity.

We honor the memory of the departed with words etched in stone, and this is as it should be.

For my enigmatic father, we left a quotation from Robert Burns:

If there's another world, he lives in bliss;
If there is none, he made the best of this.

The author's parents' headstone, Ahavai Sholom Cemetery, Portland, Oregon.

For my mother, whose untimely passing shocked us all:

So full of life even Death was caught off guard.

And for the creatures, three stones that read "Love," for what they gave unconditionally, "Peace," our hope for them, and "Courage," their lesson for us at the last.

But these words, joined with our requiems and kaddish, do not bring closure. On the contrary, as we repeat them, they twist the knife of our pain, carving a gulf of silence in our souls. And this, also, is as it should be.

The modern mental healthcare system tells us that if we are in pain, or grieve, or suffer dark thoughts, we have an illness they will help us fix. But we are not ill, we do not have a syndrome, and we do not need to be fixed. We are human—flawed, flayed, and in pain—and it is only by accepting this fact that we may go forward and, perhaps, find music, love, and life.

~~~~~ If There's Another World ~~~~~

I was raised Jewish, so I have some issues with the idea of heaven. That's not because Jews don't believe in heaven. We do—I think. The problem is we're not exactly sure *what* we believe about it. And this lack of detailed dogma doesn't apply solely to my special brand of agnostic Hebrews. I'm pretty sure it applies to most of the children of Israel.

If quizzed, most members of the tribe would tell you we believe in heaven—our spectacular level of theological inconsistency from person to person, and from one congregation to the next, notwithstanding. If you asked those same individuals *what* Judaism believes about heaven, most would be hard pressed for a coherent answer. We know we're supposed to accept that it isn't just over when we die, but beyond that things get murky.

I think this is also true of many people of other faiths, and I don't believe that's a bad thing. There are some things in the universe that simply aren't knowable, or assumable, or in any way understandable for us. We may just need to resign ourselves to the fact that this is the one thing we don't get to know.

Having already exceeded my philosophical expertise, I will climb further out on a limb and say a few words about what I'm pretty sure is *not* going to happen.

Several years ago the subject was brought into focus by a highway billboard decorated with party hats, streamers, and musical instruments, inviting, "Come to the greatest party ever . . . in heaven!" This display was, I assume, not intended literally. But even viewed as a metaphor, it is still problematic. The issue isn't what we say or write on a sign; it is what we believe. And much of the time, the fact is that we believe things we don't even admit to ourselves.

The dilemma with our preoccupation surrounding the next life is that most of us don't want the next life. We want more of this one. The culture surrounding heaven, created by Western religions, speaks volumes (literally) about what happens next. Jewish, Muslim, and Christian texts describe in detail the earthlike experiences we will encounter when we leave this world. As rational, educated people we claim we don't believe the next life is like this one. But that's just lip service.

If we don't believe, just a little, that the next life will strongly resemble our corporeal existence, then why do we keep saying it? The average Christian or Jew wouldn't tell you they think that, in heaven, they'll eat a hamburger or take a shower. But ask, instead, if we'll see departed loved ones and be free of disease and infirmity, if we'll see saints and angels or, perhaps, God. It's hard to find a believer who'll answer "no."

The text of "Das himmlische Leben" ("The Heavenly Life"), sung in the last movement of Mahler's Fourth Symphony, speaks of skipping and dancing, singing, bread-baking angels, and an abundant vegetable garden. But this poem illustrates a child's view of heaven, so its simplicity and focus on earthly joys is understandable.

We, however, are supposed to be grownups, and we can't have it both ways. It's not reasonable to believe we'll have the pleasures and familiarity of this life along with the perfection and spirituality we desire in the next. If it's a party, then we'll have to accept the strings attached: mortality, imperfection, difficult choices. If it's not a party, then we'd better stop talking about taking any of this with us.

If there's something after this, it's going to be one thing or the other. Or, more likely, it will be something no human can imagine. It's only natural that we cling to images we find comforting and familiar, because the alternative is terrifying. But if Western peoples are ever going to achieve any sanity on this subject, we need to grow up and stop insisting we can have our cake and eat it too.

Cherries

At 11:00 a.m. on August 10, 1999, the phone rang in my office at the Arkansas Symphony.

On the other end of the line, I heard my brother's quiet, strained voice. "David, I need to tell you some very bad news. Mom died this morning."

Trapped between confusion and panic—I'd spoken with my mother less than twenty-four hours earlier, and our father was the one who'd had heart trouble for more than thirty years—I replied, "I think you're confused. You mean Dad, right?"

My father was a man of many personal illusions. But after my mother died that morning, felled by an acute bacterial infection leading to cascading organ failure, I discovered what one of his illusions was not. After the shock of her unexpected death began to subside, I spoke with Dad several times about the end of our worldly existence.

My father was 79 at the time, and, naturally, my brother, sister, and I did our best to comfort and protect him. Whether we believed them or not, we used phrases like, "She's not really gone," and "I'm sure she's still with us."

In one of these exchanges, he responded curtly, "She's gone. She's not here."

Even through his pain, my father never believed he could have it both ways. Though he always remembered my mother with affection and joy, he never indulged the fantasy that someone we've lost still exists in a place we will eventually rejoin them. He did it the hard way, the honest way.

And yet . . .

When I was in second grade, my parents built a new house and moved us from the northeast side of Portland to the southwest. Dad's business was doing well, and much of our extended family had moved to the West Side. The new home had a huge yard, wrapping around two sides of the house on a big corner lot. My mother finally got the multiple rose bushes, rhododendrons, and big vegetable garden she'd always wanted, and they planted a cherry tree in the lower yard off the back deck.

Each year Mom's garden produced an abundance of fruits and vegetables worthy of the child's imagination in Mahler's Fourth, and we were constantly giving away tomatoes, cucumbers, raspberries,

The author's parents at their fiftieth wedding anniversary, 1998.

and figs to friends, neighbors, and fortunate strangers. The cherry tree, however, was a disappointment. Years, then decades, passed, and while the tree grew and produced beautiful blossoms each spring, there were no cherries. At some point Mom must have mentioned this oddity to a fellow horticulture geek, and the mystery was solved. Apparently, cherry trees come in mommy and daddy varieties, and you must have at least one of each, reasonably close together, if you plan to get baby cherries.

During a visit the summer after Mom's passing, I took a walk around the property for old time's sake, delighted to be away from the Arkansas heat and humidity. As I strolled through the lower yard, I innocently pulled several cherries from a branch and took them inside.

"Look, Dad," I said, hoping to brighten what was, by then, an unflinchingly gloomy countenance, "cherries."

I placed a couple in his hand, and he stared, dumbfounded.

"That tree can't produce cherries," he said in a flat voice. "It's impossible."

With little memory of the subject, I asked, "Why?"

He repeated the short version of the science, and then smiled as if in sudden recognition. "It's your mother."

As with so many things he said, I'm still not sure if my father had a revelation or simply saw an opportunity for high drama. Either way, it seems unlikely that a similar epiphany is coming my way anytime soon. But I keep an open mind. And who knows? Perhaps, in that moment, I'll find solace in the fact that I was wrong.

Chapter 9

In the Trenches: The Arkansas Symphony and Elsewhere, Part 2

Naked Italians on the Road to Slovenia

My first guest conducting engagement in Europe came about, like so many things, through a series of unrelated events aided by pure chance. My ongoing relationship with the Slovenska Filharmonia, and later collaborations flowing from it, proved once again that always giving our best is both the right thing to do and ultimately self-serving.

In September 1997 I worked with Italian pianist Fabio Bidini for concerts in Lake Forest. A Busoni competition medalist and Cliburn finalist, Fabio combined brilliant technique and musicianship with movie-star good looks and a Three Stooges sense of humor. We got along famously from the first moment, and I immediately engaged him for concerts in Little Rock and elsewhere.

Our bond of familiarity was cemented during our Lake Forest encounter, when we were both housed at the Deer Path Inn. A couple of hours before our second concert, I went to his room to discuss a musical detail. I tapped on the door and, receiving no answer, knocked again more firmly.

From inside the room, I heard scurrying feet, what sounded like the rustling of a towel, and then Fabio's charmingly accented voice from the opposite side of the door. "Oo ees eet?"

"Fabio, it's David," I replied.

Then, somewhat franticly, "Maestro, sono nudo!"

Telling a man you hardly know that you're standing naked on the other side of the door is a connection that cannot be severed.

In early 2000 Fabio telephoned from Italy. He had been engaged for the opening concert of the Festival Pianistico Internazionale in Bergamo, Italy, and said I'd be getting a call asking me to conduct. On the program Fabio would be playing the Chopin Piano Concerto No. 1 and the Anton Rubinstein Piano Concerto No. 5. When I enquired further, he confided that the festival's music director was a political appointee, "an okay conductor." But Fabio had told the festival he would only do the Rubinstein piece—which he didn't know and didn't want to play—with someone he completely trusted.

Flattered, I accepted, assuming the musicians would be from Bergamo or nearby Milan, but then Fabio dropped the other shoe. The orchestra for the festival was the Slovenska Filharmonia, the Slovenian national orchestra. We would rehearse first in the capital, Ljubljana, before meeting up in Bergamo for a final rehearsal and performance.

I had conducted the Chopin several times, and the Rubinstein turned out to be easy for the conductor, though taxing for the pianist. Neither of us understood why the festival insisted on this obscure, tedious work, but we were primed for an adventure and didn't much care what was on the program.

On the Adria Air flight from Zurich to Ljubljana I was seated next to a man in his 40s traveling with his teenage daughter. They were Slovenians returning home and, speaking excellent English, struck up a conversation as soon as I opened the Rubinstein score. As we landed, they asked how I planned to reach my hotel. The word "taxi" was hardly out of my mouth before they scoffed, saying it was a long, expensive trip, and that I should ride with them. Brooking no dissent, they chauffeured me to the city center, and this charming family attended every concert I conducted in Slovenia. The Ljubljana Chamber of Commerce could not have crafted a more gracious welcome.

The Slovenska Filharmonia was a fine orchestra with a few quirky habits. They played far behind my beat (not surprising for a European orchestra) but made every effort to play with me when I asked. The two things that did surprise me, however, were their civil servant work ethic—several musicians jumped to their feet to leave following the last note of a run-through despite the fact that I was not finished rehearsing—and the fact that some of them drank alcohol before and during rehearsal.

In the United States, the break in rehearsal is a sacred pact between the conductor and the musicians, but in Ljubljana "twenty minutes" was a subjective term—hence my reference to government work. But, in their defense, it *is* a government job. Adding to the likelihood of a haphazard return after break—as I discovered when I stepped next door for a quick espresso—was the fact that the coffee bar also served beer, of which some partook. Anticipating slowed reaction times and dwindling concentration, I quickly learned to accomplish as much as possible in the first half of rehearsal.

Following two rehearsals in Ljubljana, there was a nine-day interval before we met up with the orchestra in Bergamo. I had booked a hotel on the Italian coast in Cinque Terre, beginning three days later, planning to spend the intervening days in Florence en route. The rail journey from Ljubljana to Florence was a nine-and-a-half-hour odyssey including two train changes, so Fabio insisted I ride with him on his way home to Arezzo. It would be much faster in the car, he said, and far more comfortable. At least the latter was true.

We finished our second rehearsal at noon, and I assumed we'd make a speedy departure ahead of our long drive. Joining us in the car were Raniero Tazzi (our agent) and a young woman I'd never seen before—apparently Fabio's girlfriend, about whom I was discouraged from further inquiry. Foolishly anticipating an American-style, time-efficient road trip, I'd failed to account for the fact that I was traveling with three Italians, for whom a leisurely lunch before hitting the road was obligatory. We finally departed Ljubljana a few minutes before 3:00 p.m.

Hours later, having passed Trieste, Venice, and Padua, Fabio made a puzzling highway choice, saying we were making a "little detour" to Parma, to drop the girlfriend at her home. Coming from the northeast of Italy and heading to Florence, a stop in Parma is a detour of at least three hours, but there we were. We reached Parma around 8:30 in the evening, where, before depositing the girlfriend, we had to stop for a "quick" dinner. Around 3:00 a.m. I was set down in a deserted piazza in central Florence, hoping my hotel had held my room.

After two enjoyable days in my favorite city, followed by four days hiking and kayaking in Cinque Terre, I headed for Milan. My father had agreed to join me for the concert, and I traveled to the fashion capital of Italy to rendezvous with him. He was still not recovered from my mother's sudden passing seven months earlier but agreed to come because he wanted "to see Italy one more time." I scoffed at his dark inference but, sadly, he was correct.

One of Dad's most endearing delusions was that he was a wizard with foreign languages. He had, in fact, no aptitude whatsoever in that area, and his efforts in French, Spanish, Italian, and Portuguese melted into a great linguistic stew sounding like none of them. Nonetheless, he bluffed enough Italian to navigate public transportation from Malpensa, Milan's larger airport, to the city center, and the following day we took the short train ride to Bergamo.

The festival concert of Rubinstein and Chopin was a great success—more Fabio's doing than mine—and at its conclusion we headed for a celebratory dinner that included Fabio, our agent, yet another of Fabio's girlfriends, my father, and several hangers-on. It was nearly midnight when we reached the restaurant, late for my father even when not jetlagged. But he hung on gamely through the festivities, indulging in a few catnaps between courses.

Based on our success at the festival and relationships formed while in Ljubljana, in 2002 I was invited to conduct a series of subscription concerts with the Slovenska Filharmonia. Rehearsals

The author posing with the hastily revised concert poster, Ljubljana, Slovenia, 2002.

were preceded by recording sessions of a new work appearing on the program: *Cantico II*, written by the elder statesman of Slovenian composers, Lorz Lebic.

A few weeks before leaving the United States, I received the score. It was a copy of the composer's quirky, handwritten manuscript with mismatched staff paper sizes cobbled together on the same page, arrows pointing from place to place, and an array of other cut-and-paste assembly methods. For the nonmusician: imagine you are asked to read James Joyce aloud, in public, but are handed a text in which some lines are straight, some curve upward, some downward, some contain unexpected changes of font or type size, or, at times, all the above.

Based on the frustrating look of the score, I was tempted to dismiss the piece as more modern noise, but careful study proved me very much mistaken. While its idiom is thoroughly contemporary, *Cantico II* is thoughtful, emotionally charged, and overflowing with sonic variety. After meeting Lorz Lebic, I discovered how thoroughly the music matched the man. He was humble, kind, and committed—passionate about the music but never about his place in it. We maintained a friendship for many years, mostly facilitated by his daughter via email, as Lorz disdained all technology.

The element of the program that had originally attracted me was the opportunity to collaborate with pianist Alexander Toradze on the Prokofiev Piano Concerto No. 2. At the last moment we discovered that Mr. Toradze's agent had double-booked him, and he was replaced by Dimitri Alexeev. Dimitri played splendidly, though I could not help but be disappointed at losing the chance to work with the eminent Toradze.

Rounding out the program was the charming second suite from de Falla's *Three-Cornered Hat*. But coaxing the central Europeans to play Spanish music stylishly was challenging. One might imagine that, with some musicians imbibing during the break, getting the group to loosen up and find the spirit of Spanish dance music would have been easy. But the idea of connecting the music to one's body, feeling the dance within us even while seated, was utterly anathema to many of them. In the end I fell back to focusing on small musical details, attempting to manufacture what I'd hoped would grow organically. If you can't have a diamond, a cubic zirconia is better than nothing.

In 2004 I was invited for a similar concert series, again preceded by recording sessions. This time my experience with the

The Fourteenth World Saxophone Congress, Ljubljana, Slovenia, 2006.

new work was the opposite of my encounter with *Cantico II.* The immaculately typeset score arrived promptly as a PDF, but there ends the good news. The Concerto for Two Clarinets, written by the Slovenian wunderkind of the moment, was the poster child for everything audiences (and many musicians) hate about new music. The piece was emotionless, academic noise, featuring such delights as the two solo clarinets playing purposely out of tune in their highest register, and a moment when they removed their mouthpieces, squawking like panicked geese. Throughout, I fought to maintain a businesslike demeanor despite the orchestra's frequent snickers and guffaws.

In early 2006 I received a phone call from an unknown Slovenian asking if I'd be available for the opening concert of the Fourteenth World Saxophone Congress. When I asked how he came upon my name, he said his wife was a junior administrator with the Slovenska Filharmonia, and she remembered not only our successful concerts but my "particular expertise with new music." The concert, he continued, would feature three new works commissioned for the event, as well as a staple of the alto saxophone repertoire, the concerto by Henri Tomasi.

The Tomasi soloist was the French virtuoso Claude Delangle, and the opportunity to play with an artist of his stature was a big drawing card for me. In addition, one of the new works was a jazz-influenced piece featuring the Zagreb saxophone quartet, which sounded like fun. But the caller saved his big ammunition for last. Another of the commissions was written by Claude Baker, the well-known composer on the faculty of Indiana University, to be performed by the legendary Eugene Rousseau.

Claude Baker's *Lamentations (pour la fin du monde)* is a brilliant, complex, highly emotional work that Eugene Rousseau played with his usual virtuosity and interpretive depth. This fortuitous music making with Eugene was the start of a yearslong series of collaborations, including concerts in several locations and two recordings for Jeanné records.

The author with the Zagreb Saxophone Quartet and composer, Ljubljana, Slovenia, 2006.

The fact that our most innocuous choices may have far-reaching consequences was demonstrated once again. If I had not befriended a naked pianist in Chicago, I would have missed out on both an epic Italian road trip and, more important, relationships with an outstanding European orchestra and the greatest classical saxophonist of all time.

. . . and the Home of the Brave

I've worked with violinist Nadja Salerno-Sonnenberg twice. And while the second outing—a collaboration with fiddler and composer Mark O'Connor—was delightful, every moment of the first is etched indelibly on my memory. Nadja was scheduled to open the Arkansas Symphony's 2001–2002 season, playing the Mendelssohn Violin Concerto on September 15 and 16, 2001. Then, on Tuesday, September 11, everything changed.

I am not a paranoid person, nor am I prone to unreasonable existential dread. And perhaps this is why that strange week remains with me like a lingering nightmare. For days every unexpected noise, every news report, and every glace from a stranger seemed to contain the seeds of imminent, personal violence. Like many, I expected more attacks would follow, and the anticipation was almost worse than the reality.

The orchestra's first rehearsal for the cycle, scheduled for the evening of 9/11, was canceled, and plans for the weekend were up in the air. As one day blurred into the next—Tuesday, Wednesday, Thursday—it appeared increasingly unlikely the weekend could be salvaged. We mulled the obvious concerns: Should we be making music after this tragedy, and would anyone come if we did? We felt encouraged when US air traffic reopened at 11:00 a.m. on September 13, but flights were unreliable due to intermittent scares causing sudden reclosures at key airports.

Stranded literally in the middle of the chaos was Miss Salerno-Sonnenberg, hoping against hope to find a flight from New York to Little Rock. Her original Thursday flight was canceled after she arrived at La Guardia, and for the next thirty-six hours she tried a half dozen different tactics involving departures on various airlines from every New York City airport. I learned later that her travel machinations were crafted while she was at ground zero assisting families and first responders.

Between exhaustion from her volunteer work, our national state of trauma, and the fact that no sane person wanted to board an airplane, no one would have faulted her for canceling. But the tenacious Ms. Salerno-Sonnenberg wasn't about to let that happen.

On her fifth or sixth reservation and third trip to an airport, she made it to Little Rock late Friday night. I didn't want to tire her further with a meeting, so we did the Saturday afternoon rehearsal having hardly exchanged a word in advance. That afternoon, and at both performances, she played as though nothing were amiss. Following her lead, we immersed ourselves in the music and began to feel the week's accumulated tension draining from our bodies.

Despite everyone's natural urge to avoid public buildings and big crowds, we were gratified to see the audience turn out in force. Before beginning the concert, I asked the audience to rise and join us in the national anthem, which they sang with special enthusiasm.

In the twenty-three years since, I have found my relationship with "The Star-Spangled Banner" increasingly fraught. I remember that night with pride and intense emotions, but it has never been the same. Even with the mistakes and falsehoods of the post-9/11 era now apparent, for too many Americans the national anthem has become a blindfolded, oversimplified litmus test for one's patriotism. In the service of jingoism, "The Star-Spangled Banner" has been reduced to a musical version of the meaningless catchphrase "I support the troops," which allows us to avoid nuanced conversations about our foreign policy and the use of our military.

The Vietnam era slogan "Dissent is the highest form of patriotism" (often mistakenly attributed to Thomas Jefferson) still rings true. Our nation grows in strength, vitality, and morality when all voices are heard. One's patriotism is not measured by whether they stand, sit, or kneel during the national anthem. Perhaps we should consider the possibility that, sometimes, a higher patriotism is demonstrated by refusing to follow the herd.

On September 15, 2001, we all knew what "The Star-Spangled Banner" means. I wish we still did.

Here, There, and Everywhere

The decade and a half from 1990 to 2006 was the most intense period of guest conducting in my career. During these years I appeared with the San Diego Symphony (four times), the Duluth-Superior Symphony (five times), the Charleston Symphony, the Baltimore Chamber Orchestra, the Eugene Symphony, the Indianapolis Chamber Orchestra, the Delaware Symphony, the Illinois Symphony, the Reno Chamber Orchestra, the National Repertory Orchestra, the Annapolis Symphony, and the Winnipeg Symphony (four times). These engagements, and many others, in addition to those overseas, took place while I was working regularly with the Alabama Symphony, the Arkansas Symphony, the Kingsport Symphony, and/or the Birmingham Opera Theater.

I am tempted to suggest that this frenetic level of professional activity is the reason two marriages imploded, but I suspect there were more significant issues contributing to those failures. My parents' marriage lasted an amazing fifty-one years, but the numbers don't tell the whole story. Barrie Itkin and Suzanne Gevurtz were oil and water, mixing homogenously only sporadically, and when stirred vigorously. All three of their children have encountered difficulties creating long-lasting relationships, but I refuse to buy into the notion that our problems are the fault of our parents. Our mistakes and shortcomings belong to *us*, and no one else.

But let's return to the subject at hand. Some of these guest conducting engagements turned out to be ordinary, journeyman gigs. But a few are more memorable, and not always because of the music.

I conducted the San Diego Symphony four times between 1991 and 1993, twice at Copley Hall and twice in their summer venue. Despite being mildly traumatized by my first landing—planes often fly between downtown buildings on approach to the San Diego airport—I loved the city, its people, and its weather from the first moment my feet gratefully touched terra firma.

During the summer of 1992, my father and one of his oldest friends took a detour from their wine-tasting trip to attend my concert in the beautiful outdoor venue at Embarcadero Marina Park. Being reinvited to the San Diego Symphony was a big deal for me at the time, and with my father in the audience, I took special care with the preparation of my patter for this program of French light classics. While having a seasoned comedic actor in the audience added to my nerves, it also provided me with an opening for a little joke at his expense. If I remember correctly, it was something about how coming to San Diego allowed him to combine two of his passions: drinking wine and napping during my concerts.

Apparently, I did well with the comedy portion of the evening, but that was both the good news and the bad. The *San Diego Union-Tribune*'s review was glowing, suggesting that if I ever decided to give up conducting, I had a promising career ahead of me as a stand-up comedian. Unfortunately, the reviewer liked my jokes so much that he quoted nearly every word. That wouldn't have been a problem if this had been a one-off, but I still had two performances of the same concert ahead of me, and now anyone who read the paper knew my entire spiel. I'd put a lot of effort into perfecting my talking points, so I was none too happy at having to spend most of that day trying to come up with new jokes.

In the early moments of the second concert, I asked the audience who'd read that morning's paper and, big surprise, almost no one raised their hand. I probably should have seen that coming and spent my day enjoying the beautiful Southern California weather.

My four outings with the Winnipeg Symphony (2001 to 2005) all took place in November, December, or January. Looking back, I begin to wonder if they really liked me or if I'm just the only one stupid enough to repeatedly visit Winnipeg during the coldest part of the year.

My first engagement was in November, before the onset of winter, so I wasn't terribly worried about the weather. As I was dropped off at the Fairmont hotel, the symphony staffer who'd collected me at the airport pointed to the concert hall, less than two blocks away. She then told me when she'd be picking me up for rehearsal, but—not wishing to appear fragile in front of an attractive young woman—I brushed aside her offer, saying that since I could see the stage door from the hotel, I would walk.

I left the hotel at 9:30 the following morning wearing every warm garment I owned, and it wasn't enough. I had only walked to the corner and already the temperature and wind chill had rendered my fingers and toes inoperable. I began to seriously wonder if I'd be able to hold a baton a few minutes later, or if my frozen brain would be functioning when I stepped on the podium.

As I stopped to adjust my hat, gloves, and scarf, I glanced up at a plaque secured to the side of the hotel at the corner of Portage and Main, informing passers-by that this is "the windiest corner in North America." My head down against the gale, I trudged the final block, cursing my vanity and wistfully recalling the symphony staffer's kind offer.

When I was engaged to conduct the Annapolis Symphony as a music director candidate in 2004, I programmed the Khachaturian Piano Concerto, and the orchestra agreed to bring Fabio Bidini (of Chicago, Ljubljana, and Italian road trip fame) as the soloist. At baggage claim the first thing the symphony representative said after "Hello" was, "Mr. Itkin, there's a little problem."

It was not a *little* problem. While Fabio was traversing the Atlantic, his fiancée and her mother were involved in a serious car accident. Learning this shortly after touching down in New York, he immediately, and understandably, booked a flight to return to Europe.

Though we were all disappointed to lose Fabio, this would have been a "little" problem were it not for the fact that relatively few pianists have the Khachaturian concerto in their repertoire. The management asked if I wanted them to find someone who could play the Khachaturian or preferred for them to locate another soloist and let that person pick the concerto. I told them that, considering the unusual work and short time frame, we were likely to have a better result if we let a new soloist play whatever they wanted.

Either they didn't believe I could switch repertoire quickly or thought they would surprise me by doing me a favor, but the next day they told me they'd secured a local pianist who would play the Khachaturian.

Dubious, I asked, "Really? There's someone near Annapolis who has this piece at their fingertips?"

"Oh, yeah," they said. "He's played the piece and says he can get it back in his hands by Friday."

The facts, I soon learned, were somewhat different than advertised. The new soloist—who I will not name because his service in this effort was heroic even if the outcome came up a bit short—had played the piece *once*, more than ten years earlier. After all that time, he used the music (not surprising) and needed a page-turner, making the performance feel more like a rehearsal. In addition, we played the tricky final movement far slower than the composer intended, making for an overall lackluster presentation.

And the Khachaturian dominos tumbled onto the rest of the program as well. We spent so much rehearsal time on the concerto, trying make sure our brave new soloist was comfortable, that the rest of the program—including Brahms's Symphony No. 4—got rather short shrift. Sadly, what was supposed to be a joyous reunion with Fabio and a beautiful concert of Khachaturian and Brahms for my music director audition became something just short of a fiasco. After that concert, I wouldn't have hired me either.

Captain Kirk Parts the Red Sea

After ten years with the Arkansas Symphony, I took a sabbatical from May to December 2003, living in Florence, Italy, during most of that period. In addition to resting, eating good food, drinking great wine, and improving my Italian, I was writing a new composition to be premiered in April 2004. I envisioned an oratorio entitled *Exodus* for orchestra, choir, baritone soloist, and narrator, based on the story of the Israelites' departure from Egypt, with texts from the book of Exodus, the psalms, and the Passover Haggadah.

A weeks-long, transatlantic email correspondence with the assistant director of the Conservatorio Luigi Cherubini—carried out in my semifunctional Italian and his fractured English—followed by a tense, in-person meeting with the director, finally resulted in my acquisition of a studio where I could write undisturbed for a few hours each day. Most mornings I worked there until noon, by which time my unairconditioned digs had become a sweltering, humid hole in which I, usually shirtless, labored, nonetheless.

Before leaving Little Rock, I created an outline for the piece, sketching a rough idea of the overall form, which texts might be used, and in what order. Armed with limited knowledge of a work still to be written, I attempted to contact Leonard Nimoy, hoping he might be sufficiently intrigued by the newness and Jewishness of the project to consider appearing as the narrator. Following a phone conversation and document exchange with his assistant, I received a call from the man himself saying he would be delighted to take part. A contract was struck—for an absurdly small amount of money, considering the brilliance of his stardom—and the deal was done.

In my Florence hotbox, I heard his voice in my head as the notes flowed onto the sweat-stained paper. While there are many challenges in composing a work of this magnitude, the central hurdle lay in crafting a sonic universe that fulfilled multiple purposes simultaneously. The sound of the orchestra and choir, and the harmonic language utilized, needed to lure the audience into the emotional and personal content of the narrative. I'd never viewed the religious or supernatural aspects of the story as paramount but saw it as a political struggle between individuals and ideologies. And this idea needed to be conveyed through the music while not relying too heavily on older styles or film music tropes. The final product is convincing in places and less compelling in others.

When I returned to the United States, I forwarded the completed narrator's script to Mr. Nimoy with a note saying I looked forward to seeing him the following April.

In early March 2004, his assistant called unexpectedly.

"Hi, David," she began. "I need to talk with you about the concerts Leonard is supposed to do with you next month."

Is *supposed* to do? Surely, she meant *is doing*.

"Well . . . Leonard would like to see if there's some way to change the dates."

Change the dates?

Channeling all the Spock-like emotional control I could muster, I offered, "The hall was booked three years ago, there are 180 choir members ready to sing, and around 3,000 people have tickets. So, no, we can't change the dates."

"Well," she tried again, "his grandson's Bar Mitzvah is that weekend, so he just can't make those dates."

"Bar Mitzvah?" I sputtered. "And we're just talking about this now? How about maybe his kids talk to their famous father before scheduling the Bar Mitzvah? Or how about *they* change the date?"

My objections were falling on deaf ears, and I knew it. I was aware of his devotion to his faith and family, but I was disappointed in him, and disappointed for us.

With six weeks to go, we needed an actor who not only would give an outstanding performance but also had the star power to draw an audience and not disappoint the legions of fans who had purchased tickets to see Leonard Nimoy. In other words, we needed a miracle akin to the parting of the Red Sea.

Immediately, the executive director and I sat down to draft a list of possibilities. With time in such short supply, we both felt this was a fool's errand. But we had to try.

"What about William Shatner?" our executive director, Bill Vickery, suggested before leaving my office.

I immediately answered, "Absolutely not," though the star was newly trendy thanks to his hit TV show *Boston Legal*.

"Isn't he kind of a joke?" I asked. "And, besides, if we replace Leonard Nimoy with William Shatner everyone will think the project is *Star Trek* related."

Days passed, and name after name went by the wayside. Richard Dreyfus was busy, Jerry Orbach was ill, Patrick Stewart had the *Star Trek* connection and was way too expensive, and on and on.

His list exhausted, the executive director came to me again. "We're getting short on time, and shorter on names," he said. "Can I try Shatner?"

"There's no way he's free," I sighed, "and if he is, you can't afford him. But go ahead."

One day later, Bill called. "Shatner's in, if you want him."

I laid my head in my hands.

"He really loves the project," Bill encouraged, "and he's Jewish, too, you know—sort of."

The clock had run out. And so for six times Leonard Nimoy's fee, William Shatner it was.

I never spoke with Bill Shatner before he arrived. He was sent the script, the schedule, and other details through intermediaries. Suddenly it all felt commercial and transactional, whereas with Nimoy it had felt personal, a project of shared importance.

We arranged a private meeting about ninety minutes ahead of the first orchestra rehearsal, and a good thing, too. Shatner arrived without the copy of the narrator's script he had been sent, asking if we could "get another one." Annoyed, I had a copy of the script delivered from our office, but his failure to arrive with text in hand was the not the real problem. My concern was what it implied: that he had no idea what the piece was and had done no preparation. Unfortunately, all of this appeared to be correct. However, to my joyous surprise, once the orchestra began to play and the choir and baritone soloist to sing, he immersed himself in the text and revealed the actor he was capable of being.

After the rehearsal we bonded over several glasses of scotch in the lobby bar of his hotel. As we sipped and talked, he politely fended off one person after another who wanted to "come say hi." He was fun and highly entertaining, and anyone with great taste in scotch is okay in my book.

The following evening, after intermission, Bill Shatner and I were greeted onstage by a supercharged audience. As the applause began to subside, a voice shouted, "Denny Crane!" the name of his character in *Boston Legal*. A nervous ripple ran through the orchestra, as well as the audience. I checked over my shoulder to see his reaction, and he was the perfect pro. In a calm voice that nonetheless carried to the cheap seats from which the heckler had shouted, Shatner contradicted, "Not tonight."

The live recording of the performances demonstrates his commitment and talent in no uncertain terms, despite my early misgivings. Though marred by some out-of-tune brass playing, it is an elegant testament to an exciting, all-in performance by the orchestra, choir, my dear friend, baritone Paul Rowe, and, of course, William Shatner.

The recording is available on iTunes. And before anyone berates me for shameless commercialism, I have never received a dime from that recording. While I hope some will enjoy hearing it, the rights to the recording are wholly owned by Shatner's production company, as that is the only way they would agree to produce and distribute it. But that's all right. It was never about money anyway.

EXODUS

An oratorio in three parts
Music by David Itkin

William Shatner, narrator
Paul Rowe, baritone
The Arkansas Symphony Orchestra
David Itkin, conductor

Arkansas Chamber Singers - Dr. John Erwin, Director
Harding University Chorus - Dr. Cliff Ganus, Director
Henderson State University Concert Choir - Dr. Charles Rye, Director
Hendrix College Choir - Dr. Nancy Fleming, Director
Ouachita Baptist University Ouachita Singers - Dr. Charles Fuller, Director
University of Central Arkansas Concert Choir - Dr. John Erwin, Director

1. PART I: MOSES AND PHARAOH
2. PART II: TEN PLAGUES
3. PART III: REDEMPTION

CD cover for *Exodus*, 2004.

~~~~~ President Bill Clinton ~~~~~

By early 2003, two years after President Clinton left the White House, plans for the Clinton presidential library were well under way. A picturesque spot on the Arkansas River, a stone's throw from downtown Little Rock, had been selected, and fundraising was proceeding at a feverish pitch. To increase public awareness, a celebratory concert with the Arkansas Symphony was planned, featuring an appearance by the former president.

During a preliminary programming discussion, we wondered aloud if President Clinton might play the saxophone, as he had famously done on television while campaigning. The conversation with one of his staff was brief, consisting of, "Uh, no," and we moved on. Instead, he narrated Copland's *Lincoln Portrait* and Alexander Miller's *Let Freedom Ring*.

The text for *Lincoln Portrait* is divided into many small segments. The narrator reads a defined passage, then pauses, waits for a cue from the conductor, reads the next passage, and so on. Knowing rehearsal time would be brief, I carefully edited the text, making it clear when he should look for a cue and when he should stop, including large, red letters reading, "STOP."

Perhaps my document was printed on paper they considered a security threat, but when the president reached into his jacket pocket, as we sat together in his dressing room, he withdrew an entirely different document. For reasons unknown, someone on his staff had retyped the text, arranging it into neat paragraphs conforming to Lincoln's original writings. Unfortunately, this beautifully transcribed document was worthless as a narrator's script.

I remained utterly composed. And why not? I was sitting alone with a former president of the United States, ten minutes from a rehearsal for which he had no script, knowing that guys with guns were standing outside the door. I asked to borrow his script, looked it over, and saying something like, "Wow, our staff must have messed up—" drew a series of lines, arrows, and stop signs throughout his pages.

The president's charisma and oratorical skills are legendary, so one is not surprised that the orchestra was charmed in rehearsal. He was essentially flawless, despite reading from pages that now looked like a third grader's art project. One only needed to observe his effect on the room to understand why his presidency was inevitable.

His performance was captured on a live recording that is still available at the Clinton Library. And the fact that a record of the event is circulating in public makes our last-minute catch of a typo even more significant.

One sentence in Lincoln's 1862 message to Congress reads, "The fiery trial through which we pass, will light us down, in honor or dishonor, to the latest generation." Unfortunately, when the text was retyped, the word "trial" became "trail," and spellcheck did not pick up the error for obvious reasons.

During our last pass through that portion of the piece, before concluding the rehearsal, I heard the mistake I had not noticed earlier.

I stopped the orchestra, stepped over to Mr. Clinton's podium and, pushing away the mic, pointed to the spot. "Mr. President, this somehow got mistyped." I didn't mention it was his people, not ours, who were at fault, but clarified, "It's 'trial,' not 'trail.'"

"Ah," he chuckled, "you're right." Withdrawing a pen from his jacket, he made the correction. "Fiery trail doesn't make any sense."

But the former occupant of the White House was not the only part of the federal government with which I came into close contact that day.

To appreciate my encounter with the secret service, one must understand the interior of Robinson Music Hall. Performers enter the stage door through the loading dock, located a few steps from Broadway Street, arriving in the lower level of the theater where the dressing rooms are situated. Stairwells at each end of the corridor lead up to opposite sides of the stage. The only dressing room on the stage level is the star dressing room, mine during most concerts but reserved for President Clinton on this occasion.

Per the secret service, only the stage left stairway was available for the orchestra and crew. The stage right passage was reserved solely for the president and me, with agents permanently posted at the top and bottom. The rest of his security detail moved with him, except for those who were scattered around other parts of the backstage and front of house.

Just before 8:00 p.m., Mr. Clinton and I stood backstage while the patrons in the sold-out house finished taking their seats. Chatting quietly about the state of the nation, we heard a loud bang that appeared to emanate from beyond the loading dock door behind us. When there's an unexpected loud noise while you're standing near a former president, you know what everyone thinks—and by "everyone" I mean the guys with the guns.

Faster than I could process the event, four agents surrounded us. Three encircled the president, scanning the area with one hand inside their jackets. The fourth agent spoke to the president, gently checking him for damage. Despite the anxiety of his keepers, he was about as ruffled as he had been when I pointed out the typo earlier in the day.

He separated himself from the agents, checked to see if I was all right (I had been roughly brushed aside by a vigilant officer), and, nodding his head toward the big metal door facing Broadway, said, "I think it was a truck backfiring."

The author with President Bill Clinton, Little Rock, 2003.

Moments later, President Clinton strolled onstage, cool as they come. While I, two steps behind, attempted to collect my frazzled wits.

~~~~~ Footloose ~~~~~

In 2005 the Arkansas Symphony booked Kenny Loggins and his band to appear on our pops series. Many stars at his level bring their own conductor, avoiding the hassle of teaching a new guy how their show flows and so forth. I am a Kenny Loggins fan from way back, so I was a bit disappointed, if not surprised, when our operations manager was told, "Kenny's music director travels with him."

Oh, well, I thought. *I get a prime seat for the performance, and I don't have to pay for it, so I'm in no position to complain.*

For some reason the issue nagged at me over the next several weeks, and I asked our office to contact Kenny's people again. The operations manager received the same answer, word for word: "Kenny's music director travels with him."

The evening before the first performance, I dropped in on the rehearsal even though I was not, strictly speaking, needed. In truth, I wanted to be in the room while Kenny Loggins rehearsed, and my I'm-doing-diligent-music-director-oversight routine made me feel like less of a groupie.

Arriving thirty minutes before rehearsal, I found a few orchestra musicians looking over the music while Kenny's band members plugged in cables, tuned guitars, and checked sound levels.

After a few minutes, the band member who looked in charge approached me, asking, "You're David, right?"

I said I was, and he introduced himself as Kenny's music director.

"Great," I said. "I hope you don't mind if I hang around and listen for a bit, just to make sure everything is going okay."

He looked puzzled and asked, "Hang around?"

I thought, incorrectly, that I had intruded on his turf, and was searching for graceful exit when he asked, "You're leaving? Aren't you conducting?"

The lightbulb above my head began to flicker, and I replied, "What? No. You are."

"Me?" he laughed. "I'm the bass player, and Kenny's music director."

The lightbulb was fully illuminated, and I stared into it with chagrin. In the orchestral world, the terms "music director" and "conductor" are often interchangeable. In popular music, as I discovered, the star's music director is the musician who makes sure everyone in the band shows up and knows the right chords.

It took a moment to process the fact that in thirteen minutes I would conduct a rehearsal for one of my idols, despite being thoroughly unprepared. I turned to the conductor's stand and saw a pile of music as thick as the old New York City phone book. Stepping up,

I began frantically turning pages. It was rock and roll, which mostly moves under its own steam, so I looked quickly for items that might trip me up while sight-reading (sudden stops, tempo changes, etc.).

With five minutes remaining, my head down in frantic concentration, I felt a tap at my shoulder. A quick turn of my head revealed a tall, skinny guy with scraggly gray chin whiskers trying to get my attention. Obviously a roadie or another band member.

Dismissively, I muttered, "Sorry, I'm really busy. Who are you?"

The tall, skinny man with the chin whiskers put out his hand and, without a trace of sarcasm or arrogance, said, "Hi, David, I'm Kenny Loggins."

The Definition of Insanity

In a professional orchestral organization, the executive director and music director occupy lateral positions on the institutional flowchart. Each has their own sphere of authority, and both report to the board of directors. This system, very different from the old days when the conductor was God, means that a respectful relationship based on discussion and compromise, with a focus on the overall good of the organization, is vital.

For the reasons just described, the board chair and executive director could never be the same person. This situation would create a conflict of interest and imbalance of power because the executive director is the conductor's equal colleague, while the board chair is the conductor's boss. In addition, one is a volunteer leader and the other an employee.

The odds that a conductor will encounter the untenable situation where the board chair and executive director are the same person are quite low. The odds that one conductor will deal with it twice in the same career are astronomical.

I assumed my experience in Lake Forest would be my one and only. But, as outlandish as it seems, I found myself in the same position for a brief period some years later. I signed on for a three-year contract with a new orchestra, largely as a favor to an old colleague, only to have the executive director fired shortly after my arrival and replaced by the board president. Despite knowing next to nothing about our business, our new leader let me know in no uncertain terms that they planned to exert veto and sign-off authority for all programming—including inserting repertoire, solo artists, and guest conductors without my approval. Yes, it was déjà vu—all over again.

Responding to an intractable disagreement over programming, I contacted several board members with whom I had become friends. I explained the situation and requested they raise the issue of defined spheres of authority at an upcoming board meeting.

But we all know the saying: Repeatedly doing the same thing, but expecting a different result, is the definition of insanity. I'd been down this road in Lake Forest, so you'd think I'd have learned my lesson.

My so-called friends on the board spoke as one. It went something like, "Oh, David, they give so much money, why can't you just let them have their way and leave it alone?" Once again, money and cronyism overcame any thought of doing the right thing.

A man goes to his physician and, raising his arm above his head, says, "Doctor, it hurts when I do this." The doctor, of course, replies, "Then don't do that." If there's any lesson to be learned here, it is this: Repeatedly banging one's head against the same wall will be as painful as it is pointless.

Changing of the Guard

In 2006 a perfect storm brought an end to the Arkansas Symphony's glory years.

Though professional auditors repeatedly missed the signs, the organization was being systematically embezzled by its comptroller. This mild-mannered, borderline incompetent was—who would have thought?—a master thief. For several years he had been purchasing large quantities of office supplies on the orchestra's dime, directing deliveries to his home, then selling the goods, as they say, out the back door. By the time the fraud was uncovered, his home raided, and the hapless schlemiel hauled away in handcuffs, the orchestra was missing nearly $250,000—our entire cushion of operating cash.

No one said the words aloud, but nearly everyone was quietly asking, "How did our executive director fail to notice?"

There was no collusion, nor any suggestion of it. Bill Vickery was an outstanding leader who trusted his staff and our auditors, keeping his eye on the big picture rather than checking the number of paperclips in the closet. A scramble to raise funds ensued, hampered by the bad press we were receiving. We worked to right the ship, and a few angels stepped in to help. Though we had come nowhere near to replacing all the lost capital, we had finally reached a point where we knew the orchestra would survive.

Then the other shoe dropped.

About six months later, my phone rang in the middle of the night. It was Richard Wheeler, a physician, friend, enthusiastic supporter of the orchestra, and husband of our English horn player. He told me in his calm, professional manner, that I needed to come to the university medical center immediately. Bill had suffered a heart attack a couple hours earlier and was unresponsive.

Bill passed away three days later, never having regained consciousness. In the days between Bill's heart attack and his passing, Richard taught me, and demonstrated, the expression, "hanging the crepe." Now whenever I say it, I think of him, and of Bill.

This was, obviously, a catastrophe for Bill's wife and their children. He was 57 years old and so full of life it was impossible to believe he was gone. Naturally, many of us looked to the embezzlement crisis as the stress point triggering his illness. And if, by some bizarre turn of fate, our former comptroller reads this: know that you have blood on your hands.

But let us not forget "post hoc, ergo propter hoc." Bill was a chain-smoking, hard-drinking, never-exercising, I-have-no-idea-what-a-vegetable-is, type A+ personality workaholic. He was also the kindest, most lovable teddy bear of a man one could ever know.

In the months that followed, the organization was led on the executive side first by me, but I handed off the reins at my doctor's insistence when my blood pressure topped out at 160/110. Next, we were led for several months by a well-meaning but ill-equipped volunteer. And, finally, in 2007, we hired Galen Wixson.

As our new executive director, Galen had a steep hill to climb. On day one he confronted newly accumulated debt, an exhausted board, low cash reserves, and a staff in disarray. He did an outstanding job of righting the foundering ship, but, ironically, suffered the same fate his predecessor had before coming to Arkansas. After two years Galen was summarily dismissed for the offense of not fully solving a host of problems, none of which were spawned on his watch. After a bit of bouncing around to a variety of positions beneath his abilities, he is now executive director of a fine regional orchestra in Texas.

Searching for Kwai Chang Caine

I was music director of the Las Vegas Philharmonic from 2007 to 2012. The organization's budget was extremely tight, so we were not able to afford significant guest artists. One exception, however, stands out, and not for the best of reasons.

For the final concert of my first season, I planned a performance of Arthur Honegger's *King David*, featuring local choirs and soloists. The piece has been a favorite of mine since undergraduate days, when I was immediately taken with its unique vision of the characters as real human beings rather than religious archetypes.

In addition to the choir, vocal soloists, and an actress (playing the Witch of Endor), the narrator is an essential element of the work. For this role we signed Golden Globe winner Stacy Keach, who later withdrew due to other commitments. Through Mr. Keach's influence, we acquired David Carradine, an actor best known to my generation as Kwai Chang Caine in the '70s TV hit *Kung Fu*.

While Mr. Carradine's reputation caused me some concern, his career had recently been revived by his role in the *Kill Bill* films

Cover of *Las Vegas Weekly*. One of Las Vegas's most beautiful people.

(2003 and 2004), and I understood his personal life and mental health were also on a more even keel. Icing on the cake, we learned that his friend and colleague actress Jane Seymour would be attending the concert.

Our star flew into Las Vegas Friday afternoon and was met at the airport by a limousine and the philharmonic's operations manager.

At 6:45 p.m., with my new narrator late for our 6:30 meeting, I phoned the operations manager. Mr. Carradine, he told me, refused to come out of his suite despite repeated phone calls and attempts at direct conversation through the door. Minutes before the 7:00 rehearsal was scheduled to begin, the staffer phoned Carradine's agent, who in turn telephoned the suite.

With no rehearsal time to waste, I worked with the choir and orchestra while we waited. Just past 7:30 a signal from offstage alerted me that Carradine was in the building, so I called a brief break and joined the star in the green room. By 2008 I'd already spent more than thirty years with musicians and actors, so I knew what someone attempting to appear sober looked like. Chatting with David Carradine, I realized I was in the presence of a master.

But no one can disguise being as far gone and he was. We wandered through the rehearsal while he slurred his words, skipped paragraphs, and generally made a mess of the thing.

About an hour after rehearsal, a call from the operations manager informed me that Carradine had asked to stop at a liquor store en route to his hotel.

"That probably means," the staffer mused in dismay, "he already drank all the vodka he bought this afternoon."

Though I hit the pillow that night with high hopes, they were dashed the following morning. While we did not have to endure another battle to extricate him from his hotel suite, his inability to focus, keep his place in the script, and read without fumbling or skipping words was much the same.

After the rehearsal his agent was phoned again. By Hollywood standards Carradine's performance in Las Vegas was low profile. It did not threaten the future of a multimillion-dollar movie project nor place his reputation at significant risk, so the agent's response was a shoulder-shrugging, "Well, what can you do?"

In the late afternoon, Jane Seymour appeared on the scene. During a quick huddle by phone, she offered her services as intermediary and, not to mince words, babysitter. She also graciously offered to stand in as the narrator that evening should the situation warrant it. But, she added hopefully, she was certain it would not come to that.

The diminutive, elegant Ms. Seymour arrived backstage promptly at 6:45 p.m. with David Carradine in tow. Our star wore an ill-fitting, wrinkled suit and no tie, his manner calling to mind a schoolboy emerging from the principal's office.

In a private moment, Ms. Seymour assured me that her friend was "ready to go." She had been through the script with him and there was no need for her to step in. I'm certain she believed what she said and was making no attempt at deception. But they were close friends, and it's not a stretch to imagine her judgment was clouded by a desire to sugarcoat this bitter pill. Objectively, Carradine was a bit less than "ready to go."

The performance proceeded adequately, at first. Though his reading was halting and somewhat garbled at times, there were no major gaffes. Then, about halfway through the hour-long piece, he skipped a paragraph, reading a passage that had nothing to do with the music and storytelling at hand.

His podium was arm's-length from me—placed there for precisely such an eventuality—and I turned my head and muttered, "David —"

He continued reading, so I leaned toward him, my face inches from his. "David!"

He stopped and looked up, startled back into our universe.

I stepped off the podium and pointed to the preceding paragraph, saying, softly, "Here."

Instead of picking up at the spot I'd indicated, he raised his face to the audience and, without turning from the microphone, declared, "Oh, yeah, sorry."

Abashed and frustrated, I stepped back to the podium, and was only forced to descend for a similar operation one other time during the performance. We muddled through to the end and found the audience generous and forgiving.

Honegger's *King David* focuses on the vanity, greed, self-indulgence, and self-righteousness of its characters, allowing us to see them as the flawed, ordinary humans they surely were. David, for example, commits adultery with Bathsheba, the wife of one of his closest lieutenants. For this reason, among others, we cannot view him as more divine than ourselves, and we do not mourn his fall. No rational adult believes movie stars are really the people their PR would like us to see. But watching David Carradine implode alongside David the King was a bit too close for comfort.

This gifted, tormented man died one year later, under circumstances still not fully explained, while shooting a film in Bangkok. Our tribulations in Las Vegas were trifling compared with the tragedy of his wasted talent and troubled life.

~~~~~ Lone Star ~~~~~

In early 2008 my professional plans were suddenly murky. I'd initially planned to relocate to Las Vegas that summer, but this option was far less attractive after my appraisal of their shaky financial situation and general institutional dysfunction. As I considered my narrowing options, providence intervened once again.

Not long after the new year, I received an email from the University of North Texas College of Music. They were searching to replace their retiring director of orchestral studies, the well-known violinist and conductor Anshel Brusilow. I had always thought I might enjoy teaching conducting in a big university program, but at the time I was 50, younger than I'd imagined such a move, and I declined their offer to discuss the position. By chance, the next several days delivered a renewed wave of stress from Las Vegas, just in time for another email from Texas.

At the time I had no idea how one of the largest music schools in the nation had come upon my name. Not long after I discovered I had attracted the search committee's attention via two UNT graduate students who played occasionally as substitutes in my new orchestra, the Abilene Philharmonic. A principle in which I have always believed was proven true once again: Never give less than your best, because you never know who's watching.

In March I spent ten days rehearsing and conducting a concert at UNT, teaching the graduate orchestral conducting students during the same period. I was appalled by the condition of both the orchestra and the conducting students. The top orchestra's lack of preparation and discipline were perfectly reflected in the dean's body language at my first rehearsal. Seated directly in my line of sight, he spent a good deal of time staring at his shoes, head in hands. In stark contrast with the other major performance areas of the college—choirs, bands, early music, and the celebrated jazz program—orchestral studies was in disarray.

I recently mentioned my initial UNT experience to some of my conducting students, prompting one of them to ask why I'd left the Arkansas Symphony to take it on. An interesting question, and one I had not considered in some years.

Common industry wisdom suggests that a seven-year tenure with a professional orchestra is an enormous success, an epoch in musical time. In early 2008 I was completing my sixteenth season in Little Rock—two epochs and counting. The music making continued at a high level, but I could feel the wind shifting. As if overnight our board contained few faces I knew, led by a president utterly unfamiliar with our operation, history, or mission. Perhaps those sudden changes were unsettling, or maybe I was just bored, but when the UNT dean called, I accepted.

Before I heard from the dean, however, there was one more hurdle to overcome. While visiting Texas I was told that, because I was the final candidate, I would receive a response soon. But several days of silence turned into several weeks. In an uncharacteristic breach of decorum, a member of the search committee contacted me sub rosa, saying that an unsolicited, highly injurious letter had been delivered to the dean.

The letter, from a former Arkansas Symphony concertmaster who I had declined to tenure a decade earlier, accused me of a variety of ridiculous things. The accusations included that I paid student players from local colleges less than the contract rate (impossible, because

I had no authority over payroll) and a story that, in the moments preceding concerts, I paraded around backstage shirtless.

The first allegation was easy to debunk, but the latter was problematic, which the accuser undoubtedly knew. No one wants to hire a man with even a hint of sexual harassment in his past, and it is impossible to prove a negative. While considering my limited options, I received a voice mail from a major figure in the Dallas musical community who was, let's say, "well acquainted" with my former concertmaster. The message was concise and aggressive: I'm an important guy and a UNT alum, and I'll do everything in my power to keep you from getting that job.

Rather than sit on my hands, I called the chair of the Arkansas Symphony musicians' committee, a woman who had participated in and concurred with the former concertmaster's dismissal. I mentioned the story of my shirtless preconcert antics, and she laughed. Her giggling complete, she reminded me that the acoustic shell at Robinson Hall had large gaps through which the orchestra could easily see backstage. If I'd had my shirt off, the entire orchestra would have seen it. She generously offered to phone the dean, and, as if by magic, the crisis was over.

We moved to Texas in July 2008, making the 2008–2009 season a relay race between Dallas, Little Rock, Las Vegas, and Abilene. In spring 2010, exhausted and ready to slow down a bit, I bid a final farewell to Little Rock and the Arkansas Symphony. The city, its people, and, most important, the orchestra's musicians will always have a special place in my heart. I'm sure I failed to express often enough my undying gratitude for seventeen years of joy, heartbreak, smooth sailing, bumpy roads, and untold hours of great music.

ASO PROGRAM

Saturday, April 10, 2010 · 8 PM Sunday, April 11, 2010 · 3 PM
Robinson Center Music Hall Little Rock, Arkansas

windstream communications Maestro's Circle

STELLA BOYLE SMITH MASTERWORKS

Farewell, Maestro!

David Itkin, *conductor*
Marie Plette, *soprano*
Eugenie Grunewald, mezzo-*soprano*

LYON COLLEGE CONCERT CHORALE
Joel Plaag, *director*

HENDRIX COLLEGE CHOIR
Nancy Fleming, *director*

UNIVERSITY OF CENTRAL ARKANSAS CONCERT CHOIR
John Erwin, *director*

HARDING UNIVERSITY CHORUS
Cliff Ganus, *director*

MAHLER Symphony No. 2 in C minor ("Resurrection")

I. Allegro maestoso
II. Andante con moto
III. In sehr ruhig fliessender Bewegung
IV. Urlicht (Primeval Light)
V. Im Tempo des Scherzos

PLEASE SILENCE ALL ELECTRONIC DEVICES. THANK YOU.
Use of cameras and recording equipment is not permitted in the concert hall.

The Arkansas Symphony Orchestra is supported in part by a grant from the Arkansas Arts Council, an agency of the Department of Arkansas Heritage and the National Endowment for the Arts and the City of Little Rock.

All good things must come to an end.

Chapter 10

Lessons Learned

~~~~~ It's the Music, Stupid! ~~~~~

When returning to a work I've not conducted recently, I often question my earlier ideas and interpretation. With the passage of only a year or two, the page looks new. The notes are familiar, but the music seems different.

About twenty years ago, I opened the score of Tchaikovsky's Symphony No. 5 in preparation for concerts in Lake Forest. I had already known the piece for two decades and had conducted it many times. Though enormously popular with audiences, it was never a personal favorite. The work had always seemed to me a collection of A+ tunes held together by B- orchestrating and C- efforts at developing the material—a whole that was, somehow, less than the sum of its parts.

But on that occasion, twenty years ago, I had a different response. Previously, I had made the mistake of viewing the work as many others saw it: a sprawling canvas of big emotions and ideas—a kind of *War and Peace* in music. This was a youthful mistake. Tchaikovsky's Fifth Symphony is less like Tolstoy than it is like Proust—a series of vaguely interlocking, personal moments, each of which demands its own careful examination. Viewed in this way, the score suddenly made sense. More importantly, everything mattered, and I found there was far more music among those notes than I had earlier appreciated.

The key to this revelation was opening the score with fresh eyes and observing it free of both my own preconceptions and the traditions of thousands of previous performances. It is liberating to look at the music of a great composer and see only what is on the page, without assumptions inadvertently based on the ideas of others.

Do we know what our spouse will say even before they say it? Often, yes. And there is an organic, comforting connection in that knowledge. But we can also take our loved ones, or a great work of art, for granted. No matter what we think we know, there is always more to learn.

Tchaikovsky's Fifth Symphony, for example, is a beautiful, simple work. The music asks to be expressed honestly, openly, and clearly, without layers of artifice and pretense. Audiences are starving for this personal way of making music, and orchestral musicians instantly recognize a conductor who is merely regurgitating the ideas of others. And no matter how much the conductor dances about, the choreography can never replace the substance of our art.

So why does the score seem different each time? How does the music change, grow deeper and more complex? The notes have not changed. But what the music means, and the reason it exists, has.

In my 20s and early 30s, music was about perfection, ego, self. It is unlikely I would have admitted, or even realized, this at the time, but I think now that it is true. To some extent music will always be about these things, because we can never be the person we would like to be, and our highest ideals will never be fully realized. However, as years pass, we hope to make progress, and music becomes, more and more, about other things.

We live in a world driven by personality. One need only look to stories about Chopin, Liszt, Wagner, and Mozart to realize that, in the sphere of great music, this has always been so. But as our art meets the twenty-first century head-on, this phenomenon is expanding exponentially. The figure of the artist as personality, or icon, now dominates the way we view musical performers. We are still a long way from being an industry in which, Kardashian-like, some musicians are famous just for being famous. But we creep one step closer every day.

There's nothing wrong with adopting twenty-first century marketing and PR strategies in the service of great music. In fact, my belief that great music and modern marketing can comfortably coexist nearly caused a rift with my first Arkansas Symphony executive director. The question is, when does the hype end and the performance begin? When is the sexy headshot put away so the music can start?

The line between personality and music continues to blur, and this is not a new phenomenon. But the inherent difficulty of separating the performance from the performer's ego has intensified in our selfie-driven, everyone-is-an-influencer culture.

When one's person becomes as important as the performance, things have gone very wrong. When we see the individual instead of the music, the artist more than the art, then we have been cheated. Certainly, the self is part of the performance because a musician's mind, heart, and talent are the conduits for the composition. As musical artists we are asked to take the notes from the page and fashion a new, living creation. But this does not mean we place ourselves in front of the music—to stand, as it were, between the audience and the composer. In fact, the opposite is true. The performer—whether instrumental soloist, orchestral musician, conductor, or opera star—is a catalyst: the ingredient without which music cannot occur and the element that must ultimately fade into the background.

When we see and hear the performance of a great artist, we sense this balance. We feel the presence of the artist but are not blinded by it; we are not distracted from the music by the star's ego or personal eccentricities. Instead, we are allowed to bask in the presence of both the music and the talent.

Separating performance from ego, however, isn't always easy. Performing requires a certain type of personality as a starting point, and that quality can lead us down the wrong path. It requires so much self-possession to do what we do that it can be difficult to sever that tie when the moment of performance arrives.

It is always exciting to be on stage. For some it is uplifting and energizing, the tingle of nerves making the difference between rehearsal and performance. For some artists, however, it is also terrifying. But, either way, the event can become a distraction from our task of communicating the message, the meaning, and our understanding of the music.

We can weaken the ties to ego and event by focusing exclusively on the task. As audience members, we know immediately when a performer is too focused on the event. At such a moment, we feel ourselves in the presence of a show. It may be a great show, but it's still a show. Making music is not a show; it's not a game. In the presence of a great artist, we feel a purity of spirit and clarity of expression emanating from them. This clarity streams forth, unclouded by the concerns of self. We feel only the essence of the music, the mind of the composer, and the heart of the artist.

For conductors, removing the self from the performance is a unique challenge. We are the only musical artists who contribute no sound, no audible music, to the performance. Because conductors contribute no notes, it is especially tempting to offer, instead, ourselves. It seems almost irresistible for conductors to make large, dramatic gestures, sway their hips, and toss their hair even when their gyrations provide no musical benefit. In short, because we contribute no sound, we apparently need to do a dance.

Before the late seventeenth century, musical ensembles were led by one of the players, often the lead violinist. As the size of orchestras grew and orchestral music became more complex, it was necessary for the concertmaster to occasionally wave their bow in the air. Either that or a nonperformer, often the composer, beat time by either waving a small stick or beating a large one on the ground. An early example of the latter technique, Jean-Baptiste Lully (1632–1687), famously brought the heavy staff down on his toe. As a result, he developed gangrene and died—the classic cautionary tale for conductor hopefuls.

Eventually the craft of conducting was born of necessity. The conductor was needed to organize the ensemble technically and bring order and coherence to the interpretation of the work. A string quartet or chamber orchestra can perform without a conductor by agreeing in advance on matters of tempo, articulation, phrasing, and so on. But for a larger ensemble, a significant tempo change executed without a conductor is likely to wreak havoc.

Far more important, though, is the conductor's role as the unifying interpretive voice. The players in a chamber ensemble have the luxury of discussing the music among themselves, exchanging ideas, and arriving at a consensus. For a large orchestra, however, this is an unworkable process. As a result, the conductor's initial, metronomic role expanded to decision-maker for all things interpretive, artistic, and musical. Consequently, the modern orchestra became, and still is, the last great monarchy.

But conductors were never supposed to be the deity-like figures they have become. Is the conductor the leader? Yes. Is the conductor expected to know more about the score than anyone in the orchestra? Again, yes. Should the conductor be more generally knowledgeable than any musician in the orchestra? If at all possible, yes.

But the sum of leadership, technical expertise, musical background, and intimate knowledge of the score does not make one a god. I am not suggesting that the conductor should be considered literally no different than another of the orchestra's musicians. But it is important to remember that the conductor *is* one of the orchestra's musicians—simply one with a different role.

The conductor is not the instrument, the orchestra is. The conductor is not the central focus of the performance, as that role belongs to the composer's brainchild. As musicians we are all paths to music and conduits toward creation. The conductor is no more, and no less, than that.

Perhaps the most important kernel to be drawn from this discussion is that the craft of conducting grew out of legitimate musical needs. It did not spring from the audience's need to be distracted, or to have choreography added to enhance the music. The conductor's role is one of service to the music and to other musicians. Conversely, when one makes oneself the focal point of the orchestral performance, whether by design or by carelessness, one perverts the conductor's role beyond recognition.

We learn the craft, we learn the score, we distill our belief in what the music means, and we translate that knowledge into gestural and body-language choices. Then, we go and do. That's all there is.

As conducting styles go, mine is comparatively understated. So when I am approached after a concert by someone who says, "I just loved watching you," I really don't know how to feel. But I want to respond, "I wasn't the point."

I don't say it, of course. When a symphony-goer offers that compliment, I'm sure it is made with a good heart, and the patron does not deserve a lecture. I imagine they appreciated beautiful moments in the orchestra's performance, but their choice of words speaks volumes about what our culture has become. If watching what I do on the podium enhances the audience's understanding and enjoyment of the music, then it is hard to object. On the other hand, some evenings it requires every ounce of my willpower not to respond, in James Carville fashion, "It's the music, stupid!"

Herding Cats

Somewhere in their heart of hearts, most concertgoers wonder exactly what the conductor does for a living. Our role in a performance is obvious: the conductor is an overpaid crossing guard. But one feels, instinctively, there must be more. A thorough explanation is a book unto itself. But a few words are in order about the part of our craft that is, in my opinion, vastly underrated and too often ignored.

If an extraterrestrial dropped in on an orchestra concert, they might assume that the conductor is the only human onstage lacking the talent to play a musical instrument. As odd as ET's observation may seem, it contains a kernel of inescapable logic. The conductor's instrument is so complex and difficult to manage that it is easily overlooked. It is not the combination of strings, woodwinds, brass, and percussion instruments in the room; it is the people playing those instruments. And until a conductor is as proficient at getting the best from those people as he is at waving a stick, he will be as limited in his craft as a violinist who has not mastered their scales and arpeggios.

The first challenge in caring for this instrument is addressing its enormous size and diversity. The violinist has four strings, each with its own character. As difficult as mastery of the violin may be, the conductor has eighty or ninety strings on which to play. And each string, each person, has its own unique place in the whole.

When a violinist takes their instrument from the case, they can see it is the same one placed there the day before. They can depend on the fact that the bow will bounce with the same dexterity, and the violin will generally behave as expected. But the orchestra we greet on any given day may respond differently than the one we addressed a week earlier, despite containing the same individuals. Each person is different every day, and those variations create an orchestra that is entirely unique.

Unlike their instruments, the individuals of the orchestra may need the conductor to adapt to their moods or personal situations. Expressed another way, the conductor must negotiate with each string of the orchestral instrument to discover how best to coax the music from it. The conductor can take nothing for granted regarding the willingness or ability of any individual musician at any given time.

But discerning which musicians may be out of sorts or tired is not difficult. Finding a way to reinspire the uninspired and energize the exhausted is more challenging. When a singer feels their voice is not responding as they'd like, there is a temptation to solve the problem by applying pressure to the instrument. But fine singers and instrumentalists know this is not an appropriate solution. When doing so, the singer becomes hoarse, and the instrumentalist tense and fatigued. But despite this obvious logic, some conductors insist on using brute force to unravel the dilemma of an unresponsive instrument.

The conductors of old indulged in infamous tantrums and tirades. And in many cases these were fine conductors, conducting great orchestras. But just because a certain maestro behaves a certain way, and this same maestro has a great orchestra, does not necessarily mean that one is the result of the other.

We can never know for certain, but it's possible that the tantrum-throwing maestro's orchestra would have played better if they were not browbeaten into their performance. Whatever the technical outcome may have been, those orchestras would surely have risen to higher artistic levels had their motivation been connected to music rather than fear.

This doesn't mean that the conductor can succeed as a new age, warm-and-fuzzy, entirely democratic leader. It has been tried, and it doesn't work. But somewhere between these two extremes there must be a reasonable middle ground. There must be a method of leadership that allows the conductor to retain singular authority while providing for the reality that each string in their instrument is a living, breathing human whose needs and desires, musical and otherwise, must be addressed on some level. Surely there is a way to hold the instrument firmly in one's grasp without breaking it.

~~~~~ The "M" Word ~~~~~

We pause here for a word about the maestro. More specifically, about the word "maestro."

I place this overused word in the "Terms" portion of the conducting entrance exam at the University of North Texas, hoping some applicants will know what it actually means. This exercise is the beginning of a larger conversation regarding the time, commitment, and patience required to become an outstanding practitioner of our craft.

I often see the word "maestro" attached to the email addresses of prospective students (e.g., maestrojoe@gmail.com), and I sigh. When a new recruit joins the army, their rank is private. As they advance in expertise and gain more responsibility, that title will change, perhaps many times. In the orchestral world, alas, we have only one rank for a conductor. The result is that the greenest novice who can wave their arms without falling off the podium is often called "maestro."

In its original usage, the word has nothing to do with music, meaning simply "master" or "teacher." In Italian classrooms, children refer to their instructor as maestro or maestra. It is a term of respect that acknowledges the expertise and earned authority of the person to whom it refers. It is neither a synonym for conductor nor an everyday honorific like mister or miss. The key element is *earned* authority. When a university TA takes the class because the instructor of record is indisposed, we don't automatically call them professor, and for good reason.

Early in our careers, the conductor is sometimes the youngest person in the room. As a guest conductor, decades ago, I was sometimes asked how musicians should address me in rehearsal. The personnel manager would approach me with the question, "Maestro? Mr. Itkin? What would you prefer?"

In my 30s and early 40s, I always answered, "'David' is fine." How, at the age of 32, confronted with perhaps one thousand years of combined musical experience in the orchestra, was I a teacher or master? I always answered, "'David' is fine," because I figured maestro would come when, and if, I'd earned it.

In current culture many words have lost their meaning through misuse. Some words now have multiple alleged meanings or are overused as tools of a social agenda. (I will not offer examples of the latter, lest I receive for a visit from the Political Correctness Police.) But in our tiny, insignificant corner of the universe, maestro is one we can fix.

Early in my time as associate conductor of the Alabama Symphony, the principal cellist—who apparently felt I needed to be taken down a peg—addressed me in rehearsal with a snarly, sarcastic tone, "Hey, Maestro—" His behavior was unprofessional and mean-spirited, but somewhere in his dark little heart, he had a point. As an associate conductor in my second year in the professional world, I was still learning, and nobody should have referred to me as maestro.

Herbert von Karajan allegedly confided, "It took me fifteen years of conducting before I could hear what the orchestra was actually playing. It then took me an additional ten years to get to the point at which I could organize the orchestra's playing to attempt to realize the composer's vision."

James de Priest told me something similar: "I was 50 before I felt like I really knew what I was doing."

If these two great conductors can make that admission, perhaps "maestro" should wait a while for the rest of us as well.

I advise my conducting students to remove the term from their email addresses and regularly ask university musicians to refer to student conductors by their names. But it's an uphill battle.

The Balancing Act

Apart from those few musicians who were soloists practically from birth, we all came to this career along similar paths. With so much in common, why we have grown so far apart? How have some of us retained a love for what we do, no matter the ups and downs, while many become bitter, lost, and devoid of the motivations that brought us to this life? Is it the shortsightedness of orchestra managements or the players' union? Is it the fault of the individual musician, or is it the government's failure to properly support the arts? Is it the public's apathy, the conductor's arrogance, or the critic's ignorance? The answer, I believe, is yes.

There is plenty of blame to go around. And the ever-present tensions among the parties are so poorly concealed that, at one point, the subject provoked sarcasm on a national radio broadcast. At the 1996 American Symphony Orchestra League conference in Cincinnati, I renewed my acquaintance with Martin Goldsmith, author of *The Inextinguishable Symphony*, and the original host of NPR's *Performance Today*. His regular program was broadcast from Washington DC, but Martin planned a live "from the field" report on the final day of the conference.

The night before his broadcast, we found ourselves drinking wine and eating sandwiches in my hotel room, where Martin lamented that he still didn't have an angle for his piece on the conference. As we chatted about peeking into the Olympic fencing trials on the ground floor of the conference center, Martin was struck with an idea. He reported the next morning that "at the American Symphony Orchestra League's national conference, this year, for a change, the thrusting and parrying seemed to be confined to the first floor of the building."

We are all tired of everyone pointing the finger at someone else. Nonetheless, allow me to point my finger at everyone.

At one time, not so long ago, musicians were treated as servants. They served the European royalty and later the new bourgeoisie. They were expected to perform at concerts, in the salon, at the dinner table, and anywhere else instructed.

In the Prologue of Richard Strauss's opera *Ariadne auf Naxos*, a new opera is about to be premiered in the home a nobleman. The composer is seen fretting madly because, only a few minutes before the performance, the musicians are not in the orchestra pit. He is furious to discover they are still "at table," but the condescending majordomo clarifies that they are not eating, they are "bei der herrschaftigen Tafel"—they are playing dinner music for the master and his guests before heading directly to the orchestra pit.

The musicians of earlier eras were treated about the same as the cook, chambermaid, or butler. Their skill, talent, and dedication were commodities traded for the enjoyment of the privileged. For a twentieth-century illustration, note the scene in *Downton Abbey* when Lord Grantham is scandalized by the idea that opera star Nellie Melba will eat at their dinner table. Some things have changed a great deal since then, but some don't seem to have changed at all.

In many ways musicians are still second-class citizens, often in the very institutions that promote their music. They are rarely invited to receptions and parties hosted by their organization, are represented on important committees only begrudgingly, and are given little say in the future of either their orchestra or their art. I cannot count the number of times I have heard orchestra administrators, board members, or volunteers refer to their musicians as "them" or "the employees." In a great organization, there is one team and one goal; there is neither "we" nor "they."

Even the artistic advisory committee (the body tasked with advising the music director regarding programming in some orchestras) is often underpopulated by musicians and overrun with board members. A cardiologist who briefly chaired the music advisory committee in Little Rock once confided that he was not comfortable with the role he'd been given. He loved music and knew a fair bit about it but didn't see himself questioning my decisions. After all, he said, he didn't want my advice on how to treat a heart attack.

I am not suggesting that the conductor is the only person who has anything of value to contribute. On the contrary, an orchestra has the expertise of eighty or more musicians upon which to draw. But in many organizations, only one musician, the conductor, has any substantive input on programming.

This lack of active participation in the artistic development of their orchestra is a symptom of the persistent attitude about the place of musicians. But evidence of the sidelining of musicians is not only subjective. We have come to accept that a full-time musician's salary will be far less than the marketing director's, and often the executive director is paid five or ten times a musician's salary.

On the other hand, people deserve to be paid for the quality of their work. If a marketing director, executive director, or, for that matter, music director is producing stunning results, then their salary should reflect that achievement. The problem is that we accept as a point of departure the idea that entry-level staff members (often individuals in their 20s with little or no experience) begin at salaries higher than starting full-time players who often have master's degrees and years of experience.

This is clearly wrong; nonetheless, we keep doing it. Is the cause simple supply and demand, economy of scale, laziness, or America's impoverished arts culture? Take your pick.

Artist management firms occupy an unusual position in our business. They are integral to what we do and yet are not a part of what we do. They are both our partners and our antagonists. They drain our resources but cannot thrive unless we are financially stable.

Management firms (like the one that represents me) have two tasks: (1) to represent us in business matters, freeing the artist from those concerns, and (2) to act as a conduit for communication between us and the presenting organization or employer.

But management firms should also be advocates for music, promoting performances of their artists while also supporting the health of the industry and its component parts. It is in this second, more subtle role where many managers fail to perform.

In their defense, accommodating the needs of multiple constituents can be a difficult balancing act. The artists for whom the manager works want top dollar for their performances—especially when the agency is taking 20 percent off the top—and expect the manager to put their concerns above any others. Also, the manager must serve the firm. That 20 percent of fees charged to presenters must keep the business viable.

At the bottom of the priority list comes the needs of the orchestras. When many soloists are priced out of the market for all but the top orchestras, it becomes more difficult for regional and small orchestras to maintain ticket sales. It is at this point that the balancing act begins. Even from a soloist's point of view, it is better to be engaged many times each season at a lower fee than fewer times at a higher one.

But this message of balance isn't always getting through. The major firms have large rosters of soloists and conductors, only a small fraction of whom are major artists. The rest are outstanding musicians whose names are not as well-known but whose fees are inflated by virtue of sharing the roster page with star artists. This fee inflation serves neither the midlevel artist nor the musical community.

And rising fees for midlevel soloists present an issue that strikes closer to home. That soloist's fee for a pair of concerts (a two- to four-day commitment) is often between 15 and 20 percent of the annual salary for a full-time musician in that same orchestra. In a part-time professional orchestra, the same soloist's fee may equal a musician's compensation for the entire season. For a variety of reasons, some obvious and some perhaps not, soloists do deserve fees in many multiples of what an orchestral musician earns for the same concert. But even for a relatively minor name, the ratio can be as high as twenty-five-fold.

These days it is nearly impossible for smaller regional orchestras to engage genuine stars. Even at inflated ticket prices for a one-off fundraising concert, the organization will be lucky to break even without a donor willing to foot the bill. A Broadway or popular music star, a name we know will sell out the hall, will cost between $50,000 and $100,000 for one performance. In addition, the organization will be on the hook for multiple first-class airline tickets, hotel suites, technical equipment, and catering, easily amounting to another $10,000 or more.

I never cease asking myself why anyone needs to be paid that much money for an hour of singing. But the answer is simple: they demand those fees because they can get those fees. Musing about why a has-been pop singer should be paid more than $30,000 for one hour's work is foolish in a world where an average basketball player makes that much every day, 365 days a year.

With fewer affordable, well-known artists available, more orchestras will downsize or go under, reducing the number of organizations hiring soloists. In the long run, everyone loses.

Before embarking on a perilous discussion about musicians and their organizations, I offer a disclaimer that should be self-evident: I am not antiunion. I am, however, pro–common sense and civility.

No one needs a lesson from me on the founding of labor unions in the United States. And the organizations that represent musicians exist for those same, entirely sound reasons. But when we take a good idea too far, it can become divisive and destructive, and this is sometimes the case with labor unions. When protecting the rights, dignity, and health of musicians becomes a quest for power and control, then we have traveled a path leading far away from the union's mission and the music that brought us together.

My interactions with local unions have ranged from largely collegial to highly adversarial. But most of the time, I find that the character of a local musicians' organization is simply the personality of the individuals who hold its reins. Musicians are generally a cooperative group, but they are sometimes led astray by their own. This is not to suggest that the musicians' leadership should not be vigilant in protecting the rights of their colleagues. On the contrary, that is the reason they exist.

But like the management, the board, and the conductor, the musicians' leadership needs to keep one eye on the goal: the overall health of the organization and the artistic success of the orchestra. This doesn't mean caving in on vital issues or being management's doormat. Focusing on the big picture means considering every question, difficulty, or disgruntlement with an open mind instead of sticking to a one-size-fits-all response.

And it is not only our answers that matter but also our questions. Management should not always ask, "What's the cheapest way to produce a concert?" Conductors must not ask, "What pleases *me*?" And unions should not ask, "How do we make the most money while doing the least work?"

Considering scenarios that illustrate a total disregard for the big picture, two events from my time with the Alabama Symphony come to mind.

In most orchestra contracts, audio and video recording are prohibited without the express permission of the musicians. This is entirely appropriate because in years past it was common for live concert recordings to be sold without any payment to musicians. But a good idea can be carried to an illogical extreme.

Almost every orchestra requires conductor applicants to send video of their work in the initial stage of the selection process. But in those same orchestras, no video can be made without a substantial payment. While associate conductor of the Alabama Symphony, I was involved in search processes with other orchestras, and I repeatedly asked the musicians' committee to make an exception. Just once? For only ten minutes? Just in rehearsal? But it was never going to happen. I had faith that the musicians were not so unreasonable, and I repeatedly asked the committee to take my request directly to the orchestra. This they also declined, citing rules at the national level. Their responses to my frequent requests were "no," "no," and "which part of 'no' don't you understand?"

The Kafkaesque nature of the situation is plain. Eventually, the orchestra would be looking for a new associate conductor, requesting footage from candidates who were not allowed to shoot video with their current orchestras. In addition to the self-defeating nature of their position, there was also the fact that it made no objective sense. A rehearsal video, shot on a consumer-level camera or cell phone, will not create revenue, so no one is being cheated. When I floated that argument in Alabama, I was told, "That isn't the point; it's the principle of the thing." I have never figured out what principle they were talking about.

But one conductor's inability to create video is not the issue of concern. The musicians (in this as well as in more important matters) never seemed to understand that they were being manipulated.

Before each Alabama Symphony contract negotiation, the national union laid out the terms to be demanded in the new contract, specifying which issues were nonnegotiable. I've always believed that local musicians know what's best for their orchestra and their community. During my tenure as music director of the Arkansas Symphony, the musicians repeatedly declined to affiliate with the national union. And their desire not to be dictated to from above was, I believe, a big part of the reason.

Contract negotiations in any given orchestra are just one move in a larger chess game. From the national perspective, it is imperative that orchestra A receives a certain perk so that orchestra B can then demand it. Whether the item being demanded is appropriate and manageable for that organization appears to be of little concern at the national level.

The second can't-see-the-forest-for-the-trees scenario illustrates the practice of adhering to the letter of the law even when it makes everyone's life more difficult.

During the 1991–1992 Alabama Symphony season, I conducted a subscription program featuring Haydn's *Horn Call* Symphony and Carl Orff's *Carmina Burana*. The program was lopsided (twenty-five minutes before intermission and sixty-three minutes after), which can create logistical problems in rehearsal. Those problems ought to have been minor, but at the Alabama Symphony no problem was minor.

As is common in full-time, daytime orchestras, the final rehearsals with the chorus took place in the evening, three hours' duration with a twenty-minute break. The master agreement required that the break began not sooner than sixty minutes nor later than ninety minutes into the service. At its core this is a good idea, because it inhibits the conductor from making either half of the rehearsal painfully long.

At the final session, we breezed through the Haydn, rehearsing for only thirty-five minutes. It was twenty-five minutes too early to take the break, so I asked to caucus with the musicians' committee.

I suggested we take our break at that time and subtract twenty-five minutes from the end of the rehearsal, therein complying with the intent of the agreement. Even though this adjustment would have meant everyone could go home early, the musicians' committee declined to deviate from the letter of the contract. Instead, we had a forty-five-minute break and stayed until exactly 10:00 p.m.—a triumph of small minds over common sense.

Having taken orchestra managements, agents, and musicians' representation to task, it is time to ask what portion of the blame falls on the shoulders of conductors.

Some of my colleagues give their leadership role a great deal of thought, and some none. Those in the latter category continue blithely forward without considering the effect of their decisions on the orchestra, the community, or the music they serve. This doesn't mean they are doing a poor job. On the contrary, they may be excelling in nearly every way. But if so, it is by instinct, almost by accident. Some of us are not fortunate to embody the perfect balance of all qualities without working at it. Indeed, most of us just manage to keep the balancing act going, even with substantial effort.

Our goal is to establish equilibrium among the conflicting roles we are asked to play. For example, we face the daily choice between flexibility (demonstrating that we are in touch with the realities of our organization) and protecting what is sacrosanct in the music.

"We're strapped for cash, Maestro. Can we hire a few less string players for one of the pops concerts?"

With a sigh, "Okay."

"And can we do the same thing for *La Mer*?"

"Absolutely not!"

"Really? Please?"

If we say "no," administrators and board members grumble that we "don't understand the situation." If we say "yes," musicians and critics will argue that we're spineless wimps who won't stand up for what's right. The problem is that they're both correct.

The modern conductor is expected to be musician, visionary, media icon, fundraiser, spiritual leader, taskmaster, teacher, executive, negotiator, sometime psychologist, and colleague. As we attempt to sort out which aspects should dominate our thinking and actions, it's easy to get lost. We are, after all, trying to create something new from a very old set of blueprints. Making this job more difficult is the fact that the conductor is the only person in the organization who everyone thinks is on the other team. Boards tend to see the conductor as one of the musicians, and musicians often see their leader as an extension of management.

Our struggle to find a workable identity germinates from our common understanding that the old manner of being a maestro doesn't work. In earlier generations the conductor was required to be only one thing: a great musician. Only the musical and intellectual skills mattered, and beyond that all faults were forgiven. Any level of reclusive or egomaniacal behavior was tolerated, as was nearly any manner of dealing with the orchestra's musicians.

Now our efforts to redefine the craft are twofold. First, we must broaden our skillset to include things that seem far removed from our natural talents. Second, we must continue to reexamine the relationship between the conductor and the orchestra.

American conductors of my generation were not trained for many of the tasks we are called upon to perform in the professional world. I have attempted to correct some of these deficiencies in my graduate program at UNT. But in the time allotted, with so many issues to address, I can only scratch the surface. Some of these skills will come easily, based on one's personal gifts, and others will not. But easy or difficult, they are now part of the job, and we do not have the luxury of picking and choosing which tasks are to our liking.

This is not to suggest that every element of the conductor's responsibilities has equal weight and importance. The conductor is to be judged first and foremost for the artistic growth of the orchestra and the quality of its performances. But other responsibilities weigh on the scale as well. No one can reasonably expect us to be overjoyed at the prospect of pressing the flesh at cocktail parties or speaking at the chamber of commerce luncheon. But the organization can expect us to be reasonably effective at public speaking and at least look like we're having fun at a party.

Our second new task is more subtle. We cannot behave like the conductors of old, with their famous caprices and tantrums. In society at large, and as a community of musicians, we have moved beyond notions that the boss has the right to act in any manner they see fit, expecting musicians to sit still for abuses of authority by the conductor. The idea that this behavior is all part of the maestro mystique is, I hope, dead forever.

Some of my colleagues have dealt with this issue by moving, in my opinion, too far in the opposite direction. These new-age maestri are endlessly patient, effusive in praise, ceaselessly cooperative, and models of flexibility. Some of these are good qualities. In fact, it might be argued that they are all positive qualities for a conductor. But cooperativeness and flexibility, like single-mindedness and strict control, are constructive only when they exist in balance.

We have learned from the past that too little flexibility, patience, and positive reinforcement do not work. But I was the beneficiary of firsthand lessons in the fact that there can be too much flexibility, patience, and praise. In our efforts to demonstrate that we are modern conductors who are not formed from models of old, we can easily fall into the trap of giving away the vital components of authority and respect.

My first boss was a very talented, well-meaning man for whom the assertion of authority was abhorrent. His story, from the musicians' perspective, illustrates the adage that one should be careful what one wishes for. Initially, they thought he was a dream come true:

a conductor who never makes demands for personal or musical discipline. But they soon realized this was a bad bargain. What developed was a group deeply dissatisfied with the playing and discipline of their orchestra, a cadre of capable musicians who desperately wanted the music director to do his job.

In place of consistent, clear expectations and discipline, they were treated to periodic tantrums during which his frustration boiled over. That these scenes had no lasting positive effect is not surprising. But it is not fair to say that these outbursts had no consequences. The predictable result was a further diminishing of his credibility, at last becoming a leader who had lost control by refusing to take the reins handed to him.

So where does that leave us? Institutional boards with no idea what's important, management firms chasing dollars instead of supporting the art, local unions obediently toeing the line, a distracted, largely uneducated public, and conductors who can't find the middle ground between Stalin and Gandhi. We are all at fault, so if our organizations sputter and die, we will have nowhere to look but the closest mirror.

Chapter 11

All the Way Home

~~~~~ Drinking Scotch in Saigon ~~~~~

For Americans who came of age in the '60s and '70s, the word "Vietnam" carries a truckload of baggage. More than fifty thousand US soldiers, and millions of Vietnamese and Chinese, were slaughtered in this hopeless, pointless demonstration of military and ideological gamesmanship. And equally appalling, a generation of our young men returned home walking wounded, only to face the scorn that should have been directed at the leaders who sent them to southeast Asia.

The draft lottery, begun in December 1969, was an annual event during which 366 blue plastic capsules, each containing a slip of paper with a printed date, were placed in a large glass container. In a televised event, one capsule after another was drawn and the dates catalogued in numerical order. Each year young men and their families held their collective breath, hoping for a number higher than one hundred, the average yearly cutoff for those being called to active service.

The scene chillingly conjures images of a bingo game, each casual selection meaning life or death for untold numbers of 18-year-olds. Or perhaps it was more like the Powerball drawing—

a televised spectacle with everyone on the edge of their seat. But in this lottery, instead of winning millions you got blown to bits in a faraway swamp.

My brother, Hank, seven years my senior, drew number thirty-nine. His conscientious objector paperwork was denied, but as a college undergrad, he was still protected by his student deferment. Conscious of the grave injustice the student deferment system represented (an outsized percentage of the men in active service were poor and/or African American), he rejected his deferment. This meant he was eligible to be drafted in the year-end roundup of men whose status had changed.

Our mother was understandably panic-stricken, despite my brother's assurances that he would be in jail or another country before he went to Vietnam. By a stroke of luck, the last-minute collection did not occur that year, as the military had deemed its current numbers sufficient.

Our well-known, activist cousin, John Robbins, was not so fortunate. As a result, he spent a good portion of his adult life in Canada. I was spared the indignity and terror of the draft when the war ended three days before my 18th birthday.

All the emotions connected with "Vietnam" swirled as I struggled to decide whether to accept an invitation to conduct the Ho Chi Minh City Symphony in 2015. The offer to lead a concert commemorating the twentieth anniversary of renewed diplomatic ties between the two nations was communicated by a Vietnamese violinist, former UNT graduate student Chuong Vu. At length I accepted, hoping the adventure might enlighten me and broaden my perspective on a nation about which most Americans know little beyond the negative historical connections.

In keeping with the spirit of the event, the program was envisioned as a fusion of Vietnamese and American repertoire. Suggestions flowing from across the Pacific included Bernstein's *Candide* Overture and the Barber Violin Concerto. Chuong relayed this information to me, suggesting tactfully that the orchestra was not like professional groups in the United States, and I might want to be cautious about the program's difficulty. Taking his counsel to heart, I turned thumbs-down on the technically challenging *Candide* Overture. But Chuong, who would be my soloist, wanted to play the Barber concerto despite his own warning, so I offered tepid approval. Rounding out the first half of the program, they chose a Vietnamese work the orchestra had recently played.

This still left me needing an American work for the second half that would not overtax the orchestra's abilities. I chose Howard Hanson's Symphony No. 2, the *Romantic*. I've never cared for the piece, but it's popular with new audiences and is commonly played by American youth orchestras, so it checked all the boxes.

Howard Hanson's most performed work is a pillar of the American neo-Romantic movement in the mid-twentieth century. Unfortunately, like several other composers of his generation, his contributions to music are far more significant outside of his compositional output. He was a champion for new music performances and recordings, established the Eastman-Rochester Orchestra, and left an indelible mark as dean of the Eastman School of Music for four decades. I've always found Hanson's second symphony too close to movie music for my taste. But perhaps it is precisely this film score vibe that has kept the piece popular and made it his only frequently performed orchestral work.

Much of the choking Ho Chi Minh City traffic is motorbikes. Like giant, ungovernable, smog-belching schools of fish, the one- and two-occupant vehicles swarm the narrow streets and expansive intersections seemingly without reference to specific lanes or plan of any sort. In addition to human cargo, the motorbikes, which also carry goods throughout the city, are outfitted with all manner of contraptions for that purpose. Iconic to this scene are cyclists wearing wide-brimmed plywood hats atop which are piled mountains of precariously balanced bananas—a cross between Hell's Angels and Carmen Miranda.

Added to this chaos are the automobiles, like the one in which we rode to my first rehearsal, weaving like sharks through shoals of minnows. Every few seconds a motorbike threatened to collide with us, but the operator either swerved at the last second or placed a restraining hand against our car as he zipped past.

The Ho Chi Minh City Symphony rehearsed in a warehouse space, directly off a busy street. The large doors remained open throughout our rehearsals because, even with the doors parted, the space was broiling and airless by midmorning. I began with the Hanson Symphony, assuming we would work through this relatively easy piece during the first half of rehearsal, later moving on to the more difficult works with the knowledge that half the program was "in the can."

But, as they say, "Man plans, and God laughs."

The musicians were incapable of playing together in even the simplest sections of the piece and had little comprehension of the rhythms indicated. When they saw faster values or notes clustered together on the page, they played indiscriminately faster, and in longer values played much too slowly. To my amazement, almost no one in the orchestra understood what a triplet sounded like. Instead of playing the figure as intended (three notes evenly spaced across a specified unit of time), they played the three notes quickly and then waited, leaving empty space in the music before the next note—except, that is, for some musicians who couldn't wait and went on to the next beat without the rest of us.

I have mentally replayed my first hour with the orchestra many times, wondering how I could have handled the situation differently. I'm sure there was a way, but a decade later I still don't know what that would have been.

I spent about forty-five minutes on the first movement of the Hanson, during which time we achieved nothing more than the elevation of my blood pressure. We played the same passages again and again. After each repetition I explained what was wrong, often singing the correct rhythm or pitches, but little improved. Through my body language and increasingly aggravated tone, they could feel my rising frustration even without a common language. But between their shocking playing level and the ninety-degree environment, my better angels had fled.

Finally, I asked for a moment to confer privately with Chuong, who was acting as my translator, and we stepped into the doorway leading to the street. So close to an exit, I'm surprised I didn't run for it.

Instead, I asked Chuong what he thought I should do, "They can't play any of the right notes," I whined. "This is ridiculous."

Hoping to calm the situation, he suggested, "Let them practice for a while."

"Now?" I asked.

"Yeah. You take a break and give them twenty minutes to practice."

I would later learn that the orchestra, the city's only "professional" group, was made up entirely of musicians who had other jobs. For each rehearsal they were paid the equivalent of four dollars, and after each morning session they went back to their real jobs in shops, schools, and construction sites. Armed with that information, I was more sympathetic but no less agitated.

Though we never met, I felt a kinship with the guest who had preceded me, a French conductor brought in to conduct *Carmen* at the opera house. At one point in rehearsal, he apparently got down on his knees, clasped his palms together, and begged them to play some of the right notes. I know how he felt.

Adrenaline had carried Mei and me through the first full day, but by the second night the complete reversal of light and dark had worn us down. Though exhausted, I opened my eyes at around 2:30 a.m., wide awake. For several minutes I held very still, trying not to disturb her.

Then, from the dark, I heard a voice. "Are you awake, too?"

We both tried, in vain, to fall back asleep, but after a few minutes I asked, "You wanna play gin?"

"Now?" she asked. "It's the middle of the night."

For the next hour and a half, we played gin rummy and shared the scotch I'd had the foresight to buy in the duty-free shop at the Tokyo airport. At last, we slept an hour or two before I had to rise for the morning rehearsal.

The orchestra's struggles with the opening piece and the Barber concerto made the previous day's Hanson outing seem like a cakewalk.

They had allegedly performed the Vietnamese piece recently, but their playing showed no evidence of this.

The finale of the Barber concerto, a complicated perpetual motion–style movement, proved impossible. Nearing the eleventh hour, we slowed it to a crawl (approximately half the normal tempo), forcing the soloist to substantially rethink the playing technique. At this purgatorial pace, the musicians almost got through it unscathed.

But there was also good news, and plenty of it. Each day, after I'd served my 8:30 to 11:30 a.m. sentence in the mind-numbing, baking rehearsal prison, Mei and I struck out on the adventures du jour. We wandered far and wide in search of local cuisine, finding, among other delights, the most extraordinary pho we'd ever eaten at a hot, crowded, working-man's lunch spot across from the Louis Pasteur Institute.

We had nearly given up finding the Thien Hau Temple when we stumbled into it on a side street. This ancient Buddhist shrine is sandwiched between two dilapidated, half-century old apartment buildings, and we nearly walked by it without noticing. Wide meditation rooms featuring stunning iconography on the lower floor give way to individual monk's cells, narrow corridors, and balconies with sudden views of the city on the upper. I breathed deeply of the incense-laden tranquility, determined to get my priorities straight.

Less beautiful, but unforgettable, was the War Remnants Museum. This modern, multistory complex offers a detailed testimonial to what the Vietnamese generally refer to as "the American War."

There are many things we don't want to see—don't want to know—and this is one of them. And it is for precisely this reason that every American, regardless of political outlook, should visit this shrine to greed, shortsightedness, and human catastrophe. The displays begin with benign history lessons about French colonialization and other events leading to the conflict. But as we proceeded deeper, viewing information about bomb tonnage, mass executions, rape, and chemical defoliants—complete with increasingly horrific photos and testimonial—I was overcome by a wave of nausea and shame.

The author with his wife, Mei, Ho Chi Minh City, 2015.

Most Americans see war on our television sets, or through the experiences of casual acquaintances and the members of military families. At the War Remnants Museum, the experience of millions—ongoing to this day through the genetic effects of agent orange and the horror of forgotten landmines—is brought into a focus so sharp we cannot look away.

After Korea and Vietnam, Americans of my generation vowed it would never happen again. But so little is needed to stimulate American politicians into a lust for the next conflict—encouraged by their cash machines in the arms industry—that we keep forgetting.

Strolling contemplatively back to our hotel, we passed through the main open-air market and stumbled across several coffee merchants. Seizing the opportunity to acquire some of their unique brew, we asked for a half kilo. The nice lady bagged it, weighed it, and stated the price: 324,000 VND (Vietnamese dong).

Born and raised in China, Mei is no stranger to haggling. And unlike me, she enjoys it.

"No. Too much," she said, offering a lower amount.

Realizing the game was on, the coffee seller countered, budging only slightly. Back and forth it went, the combatants maneuvering their way toward middle ground while I remained happily on the sidelines.

Several minutes and multiple counteroffers later, my future wife appeared frustrated, and turned to me with a stage whisper: "Let's go. We can get it cheaper somewhere else."

At that point buyer and seller were 20,000 VND apart, and I whispered back, "You do realize you're now haggling over less than a dollar?"

Mei shrugged, flashed a mischievous smile, and the coffee was purchased at the seller's last price.

Despite our musical difficulties—which continued, unabated, through the final notes of the performance—the musicians and I enjoyed much of our time together and found common ground as human beings. And wasn't this, after all, the whole point of the endeavor?

Though I was not a participant in the diplomatic portion of the evening, I felt compelled to say a few words from the stage about being an American in Vietnam, and having been so warmly embraced by the musicians, the city, and the nation. And, I thought, wouldn't it be great if I could make my brief remarks in Vietnamese?

My handlers thought this was a wonderful idea and arranged for a tutor. I wrote out a brief paragraph that was sent to her in advance, and we met the following afternoon. Our lesson was a revelation.

Even for Mei, a native Mandarin speaker who also handles Japanese pretty well, the variety of sounds and tones in Vietnamese is mind-boggling. The language's intricacies begin with the complexity of Chinese tonal inflections layered with the nasal vowels of French. In addition, there are other sounds that neither of us could accurately reproduce. My tutor recorded the short speech on my phone, gave me a brief lesson—during which I repeated not one word to her satisfaction—and went on her way. I studied hard that evening, listening, imitating, and practicing for my captive audience of one until I thought I had the basics.

In a pause to correct a lighting issue during the final rehearsal, I told the musicians seated closest to me what I was planning, and asked if I could practice for them. They graciously agreed to be my test audience.

My opening sentence was something obvious like, "Good evening, ladies and gentlemen, it's an honor to be here and to share the stage with your orchestra."

I recited that statement in Vietnamese and was rewarded with smiles and nods. Encouraged, I plunged into the remaining sentences. Staring at my notes, I failed to notice that the smiles were fading, slowly becoming grimaces of confusion and consternation. Halfway through, I glanced up and stopped cold.

"Is it not quite right?" I asked.

The half dozen musicians glanced furtively at one another. Finally, the concertmaster spoke.

"We don't know," he said, shyly.

"You don't know if I'm pronouncing it correctly?" I asked, confused.

"No," he said, "we don't know what you're trying to say."

With only hours remaining, I concentrated on getting two or three sentences correct. Undoubtedly laughable as spoken Vietnamese, my shortened address was nonetheless greeted with surprised grins and a smattering of applause, a sincere appreciation of the effort if not the expertise.

The following morning, we rose at 4:00—not that it mattered to us, since we were still only halfway over our jetlag—to catch an 8:00 a.m. plane to Tokyo, followed by the long flight to Dallas.

As we approached the Aleutians, the pilot warned of bumpy air ahead. What followed was the worst forty-five minutes either of us has ever spent on an airplane. Wild, head-banging, side-to-side tosses alternated with sudden, engine-groaning drops, while overhead compartments popped open and passengers howled in dismay.

Post-concert with the Ho Chi Minh City Symphony, 2015.

Were more American and Chinese citizens going to die before making it home from Vietnam? Probably not. But as the plane shuddered violently—as if taking flak—and Mei held my hand in a terrified grip, the metaphor was hard to ignore: There, but for the grace of God, went my cousin, my brother, and I.

Prettiest Town I've Ever Seen

My relationship with the Abilene Philharmonic—twenty years and counting as of this writing—will undoubtedly be the longest of my career, but my thoughts here will be brief. Ask a parent to describe their favorite child and you may hear only a few words, because the full story could go on for hours.

Though knowledgeable people in our business may disagree, I am fond of dividing the orchestras of the world into two categories: those who can, and those who will.

The orchestras who *can* are the professional, usually full-time ensembles whose members are skilled and experienced and perform the most difficult repertoire at the highest level. The musicians in these orchestras are often bored, cranky, and dissatisfied, perhaps feeling they have little personal involvement in the artistic outcome. They can make great music. But too often they choose not to bother.

The orchestras who *will* are usually amateur or semiprofessional groups, including school- and university-level ensembles. The musicians in these orchestras play because they love the music and their orchestra. They will never play at, or even near, the level of the orchestras who can. But they are thoroughly invested in the success of the ensemble, giving 100 percent effort, 100 percent of the time.

Fortunately, a small subset also exists. These are the rare professional ensembles whose musicians are skilled and experienced but who still approach rehearsal with a sense of excitement about what's to come, ready and able to invest in the artistic success of the group. They don't see themselves as anonymous cogs in a machine but as vital cells in one great musical brain.

The Abilene Philharmonic is one of this rare breed.

I conducted the APO for the first time in spring 2005. During my four-day visit as a music director candidate, I stayed at a bed-and-breakfast run by a charming couple in their home near the city center. Once ensconced in a guest room that still bore traces of the child who had lived there decades earlier, I ventured out for a walk. On my way through the living room, my hosts briefed me on how the house worked.

The front door was locked at 9:00 p.m., they told me, but if I was going to be out "late" I could ask for a key. If I drank coffee they would place a pot outside my door each morning, which sounded awfully nice. Finally, they asked what I liked for breakfast. Attempting to be as little trouble as possible, as well as to tell the truth, I replied that I didn't usually eat in the morning. The look on both their faces told me I had committed an unpardonable offense. I quickly backtracked, mumbled the name of a breakfast food, and they were all smiles.

The author with "Flat Maestro" at Abilene's Paramount Theatre.

At the risk of sounding ungrateful, I detest the B&B experience. I don't like being watched, babysat, or forced to chat with strangers, even on vacation. And I find it distracting and time-consuming when working. Having confessed my prejudice, it's only fair to emphasize that my hosts were welcoming and accommodating and bear no responsibility for my bad attitude.

The following day I met with several small groups, had a tour of the town, and was scheduled for dinner with board members preceding my first rehearsal. The daytime events ran long, so when the executive director drove me to the B&B to change clothes she waited in the car. Knowing we were behind schedule, I hurried through getting ready.

We had only been seated in the dining room of the Abilene country club for about fifteen minutes when I realized I was having trouble focusing. In the multiday process endured by conducting candidates, we are "on" every second, and I fought to concentrate through my drooping eyelids. After a few minutes, I realized what was wrong. The medication I took at 5:00 p.m. daily, the one I'd tossed back hurriedly less than an hour earlier, was nearly indistinguishable from Ambien and came in an identical bottle. The signs were unmistakable: I'd taken a sleeping pill before meeting the board and conducting a rehearsal.

I held on through dinner, eating little and guzzling coffee, which only added an upset stomach to my drowsiness. On the way to rehearsal, I admitted my stupidity to the executive director, who seemed to find my clownish behavior somehow endearing. Though foggy I survived the rehearsal without appearing prematurely senile. To the best of my knowledge, the executive director never ratted me out.

The music director search in Abilene was precipitated by the ouster of a capable and, as described to me, rather difficult conductor. I'd applied for the position based on the group's reputation as a destination for some of the best freelance musicians in Central Texas, but my experience that week did not support the hype. The orchestra was a mess, and the top-level freelancers I'd heard about were few and far between.

After accepting the position, I learned that the APO's reputation had been accurate—at one time. Unfortunately, many fine players had recently fled the orchestra, citing the previous conductor's behavior as one of their major concerns.

It was orchestra building 101 starting the following fall. But together we made it happen. During the next half dozen seasons, the small group of outstanding players who had stuck with the orchestra

The author with some of his favorite guest artists, Abilene, 2019. *Left to right*: Jocelyn Hanson, Bruce Ewing, Kristi Tingle, Kristen Herzenberg, the author, Jason Forbach.

through good times and bad were augmented by dozens more, filling out the ranks as we know it today.

I am proud to lead this outstanding group made up of musicians of diverse backgrounds from every metropolitan area in Texas and several surrounding states. We come together in Abilene seven times each year, happy to see one another and excited to make excellent music together. They are a part of the miraculous subset of which I spoke earlier, those who both can and will.

They can and, I am endlessly grateful to say, they do.

~~~~~ Bill, David, and Paul ~~~~~

My approach to conducting technique, rehearsal flow and efficiency, score study, musical discipline, and creative music making were most strongly influenced by three teachers: William Dehning, David Effron, and Paul Vermel. These are three very different men with decidedly different approaches and skill sets, but each exposed me to perspectives and ideas that influence me still.

Some mentors provide a laser focus on technique, some know the repertoire like their own names, and some have singular insights into the rehearsal and music-making process, while the gifts of others are more difficult to define but no less valuable. Every great teacher brings unique lessons to the table, and if we are wise enough, we discover what they are and drain every drop from the cup.

While an undergrad at the University of the Pacific Conservatory, I spent two and a half years singing for, and studying conducting with, William Dehning. Serving as director of choral music at UOP, Bill demonstrated elegant, sophisticated conducting technique, as well as being a wizard with sound and color in the choral sphere. Coming from my self-taught conducting experiences in the theater, watching him rehearse was a revelation in how good it was possible to be. Like many first-year conservatory students, I thought I was hot stuff. After a week in his ensemble, I started to understand the cosmos-sized vacuum in my knowledge and abilities.

Every concert with Bill Dehning felt like an act of creation—a magnificent, magically organized improvisation. And I strive to create the same atmosphere in my performances. But that uninhibited spirit was, perhaps, his weakness as well as his strength. Years later I recalled things he said in the classroom that today would be unthinkable. Little did I know that those uncomfortable comments may have been my hero's true colors peeking from the shadows.

A decade after leaving UOP, a classmate told me that improprieties alleged to have taken place right under our 18-year-old noses had led to Bill's sudden divorce. But no one knows better than I that our shortcomings lend as much to our creativity as do our virtues. And we are all sinners, great or small, so far be it from me to cast the first stone.

As a senior and then graduate student at Eastman, I was admitted to David Effron's advanced conducting course, a rarified space usually reserved for masters and doctoral conducting majors. David not only is a brilliant pianist and coach but also possesses a unique, concise conducting technique that I was able to study and emulate. He taught me that while you may not be the smartest person in the room, you'd better have worked hard enough that you appear to be. In other words, if you expect the orchestra to be prepared, thoughtful, musical, and inspired, you had best show them what those qualities look like.

David is an outstanding opera conductor, and from him I learned a great deal about that part of the craft. Handling singers (in both rehearsal and performance) and understanding what they need, separating and recombining our attention between the stage and the orchestra, and knowing instinctively who needs a cue and who wants to be left alone were just a few of the items on the table.

Still intoxicated from my conquest of the theatrical world three years earlier, I was brought down many pegs when introduced to truly difficult stage conducting. Early in my time in Effron's class, we covered the ensemble passages of Verdi's *Falstaff*. I remember studying my eyes out but still feeling as though many details refused to adhere to the gray matter.

After conducting a passage adequately, but far from brilliantly, I commented privately after class, "I'm not sure I can do this. I'm just too stupid to get it all."

In an uncharacteristic display of unqualified support, David responded, "You're not stupid. This is really hard."

That was all I needed.

In the summer of 1987, it was my privilege to be accepted as a conducting fellow at the Aspen Music Festival, studying with Paul Vermel. Paul's teaching style, emphasis, and temperament were so different from anyone with whom I'd studied previously that it took me a few days to get my bearings. While Paul could be very direct and critical, when necessary, it was not his essential nature. And while he could instruct in technical matters admirably, it was not his favorite subject. A native of Paris, where he studied with Andre Cluytens, and a student of Jean Morel at the Juilliard School, Paul knew everything there is to know about the French—and pretty much all other—repertoire. He was a walking encyclopedia of stylistic and textual information, right down to the errata he had memorized.

But Paul's greatest gift was his grasp of the big picture. While there were moments in front of the festival orchestras when his gestures may have been less than technically perfect, it never mattered. His inspiring presence, thorough knowledge, gentle wisdom, and absolute conviction carried the orchestra along with him. Paul simply had that way about him that makes people believe in him and want to give their best for him. If he hadn't been a conductor, he would have made a great pope.

We remained in touch over the years, and he was kind enough to assist with French repertoire details in my first book, *Conducting Concerti*. We lost Paul in February 2024, just a few days short of his 100th birthday. Until the very end he reveled in music, lobster rolls, and sauvignon blanc—a man after my own heart. May his memory be a blessing.

To Touch the Face of God

All human beings are created, we are told, "a little lower than the angels." But a few are closer to the angels than the rest of us. Earlier I mentioned a member of the Alabama Symphony staff, Ann Robinson. Some words about Ann need to be set down, but they did not belong amid the turmoil of the Alabama narrative.

For years before I arrived in Birmingham, Ann was a symphony volunteer. After her husband passed away, she was hired to work for the orchestra, coordinating sales and seating for season ticket holders. She knew every subscriber personally, from their seat location to their children's names. When she couldn't give someone what they'd requested, she called and chatted, eventually getting around to the issue at hand. When people dealt with Ann, they didn't seem to care if they hadn't received what they'd wanted.

But Ann's greatest contribution wasn't as our audience relations expert, it was as a force for the good, the positive, and the life-affirming.

And she did it without appearing to notice. From the day I stepped into the Alabama Symphony offices to the day she passed away, Ann treated me like a son, even though we were strangers with little in common. From the first moment, she spoke to me like she'd known me all my life. Usually that sort of familiarity from a stranger strikes me as pushy and off-putting, but with Ann it never occurred to me that we didn't really know one another.

Ann was not, as one might imagine, a lonely older lady who needed a surrogate son upon whom to dote. She had adoring children and grandchildren scant blocks from her home. She simply had the gift of making a connection exactly when you needed it, in a way that few of us are able.

Ann had been diagnosed with cancer before we met, but for the first two and a half years I knew her, I was unaware of it. She never mentioned her condition, and you would never have guessed from her demeanor. She was out of the office every Wednesday for treatments, but I assumed it was simply her day off. Eventually, she was away from work more and more. Noticing this, I questioned another staff member who was surprised I didn't know about Ann's diagnosis. Quietly irritated, I could only shrug it off, because it was so like her to shield others from bad news.

She retired during my third year with the orchestra, and after that we went to lunch or dinner every few weeks. When that became too difficult, we brought dinner to her apartment. Eventually, she was admitted to the hospital. But soon after, to our surprise, she returned home. Knowing what was coming, she had no intention of letting it happen among strangers.

We visited her twice before she passed away. She was bedridden, critically thin and frail, and on our second visit could barely speak. But through it all there was never a shred of sadness or self-pity. She only wanted to be sure that her children, grandchildren, and all of us were doing well. And she was always apologizing for looking "so bad," or the fact that the effects of morphine made it difficult for her to speak clearly.

A couple days after our second visit, we called to make our next appointment. Her son told us Ann was in a coma, and she passed away two days later.

One of the last times she left her apartment, a few weeks before entering the hospital, she attended the dedication of the symphony's new conference room, named in her honor. As the Alabama Symphony collapsed, and two months later when it became apparent that my first marriage could not be salvaged, I thought that if Ann was going to leave us, I was glad it happened when it did. I was relieved she did not have to witness these two events that would have caused her such pain.

From the first day, Ann was there to support and encourage this stranger. She was an ear when my bride was ill, and a springboard when I doubted my own abilities or character. Despite my newly-anointed-professional-conductor posturing, she seemed to sense my insecurities and isolation. Ann somehow understood, even after I was married, that I was very much alone. She had unflinching confidence in me as a musician and as a person, and to this day I don't know from where those initial feelings sprang.

I have attempted to emulate her compassion and selfless humanity, to incorporate it into both my music and my life. In these ways and so many others, I haven't begun to live up to her faith in me. But I hope she knows I've done my best.

In late 2023 I gave an extended interview for a video podcast on the arts. After chatting for a half hour about music and conducting, the interviewer surprised me by closing the session with some of James Lipton's final questions from *Inside the Actors Studio*.

Interviewer: What is your favorite word?
Me: We.
Interviewer: What is your least favorite word?
Me: I.
Interviewer: What turns you on creatively, spiritually, or emotionally?

Me:	Whatever's next.
Interviewer:	What turns you off, creatively, spiritually, or emotionally?
Me:	I don't like the end of things.
Interviewer:	What sound do you love the most?
Me:	Silence.
Interviewer:	What do you want to hear God say when you arrive at the pearly gates?

I suddenly pictured Ann standing just beyond those gates, and I couldn't speak. The interviewer's innocuous question sent every bad choice, every uncharitable thought, every missed opportunity for kindness, and every moment of anger or sarcasm rushing at me like a tidal wave. Noticing my clenched jaw, the host shifted uncomfortably in her chair, uncertain how, or if, she should try to fill the empty space.

Finally, I answered, "I hope God says, 'You did better than you think.'"

Full Circle

It is April 17, 2024, 5:30 a.m. Sixty-one hours ago, as I packed my belongings in a different hotel room, the legendary pianist Misha Dichter called to ask if I would join him for a last-minute concert with the Transylvania State Philharmonic in Cluj, Romania. Eager to help my friend out of a jam, and primed for an unexpected adventure, I hurried home to pack. Now, not quite dawn in Cluj, following three flights during which I studied while others slept, I pace this hotel room, my final review of the music to be rehearsed a few hours from now.

This is Seoul 1994 redux. Exactly thirty years later it's a sudden, exhausting excursion to an exotic location and the scramble to get several hundred pages of music back in my head in a matter of hours. And, as before, it's also the thrill, the nerves, the possibilities, and the music.

Vineri, 19 aprilie 2024, ora 19
Concert simfonic
Colegiul Academic
Dirijor: David Itkin
Solist: Misha Dichter *pian*

Distribuţie:
Serghei Rahmaninov
Vocalize
2 2+1 2 2; 2 0 0 0; Archi;

Rapsodia pe o temă de Paganini
2+1 2+1 2 2; 4 2 3 1; T; P; Hp; archi;

Simfonia nr. 2 în mi minor, op. 27
3*3*2+1 2; 4 3 3 1; T; P; archi;

Repetiţii:
Miercuri: 10-14 (**10-12:45** Simfonia; **13-14** Rapsodia + solo)
Joi: 10-14 (**10-12:35** Simfonia; **12:50-13:40** Rapsodia; **13:40-14** Vocalize)
Vineri: 10-13 generală (ordinea de concert); **19-21** concert

Cordari:
Simfonie: 14 12 10 8 6
Rapsodie: 12 10 8 6 4
Vocalize: 14 12 10 8 6

Servicii: 4

Orchestra call sheet for the Transylvania State Philharmonic, April 2024.

Post-concert with the Transylvania State Philharmonic, April 2024.
Right: the author with Misha and Cipa Dichter.

And though I see the circle closing, placing me back on a familiar path, I am certainly not the same. In Seoul, glances from the über-polite orchestra seemed to say, "Impress us, youngster. Show us what you've got." In hindsight, I realize that I mostly showed them the wrong things. I delivered great technique and knowledge of the score but failed to connect with them as fellow human beings, shying away from truly challenging them as musicians and artists.

In Romania, after the first few minutes during which every orchestra sizes up a new guest conductor, their eager looks said, "Join us, help us, teach us. Show us what the music means to *you*." This time, the result was a not sterile, careful attempt at perfect Berlioz, but a singing, shouting, whispering, tear-blinking Rachmaninoff.

Backstage, one of the musicians who came to greet me offered, "Maestro, the symphony was so special. A memory I will keep with me always."

The orchestra's small inaccuracies are forgotten in an instant. But the music, and that man's joy, will live with me forever.

Right Back Where I Started

Whether rehearsing with professionals, teaching conducting students, or speaking to a preconcert audience, I often look around and wonder, "Do you not know who I am? Do you not understand that I can't be who you want me to be? How do you not see that it's all smoke and mirrors?"

The 15-year-old who played percussion for professional dinner theater in 1972, the 16-year-old drummer who was handed a baton a year later, the trumpeter who sang his way through the late '70s, the wannabe opera singer who was thrust in front of a choir, the university choral conductor who tried to make it with the big kids, and the guy with thirty-seven years in front of professional orchestras—they all still wonder when someone's going to notice.

When a second clarinetist asks how I could possibly have heard a wrong note in her part while all hell is breaking loose in Strauss or

Mahler, I shrug it off—lucky guess. When a conducting student asks how the performance of a large-scale work came together organically and logically, how the musical narrative flowed inevitably from beginning to end, I offer a knowing smile—but, honestly, I have only the faintest clue.

Are these skills the product of years of hard work and nose-to-grindstone experience? In large part, yes. But there is so much more—and so much less. Like a chalkboard-sized equation that can, at last, be condensed to a half dozen characters, we are the sum of thousands of choices, musical experiences, and influences. But equally, we are simply the person we were born to be.

If there is one thing I have learned by observing my children, my students, and myself, it is that we are who we are. With hard work and a bit of luck, we sand off the rough edges, learn the words, and acquire new tools. But the musician into whom we eventually grow, the person we become, the artist we desire to be was always there. With his simultaneous insecurities and arrogance, swaggering and fears, fragile heart, and hateful condescension, he was always there.

The author with Athena.

Honeymoon in Italy, 2018.

Every day we take the sum of it all, bearing its increasing weight on our backs, and start anew. And I wouldn't have it any other way. Each moment of music is both a synthesis of all that's come before and a fresh beginning; an opportunity to reexamine old choices while gazing forward toward the next fork in the road. One way or another, each time I bring down the baton, I am right back where I started.

Acknowledgments

The author wishes to acknowledge the invaluable assistance of friends, family members, and colleagues who contributed important memories and details.

In addition, this memoir would not have been possible without the editorial assistance and support of Heather Zullinger, Susanna Sonnenberg, and Amy Maddox.

Index